T0207154

Essential Angular for ASP.NET Core MVC 3

A Practical Guide to Successfully Using
Both in Your Projects

Second Edition

Adam Freeman

Apress®

Essential Angular for ASP.NET Core MVC 3: A Practical Guide to Successfully Using Both in Your Projects

Adam Freeman
London, UK

ISBN-13 (pbk): 978-1-4842-5283-3 ISBN-13 (electronic): 978-1-4842-5284-0
https://doi.org/10.1007/978-1-4842-5284-0

Managing Director, Apress Media LLC: Welmoed Spahr
Acquisitions Editor: Joan Murray
Development Editor: Laura Berendson
Coordinating Editor: Mark Powers

Cover designed by eStudioCalamar

Cover image designed by Freepik (www.freepik.com)

Distributed to the book trade worldwide by Springer Science+Business Media New York, 233 Spring Street, 6th Floor, New York, NY 10013. Phone 1-800-SPRINGER, fax (201) 348-4505, e-mail orders-ny@springer-sbm.com, or visit www.springeronline.com. Apress Media, LLC is a California LLC and the sole member (owner) is Springer Science + Business Media Finance Inc (SSBM Finance Inc). SSBM Finance Inc is a **Delaware** corporation.

For information on translations, please e-mail editorial@apress.com; for reprint, paperback, or audio rights, please email bookpermissions@springernature.com.

Apress titles may be purchased in bulk for academic, corporate, or promotional use. eBook versions and licenses are also available for most titles. For more information, reference our Print and eBook Bulk Sales web page at www.apress.com/bulk-sales.

Any source code or other supplementary material referenced by the author in this book is available to readers on GitHub via the book's product page, located at www.apress.com/9781484252833. For more detailed information, please visit www.apress.com/source-code.

Printed on acid-free paper

Dedicated to my lovely wife, Jacqui Griffyth.
(And also to Peanut.)

Table of Contents

About the Author

Adam Freeman is an experienced IT professional who has held senior positions in a range of companies, most recently serving as chief technology officer and chief operating officer of a global bank. Now retired, he spends his time writing and long-distance running.

About the Technical Reviewer

Fabio Claudio Ferracchiati is a senior consultant and a senior analyst/developer using Microsoft technologies. He works for BluArancio (`www.bluarancio.com`). He is a Microsoft Certified Solution Developer for .NET, a Microsoft Certified Application Developer for .NET, a Microsoft Certified Professional, and a prolific author and technical reviewer. Over the past ten years, he's written articles for Italian and international magazines and coauthored more than ten books on a variety of computer topics.

CHAPTER 1

■ ■ ■

Understanding Angular and ASP.NET Core MVC

This book is about using Angular and ASP.NET Core MVC together to create rich applications. Individually, each of these frameworks is powerful and feature-rich, but using them together combines the dynamic flexibility of Angular with the solid infrastructure of ASP.NET Core MVC.

Who Is This Book For?

This book is for ASP.NET Core MVC developers who want to add Angular to their projects but don't know where to start. Angular is a complex framework that can be overwhelming to learn, and this book provides a solid foundation by using ASP.NET Core MVC to support an Angular application. By the end of this book, you will understand how ASP.NET Core MVC and Angular can work together, and you will have gained a basic understanding of how Angular development works.

What Does This Book Cover?

This book explains how to use Angular in an ASP.NET Core MVC project. I demonstrate how to create a Visual Studio or Visual Studio Code project that contains Angular and ASP.NET Core MVC, and I show you how to get them working together. I show you how to use Entity Framework Core to store the application data and ASP.NET Core Identity to authenticate and authorize users. Each ASP.NET Core package adds its complexities, and I show you how these can be managed to deliver functionality to Angular.

This book also introduces Angular development, focusing on just those features that are required by most applications. I explain how Angular applications work, how to structure an Angular application, and how individual building blocks can collaborate to create complex features.

The examples are based around SportsStore, which will be familiar if you have read any of my other books. SportsStore is a fictional online store that contains the features that most projects need. The SportsStore examples in this book have been adapted so that I can highlight problems between Angular and ASP.NET Core MVC and explain how to solve them.

© Adam Freeman 2019
A. Freeman, *Essential Angular for ASP.NET Core MVC 3*,
https://doi.org/10.1007/978-1-4842-5284-0_1

What Doesn't This Book Cover?

This book is not a deep-dive into Angular or ASP.NET Core MVC. I assume you are already familiar with C# and ASP.NET Core MVC development, and I describe only the essential Angular features.

I have written other books that provide the deep-dive for each framework. If you are unfamiliar with ASP.NET Core MVC development, then you should read *Pro ASP.NET Core MVC* before this book. Once you have mastered the basics of Angular development, then *Pro Angular* provides a comprehensive tour of Angular features. There are different editions of both of these books, so you should take care to choose the editions that cover the Angular and ASP.NET Core MVC versions you use.

■ **Note** This book covers development on Windows. Although .NET Core supports Linux and macOS, most ASP.NET Core MVC development is done on Windows, so the instructions in this chapter—and the rest of the book—are only for that platform.

What Do You Need to Know?

Before reading this book, you should have a working knowledge of ASP.NET Core MVC development and have a good understanding of JavaScript, HTML, and CSS.

Are There Lots of Examples?

There are *loads* of examples. The best way to learn is by example, and I have packed as many of them as I can into this book. To maximize the number of examples in this book, I have adopted a simple convention to avoid listing the same code over and over again. To help you navigate the project, the caption for each listing includes the name of the file and the folder in which it can be found, like this:

Listing 1-1. The Contents of the CheckoutState.cs File in the ServerApp/Models/BindingTargets Folder

```
namespace ServerApp.Models.BindingTargets {

    public class CheckoutState  {

        public string name { get; set; }
        public string address { get; set; }
        public string cardNumber { get; set; }
        public string cardExpiry { get; set; }
        public string cardSecurityCode { get; set; }
    }
}
```

This is a listing from Chapter 9, and the caption tells you that it refers to a file called CheckoutState.cs, which can be found in the ServerApp/Models/BindingTargets folder. A project that combines Angular and ASP.NET Core MVC can have a lot of files, and it is important to change the right one. (Don't worry about the code in this listing or the folder structure for the moment.) When I make changes to a file, I show the altered statements in bold, like this:

Listing 1-2. Adding Methods in the SessionValuesController.cs File in the ServerApp/Controllers Folder

```
using Microsoft.AspNetCore.Http;
using Microsoft.AspNetCore.Mvc;
using Newtonsoft.Json;
using ServerApp.Models;
using ServerApp.Models.BindingTargets;

namespace ServerApp.Controllers {

    [Route("/api/session")]
    [ApiController]
    public class SessionValuesController : Controller {

        [HttpGet("cart")]
        public IActionResult GetCart() {
            return Ok(HttpContext.Session.GetString("cart"));
        }

        [HttpPost("cart")]
        public void StoreCart([FromBody] ProductSelection[] products) {
            var jsonData = JsonConvert.SerializeObject(products);
            HttpContext.Session.SetString("cart", jsonData);
        }

        [HttpGet("checkout")]
        public IActionResult GetCheckout() {
            return Ok(HttpContext.Session.GetString("checkout"));
        }

        [HttpPost("checkout")]
        public void StoreCheckout([FromBody] CheckoutState data) {
            HttpContext.Session.SetString("checkout",
                JsonConvert.SerializeObject(data));
        }
    }
}
```

This is another listing from Chapter 9, and the bold statements indicate the changes that you should make if you are following the example. I use two different conventions to avoid repeating code in long files. For long class files, I omit methods and properties, like this:

Listing 1-3. Restricting Access in the SupplierValuesController.cs File in the ServerApp/Controllers Folder

```
using Microsoft.AspNetCore.Mvc;
using ServerApp.Models;
using ServerApp.Models.BindingTargets;
using System.Collections.Generic;
using Microsoft.AspNetCore.Authorization;
```

```
namespace ServerApp.Controllers {

    [Route("api/suppliers")]
    [Authorize(Roles = "Administrator")]
    public class SupplierValuesController : Controller {
        private DataContext context;

        // ...methods omitted for brevity...
    }
}
```

This listing from Chapter 12 shows you that a new attribute must be applied to the
SupplierValuesController class but doesn't list the constructor or other methods, which remain
unchanged.

This is the convention that I follow to highlight changes to a region within a file, such as when new
statements are required in a single method in a long file, as shown here:

Listing 1-4. Changing the Routing Configuration in the Startup.cs File in the ServerApp Folder

```
...
app.UseEndpoints(endpoints => {
    endpoints.MapControllerRoute(
        name: "default",
        pattern: "{controller=Home}/{action=Index}/{id?}");

    endpoints.MapControllerRoute(
        name: "angular_fallback",
        pattern: "{target:regex(store|cart|checkout)}/{*catchall}",
        defaults: new  { controller = "Home", action = "Index"});

    endpoints.MapControllerRoute(
        name: "blazor_integration",
        pattern: "/blazor/{*path:nonfile}",
        defaults: new  { controller = "Home", action = "Blazor"});

    // endpoints.MapFallbackToClientSideBlazor<BlazorApp
    //     .Startup>("/blazor/{*path:nonfile}", "index.html");

    endpoints.MapRazorPages();
});
...
```

This is a listing from Chapter 10 that requires a new statement in the function passed to the
UseEndpoints method in the Startup.cs file in the ServerApp folder, while the rest of the file remains
unchanged.

Where Can You Get the Example Code?

You can download the example projects for all the chapters in this book from https://github.com/Apress/esntl-angular-for-asp.net-core-mvc-3. The download is available without charge and includes all of the supporting resources that are required to re-create the examples without having to type them in. You don't have to download the code, but it is the easiest way of experimenting with the examples and makes it easy to copy and paste code into your own projects.

Where Can You Get Corrections for This Book?

You can find corrections for this book in the Errata file in the GitHub repository for this book, https://github.com/Apress/esntl-angular-for-asp.net-core-mvc-3.

Contacting the Author

If you have problems making the examples in this chapter work or if you find a problem in the book, then you can e-mail me at adam@adam-freeman.com and I will try my best to help. Please check the errata for this book at https://github.com/Apress/esntl-angular-for-asp.net-core-mvc-3 to see whether it contains a solution to your problem before contacting me.

Summary

In this chapter, I described the purpose and content of this book, explained how you can download the project used for each chapter of the book, and described the conventions I use in the code listings. In the next chapter, I show you how to set up your development environment in preparation for creating a combined Angular and ASP.NET Core MVC project in Chapter 3

CHAPTER 2

■ ■ ■

Getting Ready

In this chapter, I explain how to set up the tool packages required for Angular and ASP.NET Core MVC development. For quick reference, Table 2-1 lists the packages and explains their purpose. Follow the instructions for your preferred operating system to install the tools that are required for the rest of this book.

> ■ **Note** This book covers development on Windows and deployment to Linux containers. .NET Core supports Linux and macOS, but most ASP.NET Core MVC development is done on Windows, so the instructions in this chapter—and the rest of the book—are only for that platform.

Table 2-1. *The Software Packages Used in This Book*

Name	Description
Visual Studio	Visual Studio is the Windows-only IDE that provides a full-featured development experience for .NET.
Visual Studio Code	Visual Studio Code is a light-weight IDE that can be used on Windows, macOS, and Linux. It doesn't provide the full range of features of Visual Studio; however, it is well-suited to Angular and ASP.NET Core MVC development and is the tool I use every day for my own projects, including this book.
.NET SDK	The .NET Core Software Development Kit (SDK) includes the .NET runtime for executing .NET applications and the development tools required to build and test applications.
Node.js	Node.js is used for many client-side development tools, delivered through its package manager, NPM. It is used to prepare the Angular code for the browser.
Git	Git is a revision control system. It is used by some of the NPM packages commonly used for client-side development.

Getting Ready

The following sections describe the setup required for Windows. All of the tools used are available for free, although some are offered in commercial versions with additional features (but these are not needed for the examples in this book).

You can use Visual Studio, which is the traditional IDE for .NET projects, or Visual Studio Code, which offers a lighter-weight alternative. Visual Studio is still the most popular choice, but I have found myself gradually switching to Visual Studio Code, which is lighter and faster and focuses on just the core development tasks, without some of the bolt-on features that can make Visual Studio feel unwieldly.

© Adam Freeman 2019
A. Freeman, *Essential Angular for ASP.NET Core MVC 3*,
https://doi.org/10.1007/978-1-4842-5284-0_2

It doesn't matter which you choose for the purposes of this book. The nature of combining Angular and ASP.NET Core MVC lends itself to working with the command line for some of the key build tools, which can feel odd if you are used to working only through Visual Studio but seems to be the direction for .NET development.

Installing .NET Core

The .NET Core Software Development Kit includes the runtime and development tools needed to start the development project and perform database operations.

To install the .NET Core SDK on Windows, download the installer from `https://dotnet.microsoft.com/download/thank-you/dotnet-sdk-3.0.100-windows-x64-installer`. This URL is for the 64-bit .NET Core SDK version 3.0.0, which is the version that I use throughout this book and that you should install to ensure that you get the expected results from the examples. Rather than type in a complex URL, you can go to `https://www.microsoft.com/net/download/core` and select the 64-bit installer for the .NET Core SDK. (Microsoft also publishes a runtime-only installer, but this does not contain the tools that are required for this book.)

Run the installer; once the install process is complete, open a new PowerShell command prompt and run the command shown in Listing 2-1 to check that .NET Core is working.

Listing 2-1. Testing .NET Core

```
dotnet --version
```

The output from this command will display the version of the latest version of the .NET Core runtime that is installed. If you have installed only the version specified earlier, this will be `3.0.100`.

Installing Node.js

Node.js is a runtime for server-side JavaScript applications and has become a popular platform for development tools. In this book, Node.js is used by the Angular build tools to compile and prepare the code that ASP.NET Core MVC will send to the browser.

It is important that you download the same version of Node.js that I use throughout this book. Although Node.js is relatively stable, there are still breaking API changes from time to time, and they may stop the examples from working. To install Node.js, download and run the installer from `https://nodejs.org/dist/v12.4.0/node-v12.4.0-x64.msi`. This is the installer for version 12.4.0. You may prefer more recent releases for your projects, but you should stick with the 12.4.0 release for the rest of this book. Run the installer and ensure that the "npm package manager" option and the two Add to PATH options are selected, as shown in Figure 2-1.

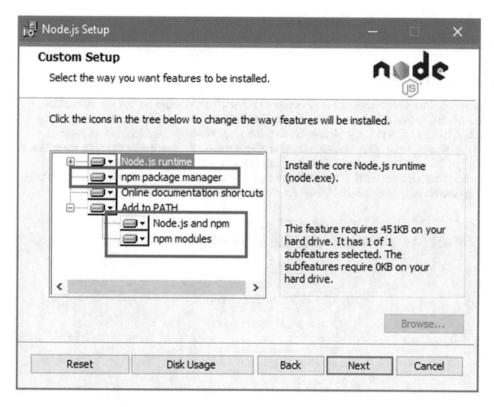

Figure 2-1. *Installing Node.js on Windows*

The NPM package manager is used to download and install Node packages. Adding Node.js to the PATH ensures that you can use the Node.js runtime at the command prompt just by typing node. Once installation is complete, open a new command prompt and run the command shown in Listing 2-2.

Listing 2-2. Checking That Node.js Is Installed Correctly

```
node -v
```

You should see the following version number displayed: v12.4.0.

Installing Git

Download and run the installer from https://git-scm.com/downloads. When the installation is complete, open a new command prompt and run the command in Listing 2-3 to check that Git is installed and working properly.

Listing 2-3. Checking the Git Install

```
git --version
```

This command prints out the version of the installed Git package. At the time of writing, the latest version of Git for Windows is 2.23.0.

Installing Visual Studio 2019

Visual Studio is the traditional development environment for ASP.NET Core and Entity Framework Core projects. It offers a full-featured development experience, but it can be resource hungry. Consider using Visual Studio Code, described in the next section, if you want a lighter-weight development experience.

Download the installer from `https://www.visualstudio.com/vs`. There are different editions of Visual Studio available, but the free Community edition is sufficient for the examples in this book.

Run the installer and ensure that the "ASP.NET and web development" workload is selected, as shown in Figure 2-2. This workload contains all the Visual Studio features required for this book.

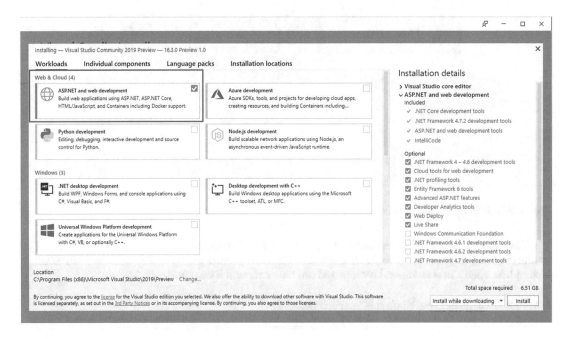

Figure 2-2. *Selecting the workload*

Click the Install button to begin the process of downloading and installing the Visual Studio features.

Installing Visual Studio Code

Visual Studio Code is a light-weight editor that doesn't have all the features of the full Visual Studio product; however, it works across platforms and is perfectly capable of handling ASP.NET Core and Angular development and can be used for the examples in this book.

To install Visual Studio code, visit `http://code.visualstudio.com` and click the download link for Windows. Run the installer and then start Visual Studio Code.

The database examples in this book require LocalDB, which is a zero-configuration version of SQL Server and which can be installed as part of the SQL Server Express edition, which is available for use without charge from `https://www.microsoft.com/en-in/sql-server/sql-server-downloads`. Download and run the Express edition installer and select the Custom option, as shown in Figure 2-3.

Figure 2-3. *Selecting the installation option for SQL Server*

When prompted, select the option to install a new SQL Server instance, as shown in Figure 2-4.

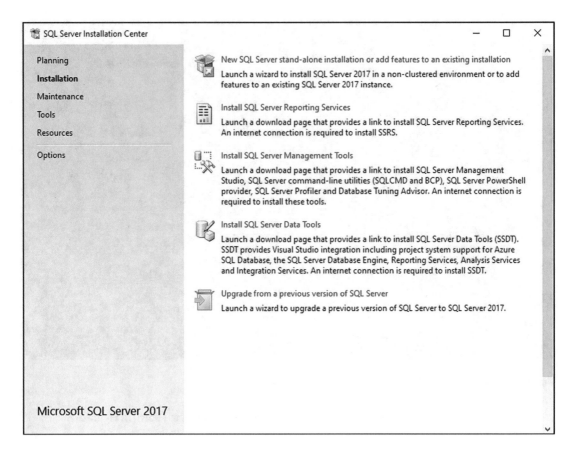

Figure 2-4. *Installing SQL Server*

Work through the installation process, selecting the default options as they are presented. When you reach the Feature Selection page, ensure that the LocalDB option is selected, as shown in Figure 2-5.

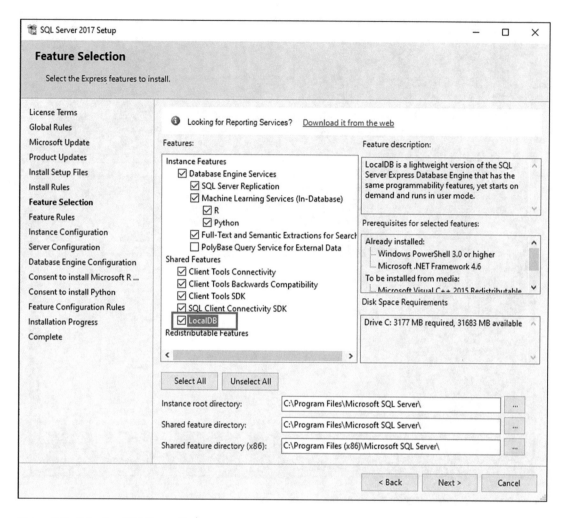

Figure 2-5. *Selecting SQL Server features*

On the Instance Configuration page, select the "Default instance" option, as shown in Figure 2-6.

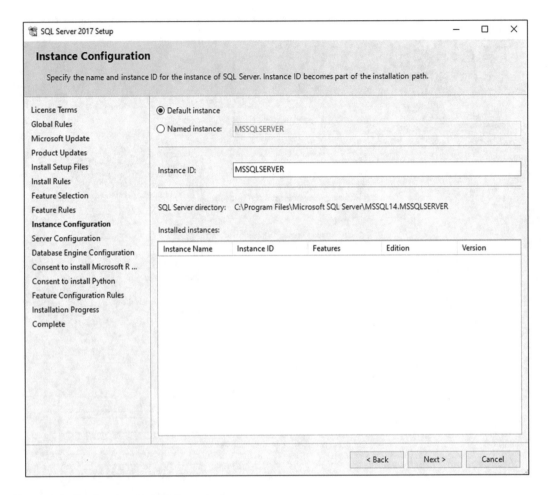

Figure 2-6. *Configuring the SQL Server instance*

Continue to work through the installation process, selecting the default values. Once the installation is complete, install the latest cumulative update for SQL Server. At the time of writing, the latest update is available at https://support.microsoft.com/en-gb/help/4498951/cumulative-update-15-for-sql-server-2017, although newer updates—or newer versions of SQL Server—may have been released by the time you read this chapter.

■ **Caution**   It can be tempting to skip the update stage, but it is important to perform this step to get the expected results from the examples in this book. As an example, the base installation of SQL Server has a bug that prevents LocalDB from creating database files, which will cause problems when you reach Chapter 3.

Summary

In this chapter, I explained how to install the tools and packages that are required to use Angular and ASP. NET Core MVC. In the next chapter, I show you how to create a project that combines them.

CHAPTER 3

■ ■ ■

Creating the Project

In this chapter, I show you how to create a project that contains ASP.NET Core MVC and Angular applications, which means that both parts of the project can be developed using Visual Studio or Visual Studio Code. This project forms the foundation for the rest of this book, as I explain how to use Angular and ASP.NET Core MVC together to create a rich web application. Table 3-1 puts the combined project in context.

■ **Tip** You can download the complete project for this chapter from `https://github.com/Apress/esntl-angular-for-asp.net-core-mvc-3`. This is also where you will find updates and corrections for this book.

Table 3-1. *Putting a Combined Project in Context*

Question	Answer
What is it?	A combined project includes Angular and ASP.NET Core MVC in a single folder structure.
Why is it useful?	A combined project makes it easy to develop both parts of an application using a single IDE, such as Visual Studio, as well as simplifying the process of using an ASP.NET Core MVC web service to provide data to Angular.
How is it used?	The Angular application is created first, followed by ASP.NET Core MVC. Additional NuGet packages are used to allow both parts of the project to work together at runtime.
Are there any pitfalls or limitations?	A combined project makes managing the development process easier, but you still need a good working knowledge of both Angular and ASP.NET Core MVC to create an effective application.
Are there alternatives?	You can develop the Angular and ASP.NET Core MVC parts of the application separately, although this tends to complicate the development process.

Preparing to Create a Project

There are several different ways to create a project that combines Angular and ASP.NET Core MVC. The approach that I use in this book relies on the @angular/cli package, used in conjunction with the .NET tools for creating a new MVC project.

© Adam Freeman 2019
A. Freeman, *Essential Angular for ASP.NET Core MVC 3*,
https://doi.org/10.1007/978-1-4842-5284-0_3

┌───┐
│ **USING THE DOTNET NEW ANGULAR COMMAND** │
└───┘

Microsoft provides a template that can be used to create a similar project structure (which you can use by running `dotnet new angular` at the command line). The process that I use in this chapter is more manual, but it means you will understand how the different building blocks fit together and therefore have a better idea of where to look when you don't get the results you expect.

The @angular/cli package provides a command-line interface that simplifies the process of creating and working with a new Angular project. During development, the Angular code is compiled, and packages are delivered to the browser automatically, making it easy to see the effect of changes immediately.

The key to combined development is to take advantage of the Angular development tools through the ASP.NET Core runtime, allowing each framework to be used with its own toolchain. To start this process, open a new PowerShell command prompt and run the command in Listing 3-1 to install the @angular/cli package.

Listing 3-1. Installing the @angular/cli Package

```
npm install --global @angular/cli@8.1.2
```

This command takes a while to run because the package has a lot of dependencies that have to be downloaded and installed.

■ **Tip** You must follow each step exactly as shown, without missing a step or changing the order. If you get stuck, then you can download a ready-made project from the source code repository, which can be found at https://github.com/Apress/esntl-angular-for-asp.net-core-mvc-3.

Creating the Angular Part of the Project

The first step is to create a new Angular project, which is done using the @angular/cli package installed in Listing 3-1. Open a new PowerShell prompt, navigate to a convenient location, and run the command shown in Listing 3-2. Put all the arguments on the same line when you enter the command.

Listing 3-2. Creating an Angular Project

```
ng new SportsStore --directory SportsStore/ClientApp --routing true --style css
--skip-tests true --skip-git true
```

The ng command is provided by the @angular/cli package, and ng new creates a new Angular project. The project is named SportsStore, and the `--directory` argument specifies the location of the project files. The name of the ClientApp folder is conventionally used when using a web application framework in an ASP.NET Core MVC project.

The --routing and --style arguments configure the project to use URL routing for navigation and regular CSS files for styling HTML elements. The --skipTests and --skipGit arguments create a project without unit tests and without a Git source code setup, neither of which are used this book.

During the installation process, you may see messages telling you that optional dependencies have been skipped. This is normal and can be ignored. When the setup is complete, the result is a folder called SportsStore/ClientApp that contains the tools and configuration files for an Angular project, along with some placeholder code to help jump-start development and check that the development tools are working.

Starting the Angular Development Tools

Use the command prompt to run the commands shown in Listing 3-3, which navigate into the project folder and start the Angular development tools.

Listing 3-3. Starting the Angular Development Tools

```
cd SportsStore/ClientApp
npm start
```

The npm start command starts the Angular development tools, which are responsible for producing the JavaScript code that is delivered to the browser for execution. The command will produce the following output as the project is prepared for use:

```
Hash: 38f7b5c53d9a2dfa3dbd

Time: 9000ms
chunk {main} main.js, main.js.map (main) 11.5 kB [initial] [rendered]
chunk {polyfills} polyfills.js, polyfills.js.map (polyfills) 248 kB [initial] [rendered]
chunk {runtime} runtime.js, runtime.js.map (runtime) 6.08 kB [entry] [rendered]
chunk {styles} styles.js, styles.js.map (styles) 16.4 kB [initial] [rendered]
chunk {vendor} vendor.js, vendor.js.map (vendor) 3.94 MB [initial] [rendered]

** Angular Live Development Server is listening on localhost:4200, open your browser on
http://localhost:4200/ **

wdm: Compiled successfully.
```

It can take a moment for the development tools to start and compile the project for its first use. Once the "Compiled successfully" message is shown, open a new browser window and navigate to http://localhost:4200 to see the placeholder content that is added to new Angular projects, shown in Figure 3-1.

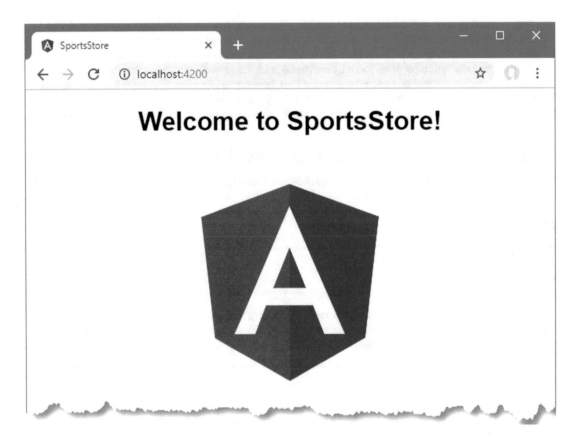

Figure 3-1. *Running the Angular development tools*

Editing the Angular Project

If you are using Visual Studio Code, you can edit the project by running code . (the word *code*, followed by a single period) from the PowerShell prompt in the SportsStore folder or by selecting File ➤ Open Folder and then selecting the SportsStore folder.

If you are using Visual Studio, choose the Open a Local Folder option when Visual Studio starts (or select File ➤ Open ➤ Folder when Visual Studio is already running) and select the SportsStore folder.

Both editors will show you the contents of the project, as illustrated by Figure 3-2, which shows the file views presented by Visual Studio Code and Visual Studio.

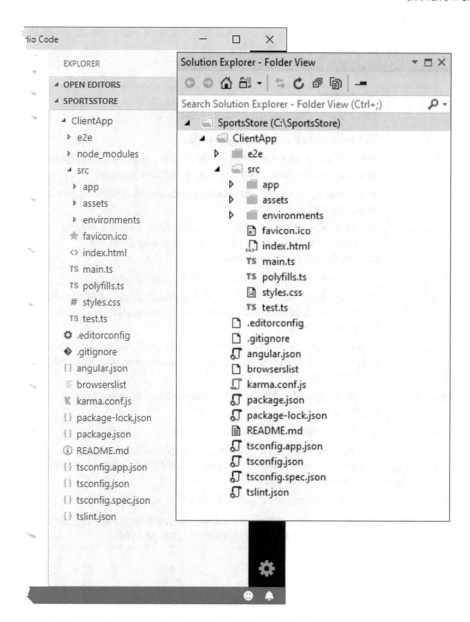

Figure 3-2. *Editing the project*

Table 3-2 describes the key files in the SportsStore project, some of which are used in later chapters as features are added to the example application.

Table 3-2. *The Key Files in the Example Project*

Name	Description
ClientApp	This is the root directory for the Angular project.
ClientApp/src	This is the directory for the application.
ClientApp/src/app	This is the directory that contains the Angular application's logic and templates and is the focus for most Angular development.
ClientApp/src/assets	This directory contains static content to be included in the application, such as images.
ClientApp/src/environments	This directory contains configuration files for different development environments. Projects are created with configurations for development and production builds.
ClientApp/src/index.html	This file contains the HTML that loads the application.
ClientApp/src/main.ts	This is the entry point for the Angular application, meaning that the statements in this file are the ones the browser executes when the application starts.
ClientApp/src/polyfills.ts	This file configures the polyfills used by the application, which provide support for modern JavaScript features that may not be supported by older browsers.
ClientApp/src/styles.css	The file defines the CSS styles that are applied throughout the application.
ClientApp/angular.json	This file configures the Angular build tools.
ClientApp/package.json	This file keeps track of the packages used by the Angular project and defines the commands that are used to start the Angular development tools and create production builds.
ClientApp/tsconfig.json	This file contains the configuration for the TypeScript compiler.
ClientApp/tsconfig.app.json	This file contains additional configuration settings for the TypeScript compiler that are applied to the code in the app folder.

Understanding the Angular Toolchain

There are three important tools used in Angular development. The first tool is the TypeScript compiler, which is responsible for compiling the TypeScript code into JavaScript that can be executed by the web browser.

The second tool is webpack. The TypeScript compiler produces a JavaScript file for each TypeScript source file that it compiles. This isn't a convenient way to distribute web applications because each file would have to be requested by the browser, leading to a series of HTTP requests for small code files. Instead, individual JavaScript files are combined into bundles that allow the application to be delivered to the browser over fewer HTTP requests. The bundles in an Angular project are created by webpack, which is the most popular bundler for web application development, regardless of the framework that is used (webpack is also used in React and Vue.js development, for example). The output from the npm start command shows the bundles that webpack creates for the example project; they are described in Table 3-3. These are the bundles that all Angular applications will contain.

Table 3-3. *The Example Application Bundles*

Name	Description
main.js	This bundle contains the application's code and content.
polyfills.js	This bundle contains code that provides support for modern JavaScript features in older browsers. The contents of this bundle are configured using the ClientApp/src/ polyfills.ts file.
runtime.js	This bundle includes the JavaScript code required to load and unpack the other bundle files.
styles.js	The bundler includes the application's CSS stylesheets in this bundle, expressed as JavaScript strings. The bundle also includes JavaScript code that processes the encoded strings and uses the browser's CSS API to add the styles to the HTML document.
vendor.js	This bundle contains the Angular runtime, which is responsible for processing the contents of the main.js bundle and presenting the application to the user.

The third important tool in Angular development is the Webpack Development Server (WDS), which provides an HTTP server that delivers the application to the browser. During development, the bundles delivered to the browser contain extra JavaScript code that opens a connection back to the server and awaits a signal. When a change to the project files is detected, the TypeScript compiler is used to compile the code, a new set of bundles is created, and the signal is sent to the browser to trigger a reload, ensuring that the effect of changes is immediately reflected. Figure 3-3 shows the Angular toolchain.

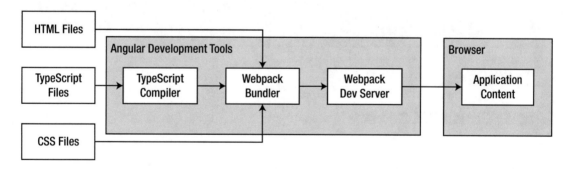

Figure 3-3. *The Angular development toolchain*

To see the update process in action, replace the contents of the app.component.html file, which can be found in the ClientApp/src/app folder, with those shown in Listing 3-4.

Listing 3-4. Replacing the Contents of the app.component.html File in the ClientApp/src/app Folder

```
<h2>SportStore</h2>
<span>Angular Content Will Go Here</span>
```

When the changes to the app.component.html file are changed, the Angular toolchain responds and produces the following output:

```
Hash: 91ce339c6f84319ad47b - Time: 160ms
4 unchanged chunks
chunk {main} main.js, main.js.map (main) 10.4 kB [initial] [rendered]
wdm: Compiled successfully.
```

The initial preparation when the npm start command is used can take a few minutes, but subsequent changes are quicker, and the Angular tools rebuild only the bundles whose contents are affected by the changed file. In this case, the main.js bundle is updated, and the reload signal is sent to the browser, which shows the content in Figure 3-4.

■ **Tip** During development, the bundle files are kept only in memory and not written to disk in order to improve performance. Disk files are created only when the application is prepared for deployment, as demonstrated in Chapter 13.

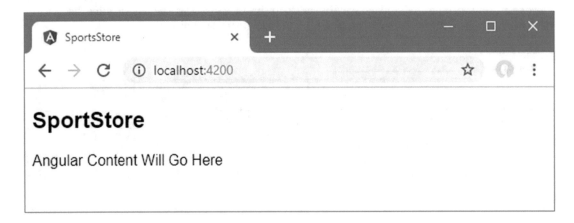

Figure 3-4. *The effect of a changed file in the Angular project*

Once you have confirmed that the live update feature is working, stop the Angular development tools using Control+C.

Creating the ASP.NET Core MVC Part of the Project

Once the Angular project has been set up, the next step is to create an ASP.NET Core project. Use a PowerShell command prompt to run the commands shown in Listing 3-5 in the SportsStore folder.

Listing 3-5. Preparing for the ASP.NET Core MVC Project

```
mkdir ServerApp
cd ServerApp
dotnet new globaljson --sdk-version 3.0.100
```

These commands create a SportsStore/ServerApp folder, which will contain the ASP.NET Core MVC project. The dotnet new globaljson command creates a file named global.json that specifies the version of the .NET Core runtime that will be used, which will help ensure the examples work as expected. By default, the latest version of the .NET Core SDK is used to create new projects, which may mean you get inconsistent results if you have a version installed that is later than the one specified in Chapter 2.

Run the command shown in Listing 3-6 in the SportsStore/ServerApp folder to create the ASP.NET Core MVC project.

Listing 3-6. Creating the ASP.NET Core Project

```
dotnet new mvc --language C# --auth None
```

The dotnet new command adds all the files required for a basic ASP.NET Core MVC project to the SportsStore/ServerApp folder, alongside the Angular project created in the previous section of this chapter. Both Visual Studio and Visual Studio Code will detect the new files and display them in the file list, as shown in Figure 3-5.

Figure 3-5. *Adding an ASP.NET Core MVC project to the SportsStore folder*

If you are using Visual Studio Code, you may be prompted to add the C# extension and you may see the prompt shown in Figure 3-6 when you open the project folder.

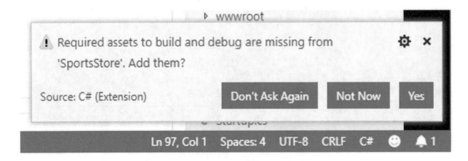

Figure 3-6. *Prompting to install the C# extension for Visual Studio Code*

Click the Yes button, and Visual Studio Code will download and install the tools required to build and debug C# code. No additions are required for Visual Studio. Table 3-4 describes the key files in the example ASP.NET Core MVC project.

Table 3-4. *The Key Files in the Example Project*

Name	Description
Controllers	This folder contains the MVC controllers, which are responsible for receiving requests and selecting the view that will be rendered to create a response.
Models	This folder contains the model classes that describe the data used by the ASP.NET Core MVC application.
Properties/ launchSettings.json	This file contains the configuration settings used to run the ASP.NET Core MVC application.
Views	This folder contains the Razor views that are used to generate HTML content.
wwwroot	This folder contains the static content used by the ASP.NET Core MVC application, such as CSS stylesheets, images, and JavaScript packages.
appsettings.json	This file contains the configuration settings for the application.
appsettings. Development.json	This file contains additional configuration settings that are used only during development. This file is nested within the appsettings.json file by the Visual Studio Solution Explorer.
Program.cs	This is the entry point for the ASP.NET Core MVC application, which is invoked when the application is started.
ServerApp.csproj	This is the project file and is used to configure the build process. This file is hidden by Visual Studio.
Startup.cs	This file contains the statements that set up ASP.NET Core at runtime, along with associated features such as MVC and Entity Framework Core.

Preparing the Project for Visual Studio

If you are using Visual Studio Code, the ServerApp project will be detected automatically and displayed in the file pane.

If you are using Visual Studio, select the File ➤ Open ➤ Project/Solution menu, navigate to the SportsStore/ServerApp folder, and select the SportsStore.csproj file. Visual Studio will open the project in .NET mode and will hide some of the files that were previously shown in the Solution Explorer window.

Right-click the Solution item at the top of the Solution Explorer window and select Add ➤ Existing Website from the popup menu. Navigate to the SportsStore folder, select the ClientApp folder, and click the Open button. Visual Studio will add the ClientApp folder to the Solution Explorer so that you can see the contents of the Angular project, as shown in Figure 3-7.

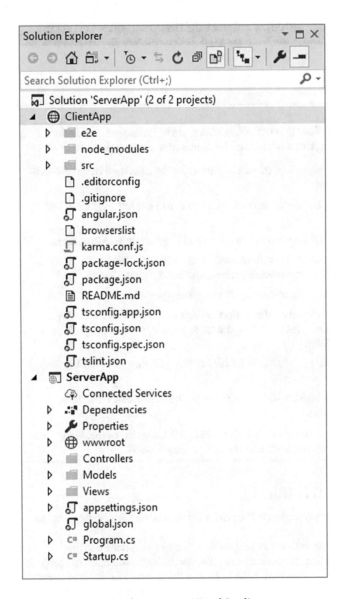

Figure 3-7. Opening the project in Visual Studio

Right-click the ClientApp item, select Property Pages from the popup menu, and navigate to the Build section. Make sure that the "Build Web site as part of solution" option is unchecked, as shown in Figure 3-8.

■ **Tip** If the option is already unchecked, toggle it on and off again just to make sure it is disabled. Visual Studio doesn't always display this setting correctly.

This configuration change prevents Visual Studio from trying to compile the code in the Angular project.

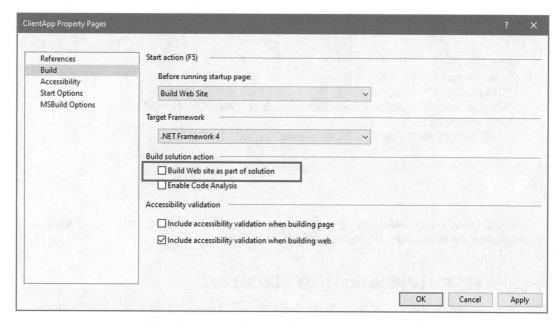

Figure 3-8. *Changing the build configuration*

Select File ➤ Save All; Visual Studio will prompt you to save the solution file, which can be used to open the Angular and ASP.NET Core MVC projects when you want to pick up a development session. Save the file in the SportsStore folder using the name SportsStore.sln. When you need to open the project again, open the SportsStore.sln file; both parts of the project will be opened and displayed in the Solution Explorer window.

Preparing to Build the ASP.NET Core MVC Application

To configure the ports used when the application is started using Visual Studio, make the changes shown in Listing 3-7 to the launchSettings.json file in the ServerApp/Properties folder.

Listing 3-7. Changing IIS Ports in the launchSettings.json File in the ServerApp/Properties Folder

```
{
  "iisSettings": {
    "windowsAuthentication": false,
    "anonymousAuthentication": true,
    "iisExpress": {
      "applicationUrl": "http://localhost:5000",
      "sslPort": 5001
    }
  },
  "profiles": {
    "IIS Express": {
      "commandName": "IISExpress",
      "launchBrowser": true,
      "environmentVariables": {
```

```
      "ASPNETCORE_ENVIRONMENT": "Development"
    }
  },
  "SportsStore": {
    "commandName": "Project",
    "launchBrowser": true,
    "applicationUrl": "https://localhost:5001;http://localhost:5000",
    "environmentVariables": {
      "ASPNETCORE_ENVIRONMENT": "Development"
    }
  }
 }
}
```

These changes ensure consistency regardless of how the application is started so that HTTP requests are received on port 5000 and HTTPS requests on port 5001.

Regenerating the Development HTTPS Certificates

The final preparatory step is to regenerate the development HTTPS certificates by running the commands shown in Listing 3-8. Select the Yes option for each prompt that Windows presents.

Listing 3-8. Regenerating the Windows Development Certificates

```
dotnet dev-certs https –clean

dotnet dev-certs https --trust
```

Building and Running the ASP.NET Core MVC Application

The ASP.NET Core MVC part of the project can be compiled and executed from the command line or using the code editor. To build and run the project from the command line, run the command shown in Listing 3-9 in the ServerApp folder.

■ **Tip** Use the dotnet build command if you want to build the project without executing it.

Listing 3-9. Building and Running the ASP.NET Core MVC Project

```
dotnet watch run
```

The ASP.NET Core MVC project will be compiled, and the runtime will start, producing the following output:

```
...
watch: Started
info: Microsoft.Hosting.Lifetime[0] Now listening on: https://localhost:5001
info: Microsoft.Hosting.Lifetime[0] Now listening on: http://localhost:5000
```

```
info: Microsoft.Hosting.Lifetime[0] Application started. Press Ctrl+C to shut down.
info: Microsoft.Hosting.Lifetime[0] Hosting environment: Development
info: Microsoft.Hosting.Lifetime[0] Content root path: C:\SportsStore
...
```

The output reports the ports that are used to listen for HTTP and HTTPS requests, which default to port 5000 for HTTP and to 5001 for HTTPS. Open a browser window and navigate to `https://localhost:5001`; you will see the placeholder content shown in Figure 3-9.

■ **Note**   You may see a security warning, which is triggered because the certificate used for development is self-signed. Most browsers will offer an "advanced" option that will allow you to continue. If you receive an ERR_SPDY_INADEQUATE_TRANSPORT_SECURITY error, then the likely cause is that you skipped over the `dotnet dev-certs` commands in Listing 3-8.

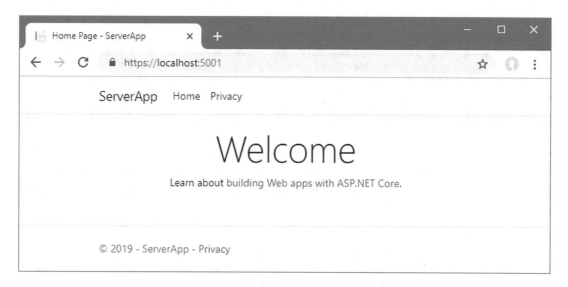

Figure 3-9. *Running the ASP.NET Core MVC application*

Understanding the ASP.NET Core MVC Toolchain

The development tools for ASP.NET Core MVC are entirely different from those used by Angular. The C# compiler processes the statements in the C# code files and generates output that can be executed by the .NET Core runtime. When the application is started, HTTP requests are received by Internet Information Services (IIS) or the stand-alone ASP.NET Core Kestrel server and handled by the ASP.NET Core request pipeline, which is the backbone of ASP.NET Core applications and allows MVC applications, RESTful web services, and other frameworks to coexist in the same application.

The template used to create the project includes the MVC framework. Requests are handled by the Home controller defined in the `ServerApp/Controllers` folder, which selects the `Index.cshtml` view file in the `ServerApp/Views/Home` folder. The MVC framework uses the Razor view engine to process the view, producing the HTML that is sent back to the browser and displayed to the user. Figure 3-10 shows the toolchain.

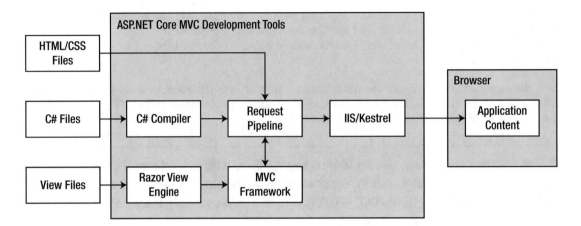

Figure 3-10. *The ASP.NET Core MVC toolchain*

The request pipeline is the heart of ASP.NET Core and is built around a series of middleware components that are able to inspect requests and either modify them or produce results. The most interesting middleware for this book integrates the MVC framework, but almost every ASP.NET Core feature relies on middleware to some extent, including serving static content and redirecting HTTP requests to the HTTPS URL.

The `dotnet watch run` command used to start the application puts .NET Core into watch mode, such that it detects changes to the files in the `ServerApp` folder and automatically recompiles the code and restarts the application. To see the update process, add a file named `Placeholder.cshtml` in the `ServerApp/Views/Home` folder with the content shown in Listing 3-10.

■ **Note**   The `dotnet watch run` command is useful, but it has limitations, the most serious of which is that it doesn't detect new files. Throughout this book, I will tell you when the ASP.NET Core runtime must be stopped using Control+C and then started again.

If you are using Visual Studio, right-click the ServerApp/Views/Home item in the Solution Explorer and select Add ➤ View from the popup menu. Set View Name to Placeholder, select the "Empty (without model)" template, ignore the other settings, and click the Add button. (You may need to stop the ASP.NET Core runtime when adding a view because Visual Studio can attempt to build the project, which requires access to files that are locked by ASP.NET Core.)

If you are using Visual Studio Code, right-click the `ServerApp/Views/Home` folder, select New File from the popup menu, and use `Placeholder.cshtml` as the file name.

Listing 3-10. The Contents of the Placeholder.cshtml File in the ServerApp/Views/Home Folder

```
@{
    ViewData["Title"] = "Placeholder";
}

<h2>SportStore</h2>
<span>ASP.NET Core MVC Content Will Go Here</span>
```

To apply the new view, change the contents of the `HomeController.cs` file in the `ServerApp/Controllers` folder, as shown in Listing 3-11.

Listing 3-11. Using a New View in the HomeController.cs File in the ServerApp/Controllers Folder

```
using Microsoft.AspNetCore.Mvc;
using ServerApp.Models;
using System.Diagnostics;

namespace ServerApp.Controllers {

    public class HomeController : Controller {

        public IActionResult Index() {
            return View("Placeholder");
        }

        public IActionResult Privacy() {
            return View();
        }

        [ResponseCache(Duration = 0, Location = ResponseCacheLocation.None,
            NoStore = true)]
        public IActionResult Error() {
            return View(new ErrorViewModel { RequestId = Activity.Current?.Id
                ?? HttpContext.TraceIdentifier });
        }
    }
}
```

The file change will be detected by the dotnet watch command, which will stop the ASP.NET Core runtime, build the project, and start the runtime again. Unlike Angular, a manual reload is required to see the effect of the changes in the browser, which are shown in Figure 3-11.

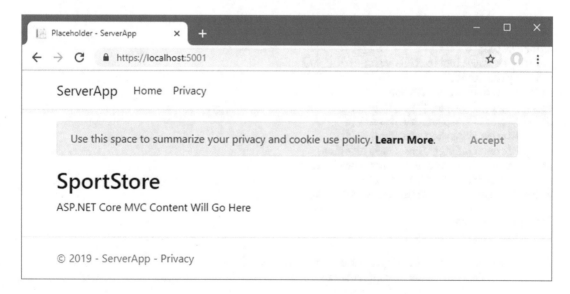

Figure 3-11. Changing the content presented by the ASP.NET Core MVC application

Connecting the Angular and ASP.NET Core Applications

The Angular and ASP.NET Core MVC applications share the same parent folder but are not connected in any way. It is possible to develop applications this way, but it is awkward. A more useful approach is to connect the two toolchains so that HTTP requests are received by ASP.NET Core and passed on to either the MVC framework or the Angular development tools based the request URL.

There are two ways to connect the toolchains, and each is useful during a different phase of the project lifecycle. I demonstrate both approaches in the sections that follow and explain when each is useful and how to switch between them. Both approaches rely on an additional .NET package. Open a new PowerShell command prompt, navigate to the SportsStore/ServerApp folder, and run the command shown in Listing 3-12.

Listing 3-12. Adding a Package to the ASP.NET Core Project

```
dotnet add package Microsoft.AspNetCore.SpaServices.Extensions --version 3.0.0
```

The Microsoft.AspNetCore.SpaServices.Extensions package is provided by Microsoft to allow single-page application (SPA) frameworks, such as Angular, to be used with ASP.NET Core.

Managing the Angular Server Through ASP.NET Core

The most commonly used connection technique is to configure the ASP.NET Core runtime so that it starts the Angular development server when the first HTTP request is received. This has the advantage of requiring only a single command to start both toolchains, which can be done via the command line or using the built-in features provided by Visual Studio and Visual Studio Code. The drawback is that restarting ASP.NET Core will also restart the Angular development server, which means the initial compilation process will be repeated for each restart, which can take 10 to 20 seconds every time.

Add the code shown in Listing 3-13 to the Startup class to configure ASP.NET Core so that it is responsible for managing the Angular development server and for selecting the connection approach based on a configuration setting.

Listing 3-13. Configuring the Application in the Startup.cs File in the ServerApp Folder

```
using System;
using System.Collections.Generic;
using System.Linq;
using System.Threading.Tasks;
using Microsoft.AspNetCore.Builder;
using Microsoft.AspNetCore.Hosting;
using Microsoft.AspNetCore.HttpsPolicy;
using Microsoft.Extensions.Configuration;
using Microsoft.Extensions.DependencyInjection;
using Microsoft.Extensions.Hosting;
using Microsoft.AspNetCore.SpaServices.AngularCli;

namespace ServerApp {
    public class Startup {

        public Startup(IConfiguration configuration) {
            Configuration = configuration;
        }
```

```
        public IConfiguration Configuration { get; }

        public void ConfigureServices(IServiceCollection services) {
            services.AddControllersWithViews();
            services.AddRazorPages();
        }

        public void Configure(IApplicationBuilder app, IWebHostEnvironment env) {
            if (env.IsDevelopment()) {
                app.UseDeveloperExceptionPage();
            } else {
                app.UseExceptionHandler("/Home/Error");
                app.UseHsts();
            }

            app.UseHttpsRedirection();
            app.UseStaticFiles();
            app.UseRouting();
            app.UseAuthorization();

            app.UseEndpoints(endpoints => {
                endpoints.MapControllerRoute(
                    name: "default",
                    pattern: "{controller=Home}/{action=Index}/{id?}");
                endpoints.MapRazorPages();
            });

            app.UseSpa(spa => {
                spa.Options.SourcePath = "../ClientApp";
                spa.UseAngularCliServer("start");
            });
        }
    }
}
```

The new code invokes the UseSpa method to add a middleware component to the ASP.NET Core request pipeline. The argument to the UseSpa method is a function that receives a configuration object; the argument is used in this example to specify the location of the Angular project and to specify the NPM command used to start the Angular development tools. The UseSpa method is used in development only and will be removed before the application is deployed in Chapter 13.

ASP.NET Core works its way through the middleware components in the sequence in which they are defined, which means that the Angular development server will receive only those requests that have not been handled by another middleware component, such as the one that applies the MVC framework.

Use Control+C to stop both the Angular development server and the ASP.NET Core runtime and then use the command prompt to run the command shown in Listing 3-14 in the ServerApp folder.

■ **Tip**   You can also select Debug ➤ Start Without Debugging in Visual Studio and Visual Studio Code. However, depending on your choice of IDE, you may find that changes to C# classes do not trigger automatic recompilation and restarts.

33

Listing 3-14. Starting the Development Servers

```
dotnet watch run
```

Open a web browser and navigate to `https://localhost:5001`; you will see the content generated by the MVC framework, as shown in the first screenshot in Figure 3-12.

Next, navigate to `https://localhost:5001/app`; you will see the output from the Angular application, as shown in the second screenshot in Figure 3-12.

The first URL is handled by the MVC framework because the default URL is translated into a request for the `Index` action on the `Home` controller by this statement in the `Startup` class:

```
...
app.UseEndpoints(endpoints => {
    endpoints.MapControllerRoute(
        name: "default",
        pattern: "{controller=Home}/{action=Index}/{id?}");
    endpoints.MapRazorPages();
});
...
```

The app segment of the second URL doesn't correspond to the name of an MVC controller, so the MVC framework can't handle the request, which is then forwarded to the Angular development server. There is no special significance of the /app URL, and any URL with a segment that doesn't match a controller name would have the same effect. (Ignore the error that you may see in the browser's JavaScript console when the Angular application is displayed.)

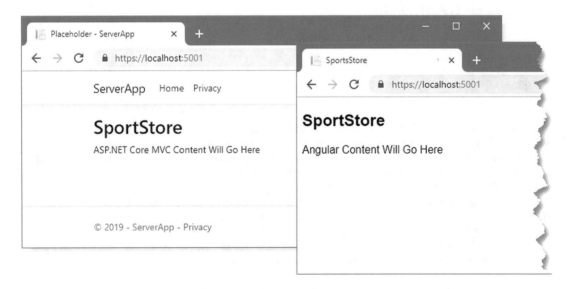

Figure 3-12. *Forwarding requests to the Angular development server*

Behind the scenes, the ASP.NET Core middleware starts the Angular development server and forwards HTTP requests that are not handled by other middleware components, such as the MVC framework, as illustrated in Figure 3-13.

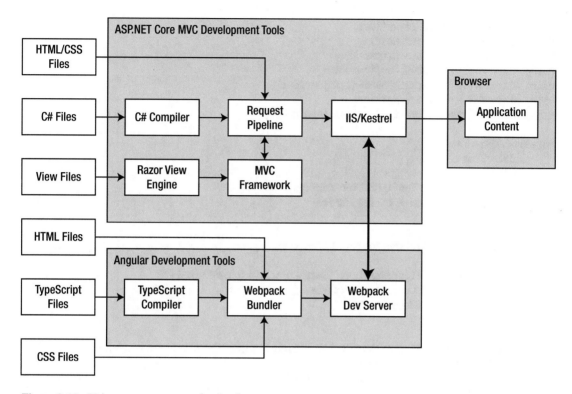

Figure 3-13. *Using separate servers for development*

Each time the ASP.NET Core runtime restarts, the Angular development server will also be restarted and won't be able to respond to requests until after the initial compilation phase has completed.

Once you have requested both of the URLs, use Control+C to stop the ASP.NET Core runtime. The Angular development server will also be terminated.

Using the ASP.NET Core MVC Proxy Feature

The alternative connection technique is to start the Angular development tools separately from the ASP.NET Core runtime. Requests are still forwarded to the Angular server, but the ASP.NET Core runtime isn't responsible for starting the Angular tools. In this approach, restarts are faster, which can create a smoother flow during iterative development. Each part of the project responds independently so that a change to a C# class, for example, doesn't affect the Angular development server. The drawback of this approach is that you need to run two commands and monitor two streams of output to see messages and errors.

Add the statements shown in Listing 3-15 to the Startup class to configure ASP.NET Core MVC to forward requests to the Angular development server, along with statements that select the connection technique based on configuration settings.

Listing 3-15. Configuring the Application in the Startup.cs File in the ServerApp Folder

```
using System;
using System.Collections.Generic;
using System.Linq;
using System.Threading.Tasks;
```

```
using Microsoft.AspNetCore.Builder;
using Microsoft.AspNetCore.Hosting;
using Microsoft.AspNetCore.HttpsPolicy;
using Microsoft.Extensions.Configuration;
using Microsoft.Extensions.DependencyInjection;
using Microsoft.Extensions.Hosting;
using Microsoft.AspNetCore.SpaServices.AngularCli;

namespace ServerApp {
    public class Startup {

        public Startup(IConfiguration configuration) {
            Configuration = configuration;
        }

        public IConfiguration Configuration { get; }

        public void ConfigureServices(IServiceCollection services) {
            services.AddControllersWithViews();
            services.AddRazorPages();
        }

        public void Configure(IApplicationBuilder app, IWebHostEnvironment env) {
            if (env.IsDevelopment()) {
                app.UseDeveloperExceptionPage();
            } else {
                app.UseExceptionHandler("/Home/Error");
                app.UseHsts();
            }

            app.UseHttpsRedirection();
            app.UseStaticFiles();
            app.UseRouting();
            app.UseAuthorization();

            app.UseEndpoints(endpoints => {
                endpoints.MapControllerRoute(
                    name: "default",
                    pattern: "{controller=Home}/{action=Index}/{id?}");
                endpoints.MapRazorPages();
            });

            app.UseSpa(spa => {
                string strategy = Configuration
                    .GetValue<string>("DevTools:ConnectionStrategy");
                if (strategy == "proxy") {
                    spa.UseProxyToSpaDevelopmentServer("http://127.0.0.1:4200");
                } else if (strategy == "managed") {
```

```
                    spa.Options.SourcePath = "../ClientApp";
                    spa.UseAngularCliServer("start");
                }
            });
        }
    }
}
```

The Configuration object is used to read the value of ConnectionStrategy in the DevTools section. If the setting is managed, then the technique from the previous section is used. If the setting is proxy, then the UseSpa method is used to specify the URL of the Angular server as an argument to the UseProxyToSpaDevelopmentServer method.

To select the managed option, add the configuration settings shown in Listing 3-16 to the appsettings. Development.json file. (If you are using Visual Studio, this file is accessed by expanding the appsettings. json file item in the Solution Explorer window.)

Listing 3-16. Adding Configuration Settings in the appsettings.Development.json File in the ServerApp Folder

```
{
  "Logging": {
    "LogLevel": {
      "Default": "Debug",
      "System": "Information",
      "Microsoft": "Information"
    }
  },
  "DevTools": {
      "ConnectionStrategy": "proxy"
  }
}
```

To start the Angular development server, open a new PowerShell command prompt, navigate to the SportsStore/ClientApp folder, and run the command shown in Listing 3-17.

Listing 3-17. Starting the Angular Development Server

```
npm start
```

To start the ASP.NET Core server, open a second PowerShell prompt, navigate to the SportsStore/ServerApp folder, and run the command shown in Listing 3-18.

Listing 3-18. Starting the ASP.NET Core Server

```
dotnet watch run
```

Once both servers are running, open a new browser and navigate to https://localhost:5001 and then https://localhost:5001/app. You will see the same results as in the previous section because requests are being forwarded in the same way. The difference is that the Angular server has been started independently.

Updating the Controller, View, and Layout

When a request cannot be handled by ASP.NET Core, it is forwarded to the Angular development server. The Angular development server falls back to returning the index.html file in the ClientApp/src folder if the request URL doesn't specify one of the bundle files or a file from the assets folder, which is where static content is usually stored in a stand-alone Angular project.

To increase the integration between Angular and the MVC framework, I am going to update the default Razor layout and the Views/Home/Index view so that only the bundle files are delivered by the Angular server. First, replace the contents of the _Layout.cshtml file in the ServerApp/Views/Shared folder with the elements shown in Listing 3-19.

Listing 3-19. Replacing the Contents of the _Layout.cshtml File in the ServerApp/Views/Shared Folder

```
<!DOCTYPE html>
<html lang="en">
<head>
    <base href="/">
    <meta charset="utf-8" />
    <meta name="viewport" content="width=device-width, initial-scale=1.0" />
    <title>SportsStore</title>
    <link rel="stylesheet" href="~/lib/bootstrap/dist/css/bootstrap.css" />
</head>
<body>
    <h2 class="bg-dark text-white p-2">SportStore</h2>
    @RenderBody()
    @RenderSection("Scripts", required: false)
</body>
</html>
```

This layout includes the Bootstrap CSS stylesheet, which I will use to style HTML elements throughout this book (Bootstrap was added to the project by the dotnet new command used to create the project). There are sections for the main body and the script elements that will contain the Angular application bundles. To provide the content and the script elements required by the application, replace the contents of the Index.cshtml file in the ServerApp/Views/Home folder with the elements shown in Listing 3-20.

Listing 3-20. Replacing the Contents of the Index.cshtml File in the ServerApp/Views/Home Folder

```
@section scripts {
    <script src="runtime.js"></script>
    <script src="polyfills.js"></script>
    <script src="styles.js"></script>
    <script src="vendor.js"></script>
    <script src="main.js"></script>
}

<app-root></app-root>
```

The scripts section includes script elements for each of the bundle files described in Table 3-3. The app-root element is the target into which the Angular application's content will be inserted when the application runs. To ensure the new view is used, change the Index action on the Home controller, as shown in Listing 3-21.

Listing 3-21. Using a Different View in the HomeController.cs File in the ServerApp/Controllers Folder

```
using Microsoft.AspNetCore.Mvc;
using ServerApp.Models;
using System.Diagnostics;

namespace ServerApp.Controllers {

    public class HomeController : Controller {

        public IActionResult Index() {
            return View();
        }

        public IActionResult Privacy() {
            return View();
        }

        [ResponseCache(Duration = 0, Location = ResponseCacheLocation.None,
            NoStore = true)]
        public IActionResult Error() {
            return View(new ErrorViewModel { RequestId = Activity.Current?.Id
                ?? HttpContext.TraceIdentifier });
        }
    }
}
```

Save the changes, allow the ASP.NET Core runtime to restart, and use the browser to navigate to https://localhost:5001. You will see that the Razor view has included the elements and bundle files that are required to display the Angular application, as shown in Figure 3-14.

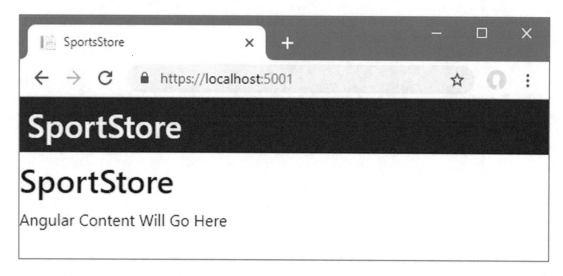

Figure 3-14. *Displaying the application using a Razor view*

Summary

In this chapter, I showed you how to create a project that combines Angular and ASP.NET Core MVC. The process is a little complicated, but the result is a solid foundation that allows the Angular and MVC parts of an application to work together while preserving the toolchain used by each of them. In the next chapter, I start work on the data model, which will underpin both the ASP.NET Core MVC and Angular parts of the project.

CHAPTER 4

■ ■ ■

Creating the Data Model

In this chapter, I start adding functionality to the ASP.NET Core MVC and Angular parts of the project to create a data model. I'll set up a SQL Server database to store the application data and define the model classes that Entity Framework Core will use to represent the data. On the Angular side, I'll define the TypeScript classes that will represent the data and define a repository that will make the data available throughout the application. Table 4-1 puts creating the data model into context.

Table 4-1. *Putting the Data Model in Context*

Question	Answer
What is it?	The data model describes the data in both parts of the application.
Why is it useful?	A consistent data model allows data to be consistently represented in Angular and ASP.NET Core MVC and to flow easily from one to the other.
How is it used?	The data model is defined as pairs of TypeScript and C# classes, with a repository in the Angular application and data context classes in the ASP.NET Core MVC application that allow the data to be stored using Entity Framework Core.
Are there any pitfalls or limitations?	The data model classes should be as simple as possible to ensure they can be represented consistently in TypeScript and C# and, for most applications, ensure they can be serialized as JSON.
Are there alternatives?	No, if an application requires both Angular and ASP.NET Core MVC, then it almost certainly requires a data model.

Preparing for This Chapter

This chapter depends on the SportsStore project that I created in Chapter 3. To prepare for this chapter, change the setting shown in Listing 4-1 in the `appsettings.Development.json` file so that the ASP.NET Core runtime will start the Angular development tools.

Listing 4-1. Changing the Configuration in the appsettings.Development.json File in the ServerApp Folder

```
{
  "Logging": {
    "LogLevel": {
      "Default": "Debug",
      "System": "Information",
```

© Adam Freeman 2019

A. Freeman, *Essential Angular for ASP.NET Core MVC 3*,

https://doi.org/10.1007/978-1-4842-5284-0_4

```
      "Microsoft": "Information"
    }
  },
  "DevTools": {
    "ConnectionStrategy": "managed"
  }
}
```

Open a new PowerShell command prompt, navigate to the SportsStore/ServerApp folder, and run the command shown in Listing 4-2 to start the ASP.NET Core runtime and the Angular development tools.

Listing 4-2. Starting the Development Tools

```
dotnet watch run
```

Open a new browser window and navigate to https://localhost:5001; you will see the content shown in Figure 4-1.

■ **Tip**　You can download the complete project for every chapter without charge from the source code repository, https://github.com/Apress/esntl-angular-for-asp.net-core-mvc-3. Run npm install in the ClientApp folder to install the packages required for Angular development and then start the development tools as instructed.

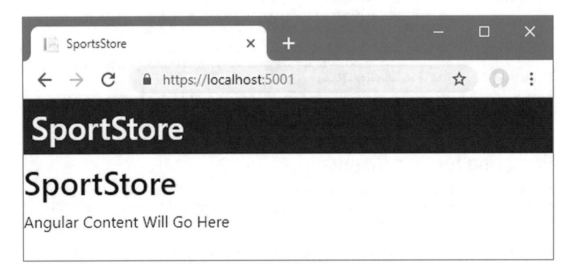

Figure 4-1. *Running the example application*

Once you have checked that the example application runs, stop the ASP.NET Core runtime using Control+C.

Starting the Data Model

Just as with a stand-alone ASP.NET Core MVC project, the best place to start is with the data model. Unlike a stand-alone project, data types for this application have to be described to both the Angular and MVC parts of the application.

Creating the ASP.NET Core MVC Data Model

The process of creating the data model for the MVC part of the application will be familiar to most MVC developers: a series of C# model classes is used to create a database schema, which is used to prepare a database to store the application's data.

An important difference from conventional ASP.NET Core development is that I do not create a repository interface and implementation class in the MVC part of the project. Instead, I create the repository in the Angular application, which is where the data is consumed. The structure of both applications will become clear as the application takes shape.

Defining the Model Data Types

Data types in a project that combines Angular and ASP.NET Core MVC should be as simple as possible so they can be described consistently using both C# and TypeScript classes and be easily serialized as JSON data, allowing them to be sent between the Angular and ASP.NET Core MVC using HTTP requests.

To get the data model started for the SportsStore application, I am going to define three classes, representing products, the suppliers of those products, and customer feedback. Add a C# class file called `Product.cs` to the `ServerApp/Models` folder and add the code shown in Listing 4-3.

If you are using Visual Studio, right-click the `Models` folder in the Solution Explorer, and select Add ➤ Class from the popup menu to add a new C# class file to the project. If you are using Visual Studio Code, right-click the `Models` folder and select New File from the popup menu.

Listing 4-3. The Contents of the Product.cs File in the ServerApp/Models Folder

```
using System.Collections.Generic;
using System.ComponentModel.DataAnnotations.Schema;

namespace ServerApp.Models {
    public class Product {

        public long ProductId { get; set; }

        public string Name { get; set; }
        public string Category { get; set; }
        public string Description { get; set; }

        [Column(TypeName = "decimal(8, 2)")]
        public decimal Price { get; set; }

        public Supplier Supplier { get; set; }
        public List<Rating> Ratings { get; set; }
    }
}
```

The ProductId property will be used as the primary key when storing Product objects in the database. The Name, Category, Description, and Price properties are regular properties that store simple data values. The Column attribute applied to the Price property tells Entity Framework Core how to set up the corresponding column in the database to ensure sufficient precision is available for the range of values that the application will store.

The Supplier and Ratings properties are *navigation properties* that Entity Framework Core uses to associate a Product object with other data in the database. The objects accessed through a navigation property are referred to as *related data*. In this case, each Product object may be related to one Supplier object and multiple Rating objects.

■ **Tip** This is a more complex data model than I used in the SportsStore examples in the *Pro ASP.NET Core MVC* and *Pro Angular* books because there are some common problems using related data when Angular and ASP.NET Core MVC are used together, which I describe in later chapters.

Add a C# class file called Supplier.cs to the ServerApp/Models folder and add the code shown in Listing 4-4.

Listing 4-4. The Contents of the Supplier.cs File in the ServerApp/Models Folder

```
using System.Collections.Generic;

namespace ServerApp.Models {
    public class Supplier {

        public long SupplierId { get; set; }

        public string Name { get; set; }
        public string City { get; set; }
        public string State { get; set; }

        public IEnumerable<Product> Products { get; set; }
    }
}
```

The SupplierId property provides the primary key when data is stored in the database, and the Name, City, and State properties are regular properties used to store simple data values. The Products property is a navigation property used to move through the related data in the database.

To complete the initial set of data model class files, add a C# class file called Rating.cs to the ServerApp/Models folder and add the statements shown in Listing 4-5.

Listing 4-5. The Contents of the Rating.cs File in the ServerApp/Models Folder

```
namespace ServerApp.Models {
    public class Rating {

        public long RatingId { get; set; }
```

```
        public int Stars { get; set; }

        public Product Product { get; set; }

    }
}
```

The `RatingId` property is used as the primary key when storing `Rating` objects in the database. The `Stars` property is a regular property used to store a rating from a customer. The `Product` property is a navigation property used to relate a `Rating` object to a `Product` object.

Adding the Entity Framework Core Packages

The data for the examples in this book will be stored in LocalDB, which is a zero-configuration version of SQL Server that was installed in Chapter 2. The data will be managed by Entity Framework Core, which is the standard data access layer for ASP.NET Core MVC applications.

To install the global tools package that provides the commands for Entity Framework Core, use a PowerShell command prompt to run the commands shown in Listing 4-6.

Listing 4-6. Installing the Entity Framework Core Tools Package

```
dotnet tool uninstall --global dotnet-ef
dotnet tool install --global dotnet-ef --version 3.0.0
```

The first command removes any existing Entity Framework Core tools package that may be installed. The second command installs the package that is used for this book.

To add the .NET packages for Entity Framework Core, use the command prompt to navigate to the `SportsStore/ServerApp` folder and run the commands shown in Listing 4-7.

Listing 4-7. Adding the Entity Framework Core Packages

```
dotnet add package Microsoft.EntityFrameworkCore.Design --version 3.0.0
dotnet add package Microsoft.EntityFrameworkCore.SqlServer --version 3.0.0
```

These commands install the Entity Framework Core features required to work with SQL Server and the command-line tools that are used for migrations, which allow database schemas to be created from C# classes.

Defining the Database Configuration Strings

Entity Framework Core needs to know how it should connect to a database, which is done using a connection string. To define the connection string for the example project, add the configuration properties shown in Listing 4-8 to the `appsettings.Development.json` file in the `ServerApp` folder.

■ **Caution**   Ensure you put the connection string, including all of its arguments, on a single line. It is shown split on two lines in the listing only because of the layout of the book page.

Listing 4-8. Defining a Connection in the appsettings.Development.json File in the ServerApp Folder

```
{
  "Logging": {
    "LogLevel": {
      "Default": "Debug",
      "System": "Information",
      "Microsoft": "Information"
    }
  },
  "DevTools": {
      "ConnectionStrategy": "managed"
  },
  "ConnectionStrings": {
    "DefaultConnection": "Server=(localdb)\\MSSQLLocalDB;Database=EssentialApp;
     MultipleActiveResultSets=true"
  }
}
```

These settings create the `ConnectionStrings` configuration section and define a connection string named `DefaultConnection`. The connection string selects LocalDB as the data store with a database named `EssentialApp`. If you have problems getting the connection string entered correctly, then go to the GitHub repository for this book, locate the folder for this chapter, and copy and paste the connection string from the `appsettings.Development.json` file directly into your project.

Creating the Database Context Class and the Seed Data

The next step is to create the database context class that provides access to the data through Entity Framework Core. Add a C# class file called `DataContext.cs` to the `ServerApp/Models` folder and add the statements shown in Listing 4-9.

Listing 4-9. The Contents of the DataContext.cs File in the ServerApp/Models Folder

```
using Microsoft.EntityFrameworkCore;

namespace ServerApp.Models {

    public class DataContext : DbContext {

        public DataContext(DbContextOptions<DataContext> opts)
            : base(opts) { }

        public DbSet<Product> Products { get; set; }
        public DbSet<Supplier> Suppliers { get; set; }
        public DbSet<Rating> Ratings { get; set; }
    }
}
```

The context class follows the standard pattern for Entity Framework Core and defines a constructor that accepts a `DbContextOptions<T>` object and that is configured during the ASP.NET Core startup sequence. The three `DbSet` properties provide access to the data in the database, allowing independent queries for each model type. You do not need to add `DbSet` properties for every model class, especially for related data types, but I find it convenient to do so.

The database is reset for every chapter to ensure you get the expected results from the examples in this book. This means it is useful to automatically populate the database with seed data so that the application always has data with which to work. Add a class file called `SeedData.cs` to the `ServerApp/Models` folder and add the statements shown in Listing 4-10.

■ **Note**   Entity Framework Core has features for managing seed data through the context class, but there are some serious limitations in this approach, and defining a custom seeding class, such as the one in Listing 4-10, provides more flexibility for most projects.

Listing 4-10. The Contents of the SeedData.cs File in the ServerApp/Models Folder

```
using System.Collections.Generic;
using System.Linq;
using Microsoft.EntityFrameworkCore;
using ServerApp.Models;

namespace ServerApp {

    public class SeedData {

        public static void SeedDatabase(DataContext context) {

            context.Database.Migrate();

            if (context.Products.Count() == 0) {
                var s1 = new Supplier { Name = "Splash Dudes",
                    City = "San Jose", State = "CA"};
                var s2 = new Supplier { Name = "Soccer Town",
                    City = "Chicago", State = "IL"};
                var s3 = new Supplier { Name = "Chess Co",
                    City = "New York", State = "NY"};

                context.Products.AddRange(
                    new Product { Name = "Kayak",
                        Description = "A boat for one person",
                        Category = "Watersports", Price = 275, Supplier = s1,
                        Ratings = new List<Rating> {
                            new Rating { Stars = 4 }, new Rating { Stars = 3 }}},
                    new Product { Name = "Lifejacket",
                        Description = "Protective and fashionable",
                        Category = "Watersports", Price = 48.95m , Supplier = s1,
                        Ratings = new List<Rating> {
                            new Rating { Stars = 2 }, new Rating { Stars = 5 }}},
```

```
                        new Product {
                            Name = "Soccer Ball",
                            Description = "FIFA-approved size and weight",
                            Category = "Soccer", Price = 19.50m, Supplier = s2,
                            Ratings = new List<Rating> {
                                new Rating { Stars = 1 }, new Rating { Stars = 3 }}},
                        new Product {
                            Name = "Corner Flags",
                            Description = "Give your pitch a professional touch",
                            Category = "Soccer", Price = 34.95m, Supplier = s2,
                            Ratings = new List<Rating> { new Rating { Stars = 3 }}},
                        new Product {
                            Name = "Stadium",
                            Description = "Flat-packed 35,000-seat stadium",
                            Category = "Soccer", Price = 79500, Supplier = s2,
                            Ratings = new List<Rating> { new Rating { Stars = 1 },
                                new Rating { Stars = 4 }, new Rating { Stars = 3 }}},
                        new Product {
                            Name = "Thinking Cap",
                            Description = "Improve brain efficiency by 75%",
                            Category = "Chess", Price = 16, Supplier = s3,
                            Ratings = new List<Rating> { new Rating { Stars = 5 },
                                new Rating { Stars = 4 }}},
                        new Product {
                            Name = "Unsteady Chair",
                            Description = "Secretly give your opponent a disadvantage",
                            Category = "Chess", Price = 29.95m, Supplier = s3,
                            Ratings = new List<Rating> { new Rating { Stars = 3 }}},
                        new Product {
                            Name = "Human Chess Board",
                            Description = "A fun game for the family",
                            Category = "Chess", Price = 75, Supplier = s3 },
                        new Product {
                            Name = "Bling-Bling King",
                            Description = "Gold-plated, diamond-studded King",
                            Category = "Chess", Price = 1200, Supplier = s3 });
                    context.SaveChanges();
                }
            }
        }
    }
}
```

The SeedDatabase method starts by calling the DataContext.Database.Migrate method, which ensures that the database has been created and updated before the seed data is applied. The rest of the SeedDatabase method creates a series of model objects, associates them with one another, and then saves them to the database using the DataContext.SaveChanges method.

To register the context class with Entity Framework Core and to ensure that the seed data is applied when ASP.NET Core starts, add the statements shown in Listing 4-11 to the Startup class in the ServerApp folder.

Listing 4-11. Registering the Context Class in the Startup.cs File in the ServerApp Folder

```
using System;
using System.Collections.Generic;
using System.Linq;
using System.Threading.Tasks;
using Microsoft.AspNetCore.Builder;
using Microsoft.AspNetCore.Hosting;
using Microsoft.AspNetCore.HttpsPolicy;
using Microsoft.Extensions.Configuration;
using Microsoft.Extensions.DependencyInjection;
using Microsoft.Extensions.Hosting;
using Microsoft.AspNetCore.SpaServices.AngularCli;
using ServerApp.Models;
using Microsoft.EntityFrameworkCore;

namespace ServerApp {
    public class Startup {

        public Startup(IConfiguration configuration) {
            Configuration = configuration;
        }

        public IConfiguration Configuration { get; }

        public void ConfigureServices(IServiceCollection services) {

            string connectionString =
                Configuration["ConnectionStrings:DefaultConnection"];
            services.AddDbContext<DataContext>(options =>
                options.UseSqlServer(connectionString));

            services.AddControllersWithViews();
            services.AddRazorPages();
        }

        public void Configure(IApplicationBuilder app, IWebHostEnvironment env,
                IServiceProvider services) {

            if (env.IsDevelopment()) {
                app.UseDeveloperExceptionPage();
            } else {
                app.UseExceptionHandler("/Home/Error");
                app.UseHsts();
            }

            app.UseHttpsRedirection();
            app.UseStaticFiles();
            app.UseRouting();
            app.UseAuthorization();
```

```
        app.UseEndpoints(endpoints => {
            endpoints.MapControllerRoute(
                name: "default",
                pattern: "{controller=Home}/{action=Index}/{id?}");
            endpoints.MapRazorPages();
        });

        app.UseSpa(spa => {
            string strategy = Configuration
                .GetValue<string>("DevTools:ConnectionStrategy");
            if (strategy == "proxy") {
                spa.UseProxyToSpaDevelopmentServer("http://127.0.0.1:4200");
            } else if (strategy == "managed") {
                spa.Options.SourcePath = "../ClientApp";
                spa.UseAngularCliServer("start");
            }
        });

        SeedData.SeedDatabase(services.GetRequiredService<DataContext>());
    }
  }
}
```

A database migration is required to create the database schema that will allow the database to store the application data. Use a command prompt to run the command shown in Listing 4-12 in the ServerApp folder. (If you receive an error that the command cannot be found, then close the PowerShell window, open a new PowerShell window and try again).

Listing 4-12. Creating the Database Migration

```
dotnet ef migrations add Initial
```

The result of running this command is that a Migrations folder is added to the project that contains C# class files with statements that generate the database schema when the migration is applied to the database.

The files created for a migration start with a timestamp. If you examine the statements in the <timestamp>_Initial.cs file in the ServerApp/Migrations folder, you will see how Entity Framework Core is going to store the application's data. The database will contain three tables, called Products, Suppliers, and Ratings, corresponding to each of the three data model types. Each table has columns that correspond to the properties defined by the equivalent data model class, while the navigation properties are translated into foreign key relationships between the tables. Figure 4-2 shows a simplified representation of the database created by the migration and the seed data. (This is not a book about Entity Framework Core, but it helps to understand how the data is stored when it comes to querying the database to provide the application with its data.)

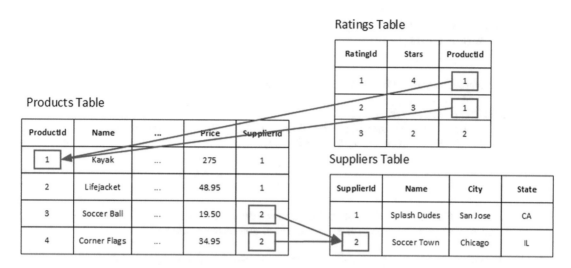

Figure 4-2. *The basic database structure*

The Products table is used to store Product objects and includes a SupplierId column that is used to capture the relationship to a Supplier object by storing the value of a SupplierId property from the Suppliers table. The Ratings table is used to store Rating objects and has a ProductId column that captures the relationship with the related Product object.

Testing the ASP.NET Core MVC Data Model

Before going further, it is worth making sure that Entity Framework Core can connect to the database and that the seed data is correctly applied. The simplest way to check the data model is to include some data in a view. Edit the Index action of the Home controller so that it receives a DataContext object through its constructor and passes on data to its view, as shown in Listing 4-13.

Listing 4-13. Working with Data in the HomeController.cs File in the ServerApp/Controllers Folder

```
using Microsoft.AspNetCore.Mvc;
using ServerApp.Models;
using System.Diagnostics;
using System.Linq;

namespace ServerApp.Controllers {

    public class HomeController : Controller {
        private DataContext context;

        public HomeController(DataContext ctx) {
            context = ctx;
        }

        public IActionResult Index() {
            return View(context.Products.First());
        }
```

```
        public IActionResult Privacy() {
            return View();
        }

        [ResponseCache(Duration = 0, Location = ResponseCacheLocation.None,
            NoStore = true)]
        public IActionResult Error() {
            return View(new ErrorViewModel { RequestId = Activity.Current?.Id
                ?? HttpContext.TraceIdentifier });
        }
    }
}
```

The data passed to the view is the first Product object stored in the database. To display the data, edit the Index.cshtml file in the ServerApp/Views/Home folder, as shown in Listing 4-14.

Listing 4-14. Displaying Data in the Index.cshtml File in the ServerApp/Views/Home Folder

```
@section scripts {
    <script src="runtime.js"></script>
    <script src="polyfills.js"></script>
    <script src="styles.js"></script>
    <script src="vendor.js"></script>
    <script src="main.js"></script>
}

<div id="data" class="p-1 bg-warning">
  @Json.Serialize(Model)
</div>

<app-root></app-root>
```

The @Json.Serialize method generates a JSON representation of the view model data provided by the action method. Save the changes to the controller and view and then start ASP.NET Core by running the command shown in Listing 4-15 in the ServerApp folder.

Listing 4-15. Starting the ASP.NET Core Runtime

```
dotnet watch run
```

■ **Tip** If you are trying to repeat the steps in this chapter, you may want to delete the database, especially if it contains changes from subsequent chapters. Run the dotnet ef database drop --force command in the ServerApp folder and then run dotnet ef database update to delete and re-create the database. Finally, run the command in Listing 4-15 to start the ASP.NET Core runtime.

Once the startup is complete, open a new browser window and navigate to https://localhost:5001. The content shown by the browser includes a block of JSON data, as shown in Figure 4-3.

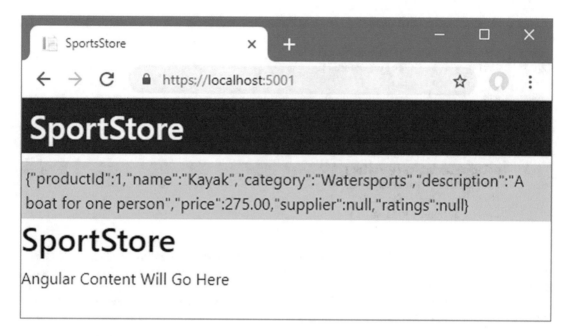

Figure 4-3. *Including JSON data in a view*

Here is the JSON data added to the HTML sent to the browser:

```
{
  "productId":1,"name":"Kayak","category":"Watersports",
  "description":"A boat for one person","price":275.00,
  "supplier":null,"ratings":null
}
```

The supplier and ratings properties are to null because I did not tell Entity Framework Core to follow the navigation properties defined by the Product class to load the related Supplier and Rating data. I show you how to work with related data in Chapter 5.

■ **Caution**   Do not continue until you see the JSON data in the view, as shown in Figure 4-3. Go back and make sure you have followed all the steps to prepare and populate the database. If you need to reset the database, stop ASP.NET Core, run the dotnet ef database drop --force command, and then start ASP.NET Core MVC again.

Starting the Angular Data Model

Creating a data model in the Angular part of the project makes it easier to work with the data received from the MVC framework. Create a ClientApp/src/app/models folder and add to it a file called product.model.ts, with the code shown in Listing 4-16. If you are using Visual Studio, right-click the models folder, select Add ➤ Add New Item from the popup menu, and use the TypeScript File template to create the product.model.ts file. If you are using Visual Studio Code, right-click the models folder and enter the file name.

Listing 4-16. The Contents of the product.model.ts File in the ClientApp/src/app/models Folder

```
import { Supplier } from "./supplier.model";
import { Rating } from "./rating.model";

export class Product {
    constructor(
        public productId?: number,
        public name?: string,
        public category?: string,
        public description?: string,
        public price?: number,
        public supplier?: Supplier,
        public ratings?: Rating[] ) { }
}
```

The convention for Angular files is to include terms like model and component in the file name to make the purpose of the file obvious. The name product.model.ts, for example, indicates that this is a TypeScript file that contains a model class called Product.

Next, create a file called supplier.model.ts in the ClientApp/src/app/models folder and add the statements shown in Listing 4-17.

Listing 4-17. The Contents of the supplier.model.ts File in the ClientApp/src/app/models Folder

```
export class Supplier {

    constructor(
        public supplierId?: number,
        public name?: string,
        public city?: string,
        public state?: string) { }
}
```

Finally, create a file called rating.model.ts in the ClientApp/src/app/models folder and add the statements shown in Listing 4-18.

Listing 4-18. The Contents of the rating.model.ts File in the ClientApp/src/app/models Folder

```
import { Product } from "./product.model";

export class Rating {

    constructor(
        public ratingId?: number,
        public stars?: number,
        public product?: Product) { }
}
```

Understanding the TypeScript Data Model Classes

Since these are the first TypeScript classes that I create in this book, I am going to dig into a little of the detail and explain what TypeScript does and how it works. TypeScript is a superset of JavaScript that adds a strong type system similar to the one you are already familiar with in C#. But TypeScript is not C#, and working on a project that combines Angular and ASP.NET Core MVC means writing code in two different languages, with two different sets of rules and features. There is a commonality between TypeScript and C#, as you might expect from two languages created by Microsoft, but there are important differences, too.

If you are new to TypeScript, you might find some of this confusing, but don't worry, TypeScript starts to make sense as you get experience using it. Don't get bogged down in the detail if you get lost; just carry on reading and try to follow along as much as you can, even if not everything makes sense right away.

As you read through the sections that follow, bear in mind that the purpose of the Angular data model classes is to mirror the C# classes from the MVC part of the project so that data sent from the server can be represented in the client and displayed to the user.

JAVASCRIPT, ECMASCRIPT, AND TYPESCRIPT

JavaScript is a broad term that describes the language and runtime used to execute code in the browser. It is the support for JavaScript that all modern browsers provide that makes it possible to create Angular applications.

The name of the technology standard that describes the JavaScript language is *ECMAScript*, also known as ES. Each version of the standard is given a version number so that version 6 of ECMAScript is known as ES6, version 7 is known as ES7, and so on. To confuse matters, ES6 and ES7 are also known as ECMAScript 2015 and ECMAScript 2016, which are usually expressed as ES2015 and ES2016. The release of ES6 marked the switch to annual updates to the language specification, which is why the 2016, 2017, and 2018 editions contain only a small number of changes.

Each new version of the language specification adds features, but it takes time for browsers to support them. It also takes time for browsers that don't support new features to fall out of use, which makes it risky to assume that a specific feature will be supported by all of the browsers used to run your Angular application.

The good news is that TypeScript provides two useful features that help navigate through the mess of JavaScript standards and implementations. The first is that TypeScript provides a type system similar to the one used by C#, which makes it easier to detect common problems when compiling TypeScript code. (The TypeScript type system is applied only when your TypeScript code files are compiled and not at runtime. The TypeScript compiler has to remove details of the C#-style types and use the JavaScript type system to generate backward-compatible JavaScript code.)

The second feature is that TypeScript allows you to use the latest JavaScript language features in your project without having to worry about whether your users have browsers that support them. When the TypeScript compiler processes a TypeScript file, it generates backward-compatible JavaScript that runs in browsers that don't support ES6 or ES7. The version of JavaScript that is targeted by the TypeScript compiler is configured in the `tsconfig.json` file and defaults to ES2015.

Examining the Product Constructor

The best place to start is with the Product class. This class contains only a constructor, which is typical for a TypeScript data model class. Here is the Product class with the constructor highlighted:

```
import { Supplier } from "./supplier.model";
import { Rating } from "./rating.model";

export class Product {
    constructor(
        public productId?: number,
        public name?: string,
        public category?: string,
        public description?: string,
        public price?: number,
        public supplier?: Supplier,
        public ratings?: Rating[] ) { }
}
```

TypeScript constructors are denoted by the constructor keyword, rather than the name of the class, but they perform the same purpose as in C#, and each parameter receives a value that can be used to configure a new instance of the class.

Using the Right Name Capitalization Convention

JavaScript uses the Camel Case convention for its property names, which means that the first letter is lowercase and the first letter of each subsequent concatenated word is uppercase. This means that the C# property ProductId in the ASP.NET Core MVC part of the project becomes productId in Angular.

Making the Parameters Optional

The question mark that follows a parameter name indicates that the parameter is optional.

```
...
public productId?: number,
...
```

Optional parameters are useful for model classes because you will not always have values for all the fields available when you create a new object. This can be because you are getting data from the user gradually through multiple HTML forms or because the data is built up over multiple HTTP requests to the server. Making all the constructor parameters optional gives you extra flexibility, allowing you to create new objects with all, some, or even no data values.

Unpacking the Properties

The reason that the Product class contains only a constructor is that TypeScript has a useful feature for avoiding a common coding pattern that is especially prevalent in model classes.

When you include an access modifier on a constructor parameter, such as public, TypeScript creates a property with the same name and access level as the parameter and assigns it the value received by the constructor. The Product class, for example, is unpacked like this:

```
...
export class Product {

        constructor(
                productId?: number,
                name?: string,
                category?: string,
                description?: string,
                price?: number,
                supplier?: Supplier,
                ratings?: Rating[]) {

                this.productId = productId;
                this.name = name;
                this.category = category;
                this.description = description;
                this.price = price;
                this.supplier = supplier;
                this.ratings = ratings;
        }

        productId: number;
        name: string;
        category: string;
        description: string;
        price: number;
        supplier: Supplier
        ratings: Rating[];
}
...
```

It is easy to make a mistake when defining properties and copying values to them manually, either forgetting to assign a value to a property or assigning the wrong value. The TypeScript feature that automates this process produces identical results but in a more concise and less error-prone way.

Understanding the Parameter Types

The type of each parameter is specified after its name using one of the built-in JavaScript types or one of the other classes defined in the project. This is known as a *type annotation*.

```
...
public productId?: number,
public name?: string,
...
```

The constructor parameters for the Product class rely on the built-in string and number types, which are used to represent character data and numbers respectively. Table 4-2 lists the basic set of types supported by JavaScript.

Table 4-2. *The JavaScript Built-in Types*

Name	Description
number	This type is used to represent numeric values. Unlike other programming languages, JavaScript doesn't differentiate between integer and floating-point values, both of which can be represented using this type.
string	This type is used to represent text data.
boolean	This type can have true and false values.
symbol	This type is used to represent unique constant values, such as keys in collections.
null	This type can only be assigned the value null and is used to indicate a nonexistent or invalid reference.
undefined	This type is used when a variable has been defined but has not been assigned a value.
object	This type is used to represent compound values, formed from individual properties and values.

TypeScript defines additional types beyond those provided by JavaScript. Of special interest is the any type, which allows a property or variable to be assigned any value.

Understanding JavaScript Modules

The most confusing term when you are new to Angular development is *module*, which is used to describe different parts of an application that are only loosely related. One use of this term is to describe a *JavaScript module*, which is a reusable piece of code that contains features that can be used elsewhere in the application.

JavaScript modules allow dependencies between the code in a JavaScript application to be determined, allowing the code in a project to be split into multiple files. When the project is built, the webpack bundler starts with the Angular application's entry point, which is conventionally the main.ts file and follows all of the dependencies to incorporate each JavaScript module into the bundles that it creates.

Each TypeScript file contains a separate JavaScript module, and the convention in an Angular application is to define each class in a separate file. The export keyword is used to make the class available outside of its file, like this:

```
...
export class Product {
...
```

Without the export keyword, the Product class would not be accessible outside of the module in which it is defined, which would mean that it could be used only by other code in the product.model.ts file.

The counterpart is the import keyword, which declares a dependency on classes exported from another JavaScript module. There are two import statements in the product.module.ts file, and they declare dependencies on two other classes, like this:

```
...
import { Supplier } from "./supplier.model";
import { Rating } from "./rating.model";
...
```

A TypeScript `import` statement specifies the type that is required and its location. These statements import `Supplier` from the `supplier.model` JavaScript module and `Rating` from the `rating.model` JavaScript module.

There are two ways to specify the location of a JavaScript module. The `import` statements in the `product.model.ts` file are *relative* imports, which means they specify a file path relative to the current file. This type of location begins with a period and includes the path to the target file but omits the file extension so that the `.ts` of the TypeScript file or the `.js` of the JavaScript file that it is compiled into is not included.

The other type of import omits the period from the target location and declares a dependency on an NPM package, such as the JavaScript modules that provide the Angular functionality. As an example, here is an `import` statement from the `app.component.ts` file from the `ClientApp/src/app` folder that declares a dependency on the `@angular/core` module:

```
...
import { Component } from '@angular/core';
...
```

This statement declares a dependency on the `Component` class defined in a package called `@angular/core`. (The @ character is part of the JavaScript module name used by Google for Angular modules.) The TypeScript compiler and the webpack tools resolve this kind of dependency by searching in the `node_modules` folder in the project.

Understanding TypeScript Access Control

TypeScript supports three levels of access control: `public`, `private`, and `protected`. The default access level is `public`, which means that a method or property can be accessed from anywhere in the application. The `private` keyword means that a method or property can be accessed only within its defining class. The `protected` keyword means that a method or property can be accessed only within its defining class or a derived class.

For most Angular development, you can ignore the access control keywords. The exception is when you want to take care of the constructor parameter unpacking feature, which works only when an access control keyword is applied to a parameter. It is for this reason that all of the constructor parameters in the `Product` class are decorated with the `public` keyword, and the result is that TypeScript automatically generates `public` properties that are accessible elsewhere in the application.

Integrating the Angular Data Model

It is not enough to simply define the classes that represent the data in the application. To complete the data model, I need to integrate those classes into the rest of the application, which I do in the sections that follow.

Defining the Repository

The repository pattern isolates the code that manages the data from the rest of the application and makes it easy to provide access to data to any part of the application that requires it. To create a repository, add a new TypeScript file called `repository.ts` in the `ClientApp/src/app/models` folder and add the code shown in Listing 4-19.

```
┌─────────────────────────────────────────────────────────────────────────┐
│              WHY ANGULAR REPOSITORIES ARE JUST CLASSES                     │
└─────────────────────────────────────────────────────────────────────────┘
```

If you have implemented the repository pattern in an ASP.NET Core MVC application, you may be surprised by how basic the Angular equivalent is. In .NET, the repository typically consists of a C# interface and one or more implementation classes. The mapping between the interface and the implementation class that provides the detail is configured using the ASP.NET Core dependency injection system and hidden away from data-consuming classes, which declare their dependency on the interface.

TypeScript does support interfaces, but the Angular dependency injection system does not support them, which means that the repository is defined as a simple class, undermining some of the benefits of the repository pattern.

Listing 4-19. The Contents of the repository.ts File in the ClientApp/src/app/models Folder

```
import { Product } from "./product.model";

export class Repository {

    constructor() {
        this.product = JSON.parse(document.getElementById("data").textContent);
    }

    product: Product;
}
```

The `Repository` class defines one property, called `product`, which returns a `Product` object. I add more features to the Angular repository later, but this is enough to get started.

The constructor for the `Repository` class sets the value of the `product` property by doing something that is helpful for a book example but that should be considered carefully in a real project, which is to interact directly with the Document Object Model (DOM) API. The DOM API is a set of JavaScript objects and functions provided by the browser that allows the HTML document to be managed programmatically. It is this API that lets frameworks like Angular present content to the user and to respond to interactions.

The `Repository` constructor uses the DOM API to locate the element that contains the JSON data and get its content. This content is then converted from a JSON string to a JavaScript object using the `JSON.parse` method and assigned to the product property.

```
...
this.product = JSON.parse(document.getElementById("data").textContent);
...
```

Using the DOM allows me to access the data included in the Razor view, but it is not how data is usually provided to an Angular application, and I replace the DOM code once I have created an HTTP web service to deliver data directly to the Angular application.

Defining the Angular Feature Module

I mentioned earlier that the term *module* has multiple meanings in an Angular application, and I explained that each TypeScript file contains a JavaScript module, managed using the `import` and `export` keywords.

The next type of module is the Angular *feature module*, which is used to group related functionality together, such as the data repository classes in the data model. Using feature modules makes Angular applications easier to manage and maintain, although the real benefits are available when working with Angular building blocks such as components, with which I start in detail in Chapter 7.

For this chapter, I am going to create a feature module so that the data model can be easily integrated into the rest of the Angular application. Add a file called model.module.ts in the ClientApp/src/app/models folder and add the statements shown in Listing 4-20.

Listing 4-20. The Contents of the model.module.ts File in the ClientApp/src/app/models Folder

```
import { NgModule } from "@angular/core";
import { Repository } from "./repository";

@NgModule({
    providers: [Repository]
})
export class ModelModule { }
```

The code in the listing defines a TypeScript class called ModelModule. The class has no properties or methods and is just a vehicle for the *decorator*, which is used to provide Angular with metadata about a building block, performing a role loosely similar to a C# attribute. This is the decorator:

```
...
@NgModule({
    providers: [Repository]
})
...
```

The decorator begins with the @ character followed by the decorator type. The type of this decorator is NgModule, which tells Angular that the ModelModule class is an Angular feature module. The decorator type is followed by the (and { characters and one or more configuration properties, followed by the } and) characters. There is only one configuration property in this decorator, called providers, which is used to register classes for dependency injection.

Just like ASP.NET Core MVC, Angular allows application building blocks to specify the services they need using their class constructors. These dependencies are resolved using dependency injection, using the classes that are registered in Angular module's providers properties. In this case, other parts of the application will be able to receive a Repository object using dependency injection.

```
...
@NgModule({
    providers: [Repository]
})
...
```

Decorators must be imported like any other TypeScript type, which is why the listing includes this statement:

```
...
import { NgModule } from "@angular/core";
...
```

The @angular/core JavaScript module includes the types that provide the most important Angular features, including decorators.

Configuring the Angular Root Module

The *root module* is a special Angular module that configures the entire application. One of its roles is to give Angular details of the feature modules that the application requires. To edit the root module, open the app. module.ts file in the ClientApp/src/app folder and make the changes shown in Listing 4-21.

Listing 4-21. Configuring the Root Module in the app.module.ts File in the ClientApp/src/app Folder

```
import { BrowserModule } from '@angular/platform-browser';
import { NgModule } from '@angular/core';
import { AppRoutingModule } from './app-routing.module';
import { AppComponent } from './app.component';
import { ModelModule } from "./models/model.module";

@NgModule({
  declarations: [AppComponent],
  imports: [BrowserModule, AppRoutingModule, ModelModule],
  providers: [],
  bootstrap: [AppComponent]
})
export class AppModule { }
```

The root module is defined by applying the @NgModule decorator to a class, called AppModule by convention, and provides the configuration of the application using four properties, which are described in Table 4-3.

Table 4-3. *The Angular Module Configuration Properties*

Name	Description
imports	This property is used to specify the Angular modules that the application requires. The BrowserModule and AppRoutingModule modules provide core Angular functionality. The ModelModule is the custom feature module that contains the data model for the example application.
providers	This property is used to specify services for the dependency injection feature. This property is empty in the root module because the only service currently in the Angular application is defined within the model feature module.
declarations	This property is used to provide Angular with a list of the building blocks used in the application. For the root module, this property specifies AppComponent, which is the only building block in the application at the moment.
bootstrap	This property specifies the root component for the application, which will be used to start the application. For the example application, this property is set to AppComponent, which is the only component in the Angular application at present.

Displaying the Data

The basic plumbing for the Angular data model is complete. There is a repository that has been configured for use with the Angular dependency injection feature. The repository will ultimately use data obtained from ASP. NET Core MVC using HTTP requests, but, for now, the repository creates its data by instantiating a TypeScript model class, which corresponds to a counterpart on the server side that has been defined using C#.

The next step is to use the repository to get the data and display it to the user. In an Angular application, the key building block is a *component*, which provides the logic and data required to display HTML content to the user. In loose terms, an Angular component is equivalent to an ASP.NET Core MVC controller, while an Angular component's template is equivalent to a Razor view. The key difference is that the MVC controllers and views are used to generate a response to an HTTP request, after which they have finished their job, but an Angular component and its template have an ongoing responsibility to manage the HTML displayed to the user and respond to user interaction and changes to the data model.

You will learn more about how components work in later examples. For the moment all I am going to do is update the existing component in the application, which was created during the project setup so that it declares a dependency on the Repository class and provides its template with the data it contains. Edit the app.component.ts file in the ClientApp/src/app folder and make the changes shown in Listing 4-22.

Listing 4-22. Working with the Repository in the app.component.ts File in the ClientApp/src/app Folder

```
import { Component } from '@angular/core';
import { Repository } from "./models/repository";
import { Product } from "./models/product.model";

@Component({
  selector: 'app-root',
  templateUrl: './app.component.html',
  styleUrls: ['./app.component.css']
})
export class AppComponent {

    constructor(private repo: Repository) { }

    get product(): Product {
        return this.repo.product;
    }
}
```

The app.component.ts file defines a class called AppComponent. You can tell that this is a component because it has been decorated with the @Component decorator, which provides Angular with the configuration settings that are required to make the component work, as described in Table 4-4.

Table 4-4. *The Component Configuration Properties*

Name	Description
selector	This property is used to specify the HTML element that the component will be responsible for managing. For this component, the selector property tells Angular that the component will manage the app-root element that can be found in the HTML file in the ClientApp/src/app folder.
templateUrl	This property is used to specify the component's template, which is the HTML content that will be displayed to the user.
styleUrls	This property is used to specify one or more CSS stylesheets that will be applied to the component's template content. I do not use this feature in this book and rely on the Bootstrap CSS framework for styling all of the content in the examples.

The goal is to provide the component's template with access to the data in the repository so that it can be displayed to the user, which is achieved by making two additions to the AppComponent class.

The first addition is a constructor. The constructor has a Repository parameter called repo, which is how dependencies are declared in an Angular application. The parameter tells Angular that the AppComponent class needs a Repository object and provides it when a new AppComponent object is created. The private keyword has been applied to the repo parameter, which means that a property with the same name will be defined and assigned the value of the constructor parameter; the repo parameter can be accessed only within the AppComponent class.

■ **Tip** You must register classes as services using the providers property of an Angular module before they can be used for dependency injection. The Repository class was registered as a service in Listing 4-20.

The second addition in Listing 4-22 is a read-only property called product that returns the value of the Repository object's product property. Notice that the this keyword is used to access the repo property, like this:

```
...
return this.repo.product;
...
```

The this keyword must be used to access TypeScript instance methods and properties. If you forget to use this, which is easy to do if you are used to the way that C# works, then you will see an error telling you that the compiler cannot find name <name>.

To display the data to the user, replace the contents of the app.component.html file with the elements shown in Listing 4-23.

Listing 4-23. The Contents of the app.component.html File in the ClientApp/src/app Folder

```
<div class="p-2">
  <table class="table table-sm">
    <tr><th>Name</th><td>{{product?.name}}</td></tr>
    <tr><th>Category</th><td>{{product?.category}}</td></tr>
    <tr><th>Description</th><td>{{product?.description}}</td></tr>
    <tr><th>Price</th><td>{{product?.price}}</td></tr>
  </table>
</div>
```

This fragment of HTML relies on an important Angular feature: the *data binding*. Data bindings incorporate data provided by a controller into a template and, in this case, display the value of properties defined by the Product object returned by the component's product property.

I have used the most basic type of data binding in this example, which is denoted by the double brace characters ({{ and }}). I demonstrate more complex bindings in later chapters, but this type of binding evaluates its contents to produce a value that is inserted into an element. This binding, for example, displays the value of the name property of the Product object provided by the component:

```
...
<tr><th>Name</th><td>{{product?.name}}</td></tr>
...
```

The question mark is the TypeScript safe navigation operator, and it has the same purpose as the C# equivalent, preventing the name property from being read when the product property has not been initialized.

Save the changes to the TypeScript files, and the browser will reload to display the static JSON data, along with the table that has been generated dynamically from the data, as shown in Figure 4-4.

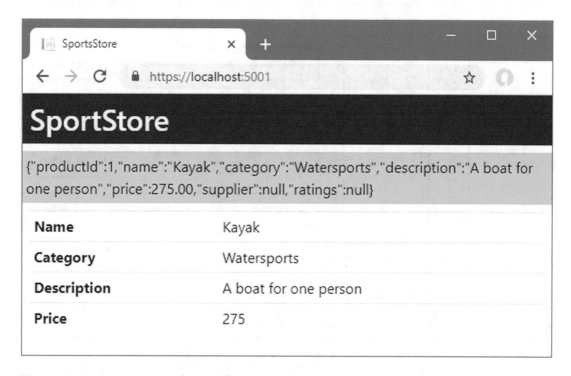

Figure 4-4. *Generating content dynamically using Angular*

Reviewing the Application Structure

The example application is taking shape. There is a data model in both the MVC and Angular parts of the project, although they are not yet connected. I remove the test data in the next chapter and replace it with an HTTP web service, but working with local data is a good way to make sure that each part of the application is working. Before moving on, it is worth taking a moment to consider the emerging structure of the SportsStore application and understand how the different features on the server and client sides have started to mesh together.

Reviewing the ASP.NET Core MVC Application Structure

When you use the browser to navigate to https://localhost:5001, the HTTP request is passed to the MVC framework, which routes it to the Index action method defined by the Home controller. This action method uses Entity Framework Core to read the Product data from the SQL Server LocalDB database using Entity Framework Core and uses it as the view model data for the Index.cshtml view.

Razor processes the Index.cshtml view and generates an HTML response for the browser that includes a JSON representation of the Product data from the database, script elements that load the JavaScript bundle files required by the Angular application, and an app-root element to which the Angular application will be applied. The browser follows the URLs in the script element to load the JavaScript files, which are forwarded to the Angular development server. The JavaScript bundle files are generated automatically from the TypeScript files by the Angular development tools. Figure 4-5 shows the structure of the application.

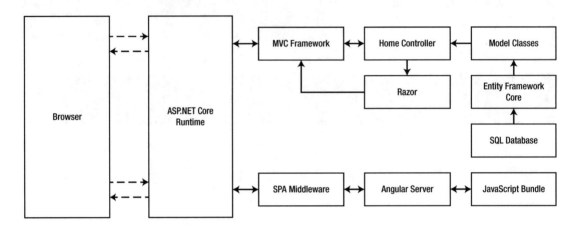

Figure 4-5. *The structure of the ASP.NET Core MVC part of the application*

The ASP.NET Core MVC part of the application is made up of familiar building blocks. A controller, action method, and Razor view work together with Entity Framework Core to generate responses for HTTP requests. The responses sent to the client contain HTML elements that provide everything the browser needs to run the Angular application, except the JavaScript bundle files. The requests for these files are forwarded to the Angular server, which provides the browser with the application's code.

The ASP.NET Core MVC part of the application has no special knowledge about the Angular application. It responds to HTTP requests by rendering views, just like any other MVC application.

Reviewing the Angular Application Structure

The Angular part of the application is rudimentary, but there is enough functionality to generate a table that displays data to the user. The HTML document received by the browser contains the app-root element into which the dynamic content produced by the Angular application is inserted and script elements for the JavaScript bundle files that contain the Angular framework and the custom application and data model classes. The HTML document also contains the JSON data used to populate the data table, although I will replace this with a web service, which is a more conventional method for delivering data to an Angular application. Figure 4-6 shows the structure of the Angular part of the application.

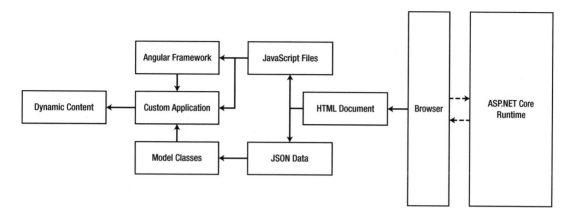

Figure 4-6. *The structure of the Angular part of the application*

The Angular part of the application has no insights into ASP.NET Core MVC. It does not know (or care) how the data is stored or represented by ASP.NET Core and Entity Framework Core. The two parts of the application work together to deliver the application and the data to the user, but they exist and run independently.

Summary

In this chapter, I started to add functionality to both the ASP.NET Core MVC and Angular parts of the application, focusing on the data model. I created a SQL Server database, populated it with seed data, and created C# data model classes so that the MVC controller and view were able to send JSON data to the application.

On the client side, I defined the TypeScript classes that represent the application data, along with a repository that is available to the rest of the Angular application through the dependency injection feature. I finished this chapter by updating the default Angular component and template to generate a table to display the JSON data. In the next chapter, I start the process of creating an HTTP web service and integrating it into the application.

CHAPTER 5

■ ■ ■

Creating a Web Service

In this chapter, I start the process of creating an HTTP web service that the Angular application can use to request data from ASP.NET Core MVC. This process is not as simple as it might be because of the way that different features interact, both in the MVC and Angular parts of the application, but the result is a solid foundation for accessing data that I build on in Chapter 6 to support a complete set of data operations.

My focus in this chapter is starting the web service and checking that each new addition works as expected. This means that I request and display data in the Angular part of the project without building the final features that will present the data to the user. In this chapter, I write just enough code to get the data and display it in the browser. Table 5-1 puts the chapter in context.

■ **Note** The web service features in this chapter and Chapter 6 are unsecured, which means that any client can access the data and make changes. I show you how to add authentication and authorization to the web service in Chapter 12 and how to protect your application from cross-site request forgery (CSRF) attacks in Chapter 13.

Table 5-1. *Putting a Web Service in Context*

Question	Answer
What is it?	An HTTP web service provides Angular with access to the data managed by ASP.NET Core MVC and Entity Framework Core.
Why is it useful?	A web service exposes the data in a format that is easily requested and consumed by the Angular application.
How is it used?	The Angular application sends HTTP requests to the ASP.NET Core MVC application and receives data responses in return. The responses typically represent data using the JSON data format, which is easy to create in ASP.NET Core MVC and easy to consume in Angular.
Are there any pitfalls or limitations?	Getting Entity Framework Core, ASP.NET Core MVC, and Angular to work together requires careful development and testing to get the right results. There are pitfalls for the unwary, especially when handling GET requests.
Are there any alternatives?	You don't have to use a web service, but doing so makes it difficult to send data between the Angular and ASP.NET Core MVC parts of the project.

© Adam Freeman 2019
A. Freeman, *Essential Angular for ASP.NET Core MVC 3*,
https://doi.org/10.1007/978-1-4842-5284-0_5

Preparing for This Chapter

This chapter uses the SportsStore project that I created in Chapter 3 and modified in Chapter 4. No changes are required to prepare for this chapter. Open a new PowerShell command prompt, navigate to the SportsStore/ServerApp folder, and run the command shown in Listing 5-1 to remove the database.

Listing 5-1. Resetting the Database

```
dotnet ef database drop --force
```

Run the command shown in Listing 5-2 in the ServerApp folder to start the Angular development server and the ASP.NET Core runtime.

Listing 5-2. Starting the Development Tools

```
dotnet watch run
```

After the initial startup sequence, open a new browser window and navigate to https://localhost:5001; you will see the content shown in Figure 5-1.

■ **Tip** You can download the complete project for every chapter without charge from the source code repository, https://github.com/Apress/esntl-angular-for-asp.net-core-mvc-3. Run npm install in the ClientApp folder to install the packages required for Angular development and then start the development tools as instructed.

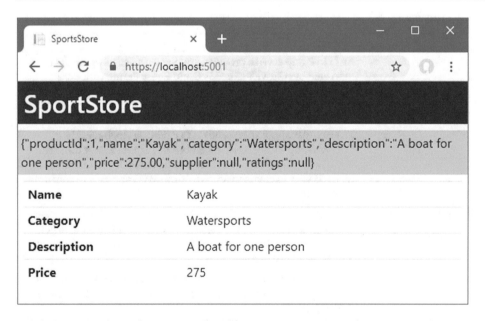

Figure 5-1. *Running the example application*

Introducing a Web Service

The Angular part of the project is getting data from the MVC framework through the HTML response sent by the Home controller. This was helpful when putting the plumbing for the data model into place because it lets me focus on the model classes and repository, but including JSON data in HTML documents has some shortcomings. The first, and most obvious, is that users don't typically expect to have to see the application data alongside the regular content. The second shortcoming is that getting that data into Angular required using the browser's DOM API, which restricts the application to running in browsers, even though Angular has the potential to work on a range of platforms.

To improve the application, I am going to introduce an HTTP web service. In this arrangement, the Angular application will start without any data and then make an HTTP request back to the ASP.NET Core MVC application. The HTTP request will be made asynchronously and is known as an *Ajax request*, which used to stand for Asynchronous JavaScript and XML but which has become a term in its own right, not least because XML is rarely used and has been largely replaced by JSON as the standard data format for HTTP data requests. In the sections that follow, I show you how to plan and create a web service using ASP.NET Core MVC and integrate it into Angular.

Understanding RESTful Web Services

There are no hard-and-fast rules for how web services should work, but the most common approach is to adopt the Representational State Transfer (REST) pattern. There is no authoritative specification for REST, and there is no consensus about what constitutes a RESTful web service, but there are some common themes that are widely used for web services.

The lack of a detailed specification leads to endless disagreement about what REST means and how RESTful web service should be created, all of which can be safely ignored just as long as the web services you create work for your projects.

The core premise of REST—and the only aspect for which there is broad agreement—is that a web service defines an API through a combination of the URLs and HTTP methods such as GET and POST, which are also known as the *HTTP verbs*. The verb specifies the type of operation, while the URL specifies the data object or objects that the operation applies to.

As an example, here is a URL that might identify a Product object in the example application:

```
/api/products/1
```

This URL may identify the Product object that has a value of 1 for its ProductId property. The URL identifies the Product, but it is the HTTP method that specifies what should be done with it. Table 5-2 lists the HTTP methods that are commonly used in web services and the operations they conventionally represent.

Table 5-2. *HTTP Methods and Operations*

HTTP Method	Description
GET	This method is used to retrieve one or more data objects.
POST	This method is used to create a new object.
PUT	This method is used to update an existing object.
PATCH	This method is used to update part of an existing object.
DELETE	This method is used to delete an object.

It is a good idea to give some thought to the API you are going to present through your web service before starting development. It is worth paying special attention to the operations that can be performed with the GET method because they can be more complicated than you might expect.

UNDERSTANDING GRPC

ASP.NET Core 3 has introduced support for gRPC, which is an alternative to conventional HTTP web services that addresses some of the inefficiencies and inconsistencies that arise in conventional HTTP web services. At the time of writing, gRPC isn't suitable for web applications because it requires HTTP/2, which isn't widely supported by browsers.

For the foreseeable future, regular web services are the best way to deliver data to web applications.

Creating the Web Service

Once you become experienced in designing and implementing web services, you will reach the point where you can write all of the C# code first and only then add the code to the Angular application to consume the services you have created. For this book, I am going to take a more iterative approach, integrating each new feature in both parts of the application to emphasize how the different parts of the application work together and to check that everything functions as expected. In the sections that follow, I set up a web service and integrate it into the Angular application.

Creating the Web Service Controller

ASP.NET Core MVC makes it easy to add web services to an application using standard controller features. Create a C# class file called ProductValuesController.cs in the ServerApp/Controllers folder and add the code shown in Listing 5-3.

Listing 5-3. The Contents of the ProductValuesController.cs File in the ServerApp/Controllers Folder

```
using Microsoft.AspNetCore.Mvc;
using ServerApp.Models;

namespace ServerApp.Controllers {

    [Route("api/products")]
    [ApiController]
    public class ProductValuesController : Controller {
        private DataContext context;

        public ProductValuesController(DataContext ctx) {
            context = ctx;
        }

        [HttpGet("{id}")]
        public Product GetProduct(long id) {
            return context.Products.Find(id);
        }
    }
}
```

This is a regular ASP.NET Core MVC controller, derived from the `Controller` class in the `Microsoft.AspNetCore.Mvc` namespace, just like the existing `Home` controller that has been rendering Razor views for the examples so far. The name of this new controller class is `ProductValuesController`, which follows the convention of including the word `Values` in the name to indicate that the controller will return data to its clients rather than HTML.

Another convention for web service controllers is to create a separate part of the routing schema dedicated to handling requests for data. The most common way to do this is to create URLs for web services that start with `/api`, followed by the plural form of the name of the data type that the web service handles. For a web service handling `Product` objects, this means that HTTP requests should be sent to the `/api/products` URL, which I have configured using the `Route` attribute, like this:

```
...
[Route("api/products")]
...
```

The `ApiController` attribute tells the MVC framework to configure the controller only for web service requests. This is an optional attribute that sets up some useful behaviors, especially for dealing with parameter data.

The only action defined by the controller is the `GetProduct` method, which returns a single `Product` object based on its primary key, which is the value assigned to its `ProductId` property. The action method is decorated with the `HttpGet` method, which will allow ASP.NET Core MVC to use this action to handle HTTP GET requests.

```
...
[HttpGet("{id}")]
public Product GetProduct(long id) {
...
```

The attribute's argument extends the URL schema defined by the `Route` attribute so that the `GetProduct` method can be reached by a URL in the form `/api/products/{id}`.

Action methods for web services can return .NET objects, which are automatically serialized and sent to the client. The result of the `GetProduct` method is a `Product` object.

Testing the Web Service

To test the new web service, stop the ASP.NET Core runtime using Control+C and start it again by running the command in Listing 5-4 in the `ServerApp` folder.

Listing 5-4. Starting the ASP.NET Core Runtime

```
dotnet watch run
```

Once the runtime has started, open a web browser and request the URL shown in Listing 5-5.

Listing 5-5. Testing the Web Service

```
https://localhost:5001/api/products/1
```

The HTTP request from the browser is received by ASP.NET Core, which passes it on to the MVC framework. The combination of the Route and HttpGet attributes indicates that the GetProduct method in the ProductValues controller can handle the request. The GetProduct method uses the Find method defined by the database context's DbSet property to retrieve a Product object from the database and return it as the result. The Product object is serialized and returned to the browser, which will display the data it receives.

```
{
  "productId":1,"name":"Kayak","category":"Watersports",
  "description":"A boat for one person","price":275.00,
  "supplier":null,"ratings":null
}
```

The Product object is serialized into JSON, which is the standard data format used for web services. Each property is automatically converted from the C# capitalization convention (ProductId) to the JavaScript convention (productId).

Notice that the navigation properties for the related Supplier and Rating objects have been included in the JSON data but set to null. This is because Entity Framework Core doesn't load related data unless specifically asked to, and no objects were assigned to the Supplier and Ratings products of the Product objects that Entity Framework Core created when it read the data from the database. I show you how to work with related data later in this chapter.

Using Swagger to Explore the Web Service

Sending HTTP GET requests is a simple way to test a web service, but it can be harder to test other request types. A more elegant way to test the web service is to use Swagger, which is also known as OpenAPI. Swagger provides a standard description of a web service that can be displayed by a range of add-on packages. For this book, I am going to use the Swashbuckle package, which is one of the most established Swagger implementations available for ASP.NET Core MVC. To install the package, open a new command prompt, navigate to the SportsStore/ServerApp folder, and run the command shown in Listing 5-6.

Listing 5-6. Installing the Swashbuckle Package

```
dotnet add package Swashbuckle.AspNetCore --version 5.0.0-rc2
```

To enable and configure Swashbuckle, add the statements shown in Listing 5-7 to the Startup class.

Listing 5-7. Configuring the Package in the Startup.cs File in the ServerApp Folder

```
using System;
using System.Collections.Generic;
using System.Linq;
using System.Threading.Tasks;
using Microsoft.AspNetCore.Builder;
using Microsoft.AspNetCore.Hosting;
using Microsoft.AspNetCore.HttpsPolicy;
using Microsoft.Extensions.Configuration;
using Microsoft.Extensions.DependencyInjection;
using Microsoft.Extensions.Hosting;
```

```
using Microsoft.AspNetCore.SpaServices.AngularCli;
using ServerApp.Models;
using Microsoft.EntityFrameworkCore;
using Microsoft.OpenApi.Models;

namespace ServerApp {
    public class Startup {

        public Startup(IConfiguration configuration) {
            Configuration = configuration;
        }

        public IConfiguration Configuration { get; }

        public void ConfigureServices(IServiceCollection services) {

            string connectionString =
                Configuration["ConnectionStrings:DefaultConnection"];
            services.AddDbContext<DataContext>(options =>
                options.UseSqlServer(connectionString));

            services.AddControllersWithViews();
            services.AddRazorPages();

            services.AddSwaggerGen(options => {
                options.SwaggerDoc("v1",
                    new OpenApiInfo { Title = "SportsStore API", Version = "v1" });
            });
        }

        public void Configure(IApplicationBuilder app, IWebHostEnvironment env,
                IServiceProvider services) {

            if (env.IsDevelopment()) {
                app.UseDeveloperExceptionPage();
            } else {
                app.UseExceptionHandler("/Home/Error");
                app.UseHsts();
            }

            app.UseHttpsRedirection();
            app.UseStaticFiles();
            app.UseRouting();
            app.UseAuthorization();

            app.UseEndpoints(endpoints => {
                endpoints.MapControllerRoute(
                    name: "default",
                    pattern: "{controller=Home}/{action=Index}/{id?}");
                endpoints.MapRazorPages();
            });
```

```
app.UseSwagger();
app.UseSwaggerUI(options => {
    options.SwaggerEndpoint("/swagger/v1/swagger.json",
        "SportsStore API");
});

app.UseSpa(spa => {
    string strategy = Configuration
        .GetValue<string>("DevTools:ConnectionStrategy");
    if (strategy == "proxy") {
        spa.UseProxyToSpaDevelopmentServer("http://127.0.0.1:4200");
    } else if (strategy == "managed") {
        spa.Options.SourcePath = "../ClientApp";
        spa.UseAngularCliServer("start");
    }
});

SeedData.SeedDatabase(services.GetRequiredService<DataContext>());
        }
    }
}
```

There are two parts to the configuration changes. The first is to generate a description of the web service. Save the changes to the Startup class, open a new browser window, and request the https://localhost:5001/swagger/v1/swagger.json URL. The response is a JSON representation of the data types and request types that the web service supports, which starts like this:

```
...
{
  "openapi": "3.0.1",
  "info": { "title": "SportsStore API", "version": "v1" },
  "paths": { "/api/products/{id}": {
      "get": {
        "tags": ["ProductValues" ],
        "parameters": [
          {
            "name": "id", "in": "path",
            "required": true,
            "schema": { "type": "integer", "format": "int64" }
          }
        ],
        "responses": {
          "200": {
            "description": "Success",
            "content": {
              "text/plain": { "schema": { "$ref": "#/components/schemas/Product" }
              },
              "application/json": {
                "schema": { "$ref": "#/components/schemas/Product" }
              },
```

```
        "text/json": { "schema": { "$ref": "#/components/schemas/Product" }
      }
    }
...
```

The description is comprehensive but difficult to make sense of. The second part of the configuration in Listing 5-7 sets up a friendlier interface. Open a new browser window and navigate to `https://localhost:5001/swagger`; you will see the interface presented by the `SwaggerUI` middleware, which shows a more easily understood representation of the web service and allows each type of request to be tested. Click the GET button, click the Try It Out button, enter **1** in the `id` text field, and click the Execute button. A GET request will be sent, and the results will be displayed in the browser window, as shown in Figure 5-2.

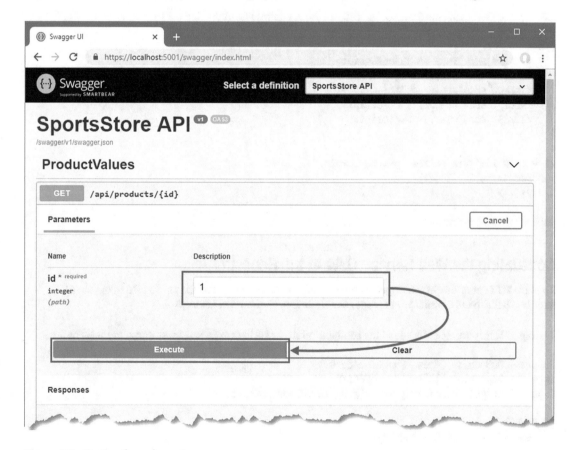

Figure 5-2. *Testing the web service*

Using the Web Service in the Angular Application

The web service doesn't do much at the moment, but there is just enough functionality to integrate it into the Angular application, which I demonstrate in the sections that follow.

Removing the Static Data from the Razor View

The first step is to remove the static data from the Razor view, which is no longer required now that the web service will provide data directly to the Angular application. Comment out the statements that generated the JSON data in the Index.cshtml view, as shown in Listing 5-8.

Listing 5-8. Removing the Static Data from the Index.cshtml File in the ServerApp/Views/Home Folder

```
@section scripts {
    <script src="runtime.js"></script>
    <script src="polyfills.js"></script>
    <script src="styles.js"></script>
    <script src="vendor.js"></script>
    <script src="main.js"></script>
}

<!-- <div id="data" class="p-1 bg-warning">
  @Json.Serialize(Model)
</div> -->

<app-root></app-root>
```

Consuming the Web Service Data in the Repository

To make HTTP requests in the Angular application, I need to import HttpClientModule in the model. module.ts file in the ClientApp/src/app/models folder, as shown in Listing 5-9.

Listing 5-9. Importing a Module in the model.module.ts File in the ClientApp/src/app/models Folder

```
import { NgModule } from "@angular/core";
import { Repository } from "./repository";
import { HttpClientModule } from '@angular/common/http';

@NgModule({
    imports: [HttpClientModule],
    providers: [Repository]
})
export class ModelModule { }
```

This module contains the Angular functionality for making HTTP requests and processing the responses. Next, update the Angular Repository class so that it gets its data from the web service and not from the static HTML element, as shown in Listing 5-10.

Listing 5-10. Getting Web Service Data in the repository.ts File in the ClientApp/src/app/models Folder

```
import { Product } from "./product.model";
import { Injectable } from "@angular/core";
import { HttpClient } from "@angular/common/http";

@Injectable()
export class Repository {
    product: Product;

    constructor(private http: HttpClient) {
        this.getProduct(1);
    }

    getProduct(id: number) {
        this.http.get<Product>("/api/products/" + id)
          .subscribe(p => this.product = p);
    }
}
```

Understanding the HttpClient Class

Support for making HTTP requests in Angular applications is provided by the HttpClient class, which is defined in the @angular/common/http module that was added to the application in Listing 5-9. The new constructor for the Repository class declares a dependency on the HttpClient class like this:

```
...
constructor(private http: HttpClient) {}
...
```

Angular will provide an HttpClient object as the constructor argument when a new Repository object is created, which will be assigned to a private instance variable called http. The HttpClient class provides methods for making HTTP requests, including the get method, which sends an HTTP GET request and which the getProduct method uses, like this:

```
...
getProduct(id: number) {
    this.http.get<Product>("/api/products/" + id)
        .subscribe(p => this.product = p);
}
...
```

The get method accepts a URL as its argument. The URL specified in the listing is a relative URL, which will be requested from the same location that the application was loaded from. This means that the request will be sent to https://localhost:5001/api/products/1, which is the same URL used to test the web service earlier in the chapter.

The data type that the web service is expected to return is specified using a generic type argument. In this case, the type argument is Product, which tells Angular that it should use the data returned by the server to create a Product object.

Understanding Observables

The result of the get method is an Observable<Product> object, which is an example of an *observable*. Observables are part of a library called Reactive Extensions, which is used by Angular to connect different parts of the application. For the most part, you don't work directly with observables in an Angular application because they are used behind the scenes, but one exception is when you need to introduce data into the application, such as from a web service.

An observable represents an item of work that will be performed asynchronously and produce a result at some point in the future, loosely equivalent to a .NET Task. The Observable<Product> result returned by the HttpClient.get method, for example, represents an asynchronous activity that will produce a Product object when it is complete.

The subscribe method is used to invoke a function when the work represented by the Observable has completed. The function receives the Observable result, which is a Product object in this case, and assigns it to the product property, like this:

```
...
getProduct(id: number) {
    this.http.get<Product>("/api/products/" + id)
        .subscribe(p => this.product = p);
}
...
```

The overall effect is that when a new instance of the Repository class is created, the constructor calls the getProduct method, which sends an HTTP request to the web service and uses the JSON data received in response to set the product property, which can be accessed by the rest of the application.

■ **Tip**   You only need to understand enough about how observables work to get data into the Angular application, but if you want to know more about the features that are available, then you can consult the Reactive Extensions project web site: https://github.com/Reactive-Extensions/RxJS.

Understanding the @Injectable Decorator

You must apply the @Injectable decorator if you are defining a class that will be instantiated using the Angular dependency injection feature and that class's constructor has its own dependencies. I didn't need to apply this decorator to the Repository class in Chapter 4 because there was no constructor, but now that there is a dependency on an HttpClient object, the @Injector decorator must be applied.

```
...
@Injectable()
export class Repository {
...
```

When you save the changes and navigate to https://localhost:5001, the Angular application will display the data, as shown in Figure 5-3.

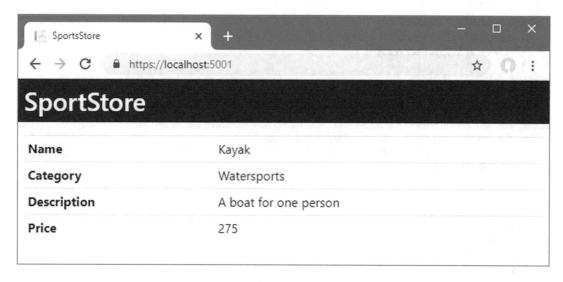

Figure 5-3. *Getting the data from the web service*

Understanding Live Data and Asynchronous Responses

The way that the Respository class handles its data may seem odd: the constructor calls the getProduct method, and the data that is received is assigned to a property.

You might be tempted to simplify the structure of the Repository class so that the HTTP request is sent when the value of the product property is read, but, if you do, you will end up sending repeated HTTP requests to the web service, all of which ask for the same data. To understand why this is the case, add the statements shown in Listing 5-11 to the Repository class.

Listing 5-11. Adding Logging Statements in the repository.ts File in the ClientApp/src/app/models Folder

```
import { Product } from "./product.model";
import { Injectable } from "@angular/core";
import { HttpClient } from "@angular/common/http";

@Injectable()
export class Repository {
    productData: Product;

    constructor(private http: HttpClient) {
        this.getProduct(1);
    }

    getProduct(id: number) {
        this.http.get<Product>("/api/products/" + id)
          .subscribe(p => {
            this.productData = p;
            console.log("Product Data Received");
          });
    }
}
```

```
get product(): Product {
    console.log("Product Data Requested");
    return this.productData;
}
}
```

The console.log statements write messages to the browser's JavaScript console, indicating when the HTTP request delivers data to the application and when Angular reads the value of the product property to get the data it needs to display in the application's data bindings.

When you save the changes, the browser will reload, and you will see a sequence of messages like this displayed in the browser JavaScript console:

```
...
Product Data Requested
Product Data Requested
Product Data Received
Product Data Requested
Product Data Requested
...
```

The data model in an Angular application is *live*, meaning that changes to the data model are automatically reflected in the content displayed to the user. This is a powerful feature, as you will see as features are added to the example in later chapters, but the process by which Angular deals with changes means that data bindings are evaluated repeatedly, which is why there are so many Product Data Requested messages shown in the JavaScript console.

If I had placed the code that leads to the HTTP request in the getter of the product property, then a new HTTP request would have been sent to the web service each time that Angular evaluated its data bindings, each of which would request the same data.

Notice also that some of the Product Data Requested messages appear before the Product Data Received message, showing that Angular starts evaluating its data bindings before the HTTP response from the web service is received and processed.

Adding Placeholder Content

A consequence of using asynchronous requests to get data is that there is a period where there is no data to display to the user. You may not have noticed this interval because the response from the web service is immediate when the browser and the ASP.NET Core runtime are on the same machine. But once an application is deployed and clients connect to the server over public networks, the effect can be obvious to the user. To simulate a substantial delay, add the statement shown in Listing 5-12 to the web service controller to introduce a five-second delay to handling data requests.

Listing 5-12. Adding a Delay in the ProductValuesController.cs File in the ServerApp/Controllers Folder

```
using Microsoft.AspNetCore.Mvc;
using ServerApp.Models;

namespace ServerApp.Controllers {

    [Route("api/products")]
    [ApiController]
```

```
public class ProductValuesController : Controller {
    private DataContext context;

    public ProductValuesController(DataContext ctx) {
        context = ctx;
    }

    [HttpGet("{id}")]
    public Product GetProduct(long id) {
        System.Threading.Thread.Sleep(5000);
        return context.Products.Find(id);
    }
}
}
```

Save the changes, let the ASP.NET Core runtime restart, and use the browser to navigate to https://localhost:5001. Once the Angular application has loaded, an HTTP request will be sent to the web service to get the data that will be displayed to the user. You will see that the table is displayed without content for a few seconds and then populated, as shown in Figure 5-4.

Figure 5-4. *The effect of a delay in receiving the web service data*

The delay emphasizes the dynamic nature of data in Angular. When the HTTP request completes and the data is introduced into the application, Angular automatically updates the content it displays to the user, reflecting the change without needing any explicit instruction. But the delay in receiving the data leaves the user looking at an empty table, so it is good practice to introduce some placeholder content to display to the user while waiting for data to load. To make it obvious to the user that the application is waiting for data, make the changes to the HTML template shown in Listing 5-13.

Listing 5-13. Displaying a Placeholder in the app.component.html File in the ClientApp/src/app Folder

```
<div class="p-2">
  <table class="table table-sm">
    <tr><th>Name</th><td>{{product?.name || 'Loading Data...'}}</td></tr>
    <tr><th>Category</th><td>{{product?.category || 'Loading Data...'}}</td></tr>
    <tr><th>Description</th>
        <td>{{product?.description || 'Loading Data...'}}</td>
    </tr>
```

```
    <tr><th>Price</th><td>{{product?.price  || 'Loading Data...'}}</td></tr>
  </table>
</div>
```

The expressions in data bindings, which appear between the {{ and }} characters, are fragments of JavaScript code that are evaluated to produce the content that will be presented to the user. This listing uses the JavaScript logical OR operator (||) in a way that is loosely equivalent to the C# null coalescing operator, like this:

```
...
<td>{{product?.name || 'Loading Data...'}}</td>
...
```

This effect is to display the value of the name property if the product property has been assigned and the Loading Data message when it hasn't. The product property is assigned only when the HTTP request has completed, which has the effect of displaying the loading message until the data is available, as shown in Figure 5-5.

Figure 5-5. *Displaying a loading message*

Loading Related Data

To avoid loading data that may not be needed, Entity Framework Core doesn't load related data unless specifically instructed to do so. To include the Supplier and Rating objects that are associated with a Product object, change the query performed by the web service controller, as shown in Listing 5-14.

Listing 5-14. Query for Data in the ProductValuesController.cs File in the ServerApp/Controllers Folder

```
using Microsoft.AspNetCore.Mvc;
using ServerApp.Models;
using Microsoft.EntityFrameworkCore;
using System.Linq;

namespace ServerApp.Controllers {

    [Route("api/products")]
    [ApiController]
    public class ProductValuesController : Controller {
        private DataContext context;
```

```
public ProductValuesController(DataContext ctx) {
    context = ctx;
}

[HttpGet("{id}")]
public Product GetProduct(long id) {
    //System.Threading.Thread.Sleep(5000);
    return context.Products
        .Include(p => p.Supplier)
        .Include(p => p.Ratings)
        .FirstOrDefault(p => p.ProductId == id);
}
}
}
```

The Include method tells Entity Framework Core to follow a navigation property and load the related data. In the listing, the Include method is used to select the Product.Supplier and Product.Ratings properties and load the related Supplier and Rating objects.

The Include method is called on the IQueryable<T> interface, which is implemented by the DbSet properties defined by the database context class. The IQueryable<T> interface is derived from IEnumerable<T> but represents a database query that will be evaluated by the Entity Framework Core database provider to minimize the amount of data that will be read from the database. The Include method can be chained together to select multiple navigation properties but cannot be used with the Find method. As a consequence, selecting the Product object with the specified key must be done with the FirstOrDefault method, which selects the first object that matches the query and returns null if there are no matches in the database.

Understanding the Circular Reference Problem

The code in Listing 5-14 contains a problem that causes so much confusion that it is worth exploring in detail. Reload the browser window after saving the changes in Listing 5-14 and allowing the ASP.NET Core runtime to restart. When the Angular application sends the HTTP request, the ASP.NET Core MVC application will report the following exception:

```
...
System.InvalidOperationException: CurrentDepth (32) is equal to or larger than the maximum
allowed depth of 32. Cannot write the next JSON object or array.
   at System.Text.Json.ThrowHelper.ThrowInvalidOperationException(String message)
   at System.Text.Json.ThrowHelper.ThrowInvalidOperationException(Int32 currentDepth)
...
```

The exception is reported by the package responsible for JSON serialization in ASP.NET Core. As the serializer processes an object, it follows its properties and serializes the values it finds. If a property returns an object, then that is serialized in the same way. In this case, the serializer has reported an error when it has attempted to serialize the Product object returned by the query in the ProductValues controller and generated serialized data for 32 objects. The cause of the problem is a circular reference between objects, and the serializer doesn't keep track of objects that it has already processed.

■ **Tip** Earlier versions of ASP.NET Core MVC used a different JSON serializer that detected circular references and threw a different exception. The result was the same, but you may be familiar with a different error message when encountering this issue.

Looking at the code in Listing 5-14, you might struggle to see why using the Include method has created a circular reference. The problem is caused by a well-intentioned Entity Framework Core feature that attempts to minimize the amount of data read from the database but that causes problems in ASP.NET Core MVC applications.

When Entity Framework Core creates objects, it populates navigation properties with objects that have already been created by the same database context. This can be a useful feature in some kinds of applications, such as desktop apps, where a database context object has a long life and is used to make many requests over time. It isn't useful for ASP.NET Core MVC applications where a new context object is created for each HTTP request.

In the example application, the only objects that Entity Framework Core creates are the ones for the current query, which starts with a Product object and includes the related Supplier and Rating objects.

It is easy for Entity Framework Core to populate the supplier navigation property on the Product object because the value of the supplierId property corresponds to that defined by the Supplier object. This is a sensible action because the query in Listing 5-14 uses the Include method to explicitly request the Supplier related to the Product object.

The problem arises when Entity Framework Core populates the products navigation property on the Supplier object, which it does using any Product objects returned by the query whose supplierId property matches that of the Supplier. For an ASP.NET Core MVC application, this is an unhelpful step to take because it creates a circular reference between the navigation properties of the Product and Supplier objects, as shown in Figure 5-6.

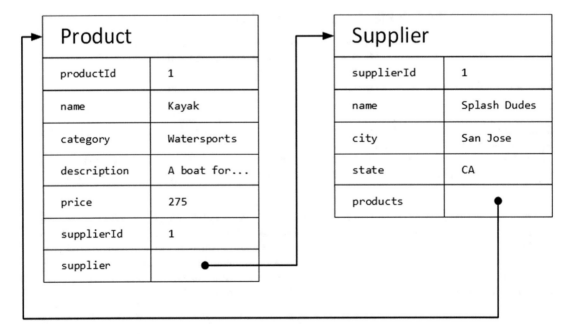

Figure 5-6. Understanding how Entity Framework Core uses objects

When the Product object is returned by the controller's action method, the JSON serializer works its way through the properties and follows the reference to the Supplier object, which has a reference back to the Product object and so on until the maximum depth is reached and the exception is thrown.

Breaking the Circular References

There is no way to stop Entity Framework Core from using existing objects for navigation properties. Preventing the problem means presenting the JSON serializer with data that doesn't contain circular references. The simplest approach is to alter the data objects before they are returned by the action method, as shown in Listing 5-15.

Listing 5-15. Fixing References in the ProductValuesController.cs File in the ServerApp/Controllers Folder

```
using Microsoft.AspNetCore.Mvc;
using ServerApp.Models;
using Microsoft.EntityFrameworkCore;
using System.Linq;

namespace ServerApp.Controllers {

    [Route("api/products")]
    [ApiController]
    public class ProductValuesController : Controller {
        private DataContext context;

        public ProductValuesController(DataContext ctx) {
            context = ctx;
        }

        [HttpGet("{id}")]
        public Product GetProduct(long id) {
            Product result = context.Products
                .Include(p => p.Supplier)
                .Include(p => p.Ratings)
                .FirstOrDefault(p => p.ProductId == id);

            if (result != null) {
                if (result.Supplier != null) {
                    result.Supplier.Products = null;
                }

                if (result.Ratings != null) {
                    foreach (Rating r in result.Ratings) {
                        r.Product = null;
                    }
                }
            }
            return result;
        }
    }
}
```

To break the relationships, the listing sets the `Supplier.Products` property to `null`. There is also a circular reference between the `Product` and `Rating` objects, so the listing enumerates the `Rating` objects returned by the `Product` object's `Ratings` property to set their `Product` property to `null`.

To see the effect, save the changes to the controller, allow the ASP.NET Core runtime to restart, and use a browser to request the `https://localhost:5001/api/products/1` URL, which will produce the following data:

```
...
{"productId":1,"name":"Kayak","category":"Watersports",
  "description":"A boat for one person","price":275.00,
    "supplier":{"supplierId":1,"name":"Splash Dudes","city":"San Jose",
        "state":"CA","products":null},
    "ratings":[{"ratingId":1,"stars":4,"product":null},
                {"ratingId":2,"stars":3,"product":null}]}
...
```

I have emphasized the properties that were set to `null` in Listing 5-15 and that ensure that the JSON serializer is able to process the `Product` object and its relayed `Supplier` and `Rating` objects.

Breaking Circular References in Additional Related Data

One of the odd effects of the way that Entity Framework Core populates navigation properties is that the related data is often incomplete. In the previous example, the only `Product` object that Entity Framework Core had to work with was the one that was being queried, which meant that all of the other `Product` objects associated with that `Supplier` were simply not available and so were not included in the result.

If you want to include additional related data, you can load it using the `ThenInclude` method, which will ensure that all the data in the database will be used and not just whatever has been loaded so far. For example, to include all the `Product` objects associated with a `Supplier`, add the `ThenInclude` method to the web service query, as shown in Listing 5-16.

Listing 5-16. Including Data in the ProductValuesController.cs File in the ServerAppControllers Folder

```
using Microsoft.AspNetCore.Mvc;
using ServerApp.Models;
using Microsoft.EntityFrameworkCore;
using System.Linq;

namespace ServerApp.Controllers {

    [Route("api/products")]
    [ApiController]
    public class ProductValuesController : Controller {
        private DataContext context;

        public ProductValuesController(DataContext ctx) {
            context = ctx;
        }

        [HttpGet("{id}")]
        public Product GetProduct(long id) {
            Product result = context.Products
```

```
            .Include(p => p.Supplier).ThenInclude(s => s.Products)
            .Include(p => p.Ratings)
            .FirstOrDefault(p => p.ProductId == id);

        if (result != null) {
            if (result.Supplier != null) {
                result.Supplier.Products = result.Supplier.Products.Select(p =>
                    new Product {
                        ProductId = p.ProductId,
                        Name = p.Name,
                        Category = p.Category,
                        Description = p.Description,
                        Price = p.Price,
                    });
            }

            if (result.Ratings != null) {
                foreach (Rating r in result.Ratings) {
                    r.Product = null;
                }
            }
        }
        return result;
    }
}
```

This example requires a different technique for dealing with circular references. Rather than set a property to null, new Product objects without the circular reference to the Supplier are created using the LINQ Select method.

To understand why this is important, restart the ASP.NET Core MVC application and use a browser to navigate to the https://localhost:5001/api/products/1 URL. The JSON data returned by the web service includes the Product object, the Product object's related Supplier, and the Supplier object's related Product objects (and the Rating objects, but they are not important for this example).

```
{
  "productId":1,"name":"Kayak","category":"Watersports",
  "description":"A boat for one person","price":275.00,
  "supplier":{"supplierId":1,"name":"Splash Dudes","city":"San Jose",
  "state":"CA",
  "products":[
    { "productId":1,"name":"Kayak","category":"Watersports",
      "description":"A boat for one person", "price":275.00,
      "supplier":null,"ratings":null},
    { "productId":2,"name":"Lifejacket","category":"Watersports",
      "description":"Protective and fashionable","price":48.95,
      "supplier":null,"ratings":null}]},
  "ratings":[{"ratingId":1,"stars":4,"product":null},
            {"ratingId":2,"stars":3,"product":null}]
}
```

The highlighting shows that the same Product object appears twice in the JSON data, which is typical when the Include and ThenInclude methods are used to get data on both ends of a navigation property.

Entity Framework Core creates only one Product object for the Kayak product, and this means that setting its Supplier property to null wouldn't just break the relationship for the nested related data; it would also break the relationship between the main Product object that has been queried and its Supplier, which would exclude all the related data.

Omitting Null Properties

A consequence of using navigation properties, whether they are followed or not, is that the JSON data sent to the client contains properties whose values are null. This doesn't often cause problems, but it does consume bandwidth, and it is good practice to omit them. Add the configuration statement shown in Listing 5-17 to the Startup class to tell the JSON serializer to omit properties that are null.

Listing 5-17. Configuring the JSON Serializer in the Startup.cs File in the ServerApp Folder

```
...
public void ConfigureServices(IServiceCollection services) {

    string connectionString =
        Configuration["ConnectionStrings:DefaultConnection"];
    services.AddDbContext<DataContext>(options =>
        options.UseSqlServer(connectionString));

    services.AddControllersWithViews()
        .AddJsonOptions(opts => {
            opts.JsonSerializerOptions.IgnoreNullValues = true;
        });
    services.AddRazorPages();

    services.AddSwaggerGen(options => {
        options.SwaggerDoc("v1",
            new OpenApiInfo { Title = "SportsStore API", Version = "v1" });
    });
}
```

Let the ASP.NET Core MVC restart and use a browser to request https://localhost:5001/api/products/1; you see that the null properties are no longer included in the JSON returned by the web service, like this:

```
{
  "productId":1,"name":"Kayak","category":"Watersports",
  "description":"A boat for one person","price":275.00,
  "supplier":{
    "supplierId":1,"name":"Splash Dudes","city":"San Jose","state":"CA",
    "products":[{"productId":1,"name":"Kayak","category":"Watersports",
                "description":"A boat for one person","price":275.00},
```

```
            {"productId":2,"name":"Lifejacket","category":"Watersports",
                "description":"Protective and fashionable","price":48.95}]},
    "ratings":[{"ratingId":1,"stars":4},{"ratingId":2,"stars":3}]
}
```

Displaying Related Data

No special steps are required to display the related data in the Angular part of the project, which is handled automatically when the JSON data is processed. To display the related data, add the elements shown in Listing 5-18 to the Angular component's template.

Listing 5-18. Displaying Related Data in the app.component.html File in the ClientApp/src/app Folder

```html
<div class="p-2">
    <table class="table table-sm">
        <tr><th colspan="2" class="bg-info">Product</th></tr>
        <tr><th>Name</th><td>{{product?.name || 'Loading Data...'}}</td></tr>
        <tr><th>Category</th><td>{{product?.category || 'Loading Data...'}}</td></tr>
        <tr>
                <th>Description</th>
                <td>{{product?.description || 'Loading Data...'}}</td>
        </tr>
        <tr><th>Price</th><td>{{product?.price  || 'Loading Data...'}}</td></tr>
        <tr><th colspan="2" class="bg-info">Supplier</th></tr>
        <tr><th>Name</th><td>{{product?.supplier?.name}}</td></tr>
        <tr><th>City</th><td>{{product?.supplier?.city}}</td></tr>
        <tr><th>State</th><td>{{product?.supplier?.state}}</td></tr>
        <tr><th>Products</th><td>{{product?.supplier?.products?.length}}</td></tr>
    </table>
</div>
```

The new elements use data bindings with expressions that use the safe navigation operator to select properties from the related Supplier object. When you save the change to the template and navigate to https://localhost:5001, the browser will display the content shown in Figure 5-7. (You may have to manually reload the browser to see the changes.)

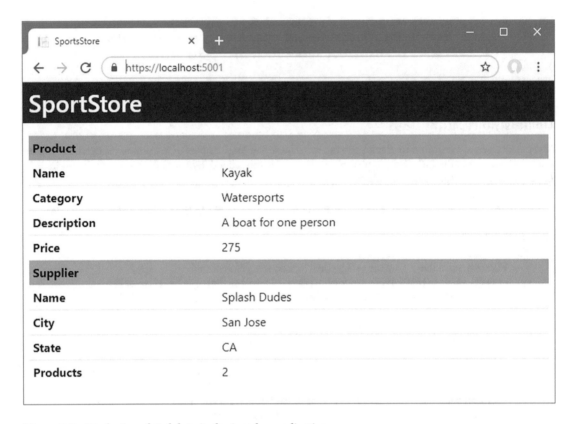

Figure 5-7. *Displaying related data in the Angular application*

Implementing the GET Method for Multiple Objects

In a RESTful web service, the HTTP GET method typically does double duty and is used to denote queries for one object as well as queries for multiple objects, with the request URL being used to specify the purpose of the query. In this section, I demonstrate how to support queries for multiple objects and how to display the data in an Angular application. The result will be to expand the API provided by the web service, as shown in Table 5-3.

Table 5-3. *The Web Service API with GET for Multiple Objects*

Method	URL	Description
GET	/api/products/<id>	Retrieves a single Product object
GET	/api/products	Retrieves multiple Product objects

Implementing the Web Service Action Method

It took a long time to explain how to implement the GET method for single objects because of the complexities of serializing related data. But once you understand how to deal with circular references, the process for dealing with multiple objects is simpler. To add support for querying for multiple objects, add the action method shown in Listing 5-19 to the ProductValues controller.

Listing 5-19. Adding an Action in the ProductValuesController.cs File in the ServerApp/Controllers Folder

```
using Microsoft.AspNetCore.Mvc;
using ServerApp.Models;
using Microsoft.EntityFrameworkCore;
using System.Linq;
using System.Collections.Generic;

namespace ServerApp.Controllers {

    [Route("api/products")]
    [ApiController]
    public class ProductValuesController : Controller {
        private DataContext context;

        public ProductValuesController(DataContext ctx) {
            context = ctx;
        }

        [HttpGet("{id}")]
        public Product GetProduct(long id) {
            Product result = context.Products
                .Include(p => p.Supplier).ThenInclude(s => s.Products)
                .Include(p => p.Ratings)
                .FirstOrDefault(p => p.ProductId == id);

            if (result != null) {
                if (result.Supplier != null) {
                    result.Supplier.Products = result.Supplier.Products.Select(p =>
                        new Product {
                            ProductId = p.ProductId,
                            Name = p.Name,
                            Category = p.Category,
                            Description = p.Description,
                            Price = p.Price,
                        });
                }

                if (result.Ratings != null) {
                    foreach (Rating r in result.Ratings) {
                        r.Product = null;
                    }
                }
            }
```

```
            return result;
        }

        [HttpGet]
        public IEnumerable<Product> GetProducts(bool related = false) {
            IQueryable<Product> query = context.Products;
            if (related) {
                query = query.Include(p => p.Supplier).Include(p => p.Ratings);
                List<Product> data = query.ToList();
                data.ForEach(p => {
                    if (p.Supplier != null) {
                        p.Supplier.Products = null;
                    }
                    if (p.Ratings != null) {
                        p.Ratings.ForEach(r => r.Product = null);
                    }
                });
                return data;
            } else {
                return query;
            }
        }
    }
}
```

The GetProducts method is decorated with the HttpGet attribute, which tells the MVC framework that it can be used to handle GET requests. The action method defines a related parameter that is used to indicate whether related data should be included in the response; the parameter defaults to false.

Within the action method, if the related data is not required, then the result is the IQueryable<Product> object obtained by reading the database context object's Product property. If related data is required, then I use the ToList method to force the execution of the query and create a List<Product> on which I can use the ForEach method to break the circular references before the data is serialized.

To test the new action, restart the ASP.NET Core MVC application and use a browser to request https://localhost:5001/api/products. This URL requests the products without related data and will produce a result with data like this (I have shown just two Product objects for brevity):

```
...
[{"productId":1,"name":"Kayak","category":"Watersports",
  "description":"A boat for one person","price":275.00},
 {"productId":2,"name":"Lifejacket","category":"Watersports",
  "description":"Protective and fashionable","price":48.95},
...
```

To include related data in the request, use a browser to request https://localhost:5001/api/products?related=true, which will produce data like this:

```
...
[{"productId":1,"name":"Kayak","category":"Watersports",
  "description":"A boat for one person","price":275.00,
  "supplier":{"supplierId":1,"name":"Splash Dudes",
            "city":"San Jose","state":"CA"},
```

```
  "ratings":[{"ratingId":1,"stars":4},{"ratingId":2,"stars":3}]},
{"productId":2,"name":"Lifejacket","category":"Watersports",
  "description":"Protective and fashionable","price":48.95,
  "supplier":{"supplierId":1,"name":"Splash Dudes",
  "city":"San Jose","state":"CA"},
  "ratings":[{"ratingId":3,"stars":2},{"ratingId":4,"stars":5}]},
...
```

■ **Tip** You can extend the ASP.NET Core MVC routing configuration so that you don't have to use query parameters in your URLs. I have not done so because I add some additional features to this action method that would make for a complicated routing configuration. I tend to use query parameters for simplicity in my own projects, especially when the Angular application is the only client of the web service.

Querying Multiple Objects in the Angular Application

The process of sending a request from the Angular application to get multiple objects follows the same pattern as for a single object. The first step is to define a new method in the Repository class to send the request and process the response, as shown in Listing 5-20. I have also taken the opportunity to simplify the Repository class to remove the console.log statements and the property getter I used earlier.

Listing 5-20. Adding a Method in the repository.ts File in the ClientApp/src/app/model Folder

```
import { Product } from "./product.model";
import { Injectable } from "@angular/core";
import { HttpClient } from "@angular/common/http";

const productsUrl = "/api/products";

@Injectable()
export class Repository {
    product: Product;
    products: Product[];

    constructor(private http: HttpClient) {
        this.getProducts(true);
    }

    getProduct(id: number) {
        this.http.get<Product>(`${productsUrl}/${id}`)
            .subscribe(p => this.product = p);
    }

    getProducts(related = false) {
        this.http.get<Product[]>(`${productsUrl}?related=${related}`)
            .subscribe(prods => this.products = prods);
    }
}
```

The getProducts method sends an HTTP request to the /api/products URL, which gets all of the Product data that is available. The method defines an optional parameter that is used to set the related query string parameter in the request URL to specify whether the response should include related data.

Updating the Component

The next step is to update the component so that it defines a property that the template can use to access the product data, as shown in Listing 5-21. Templates can only access data through their component, which is why these mapping properties are useful. I could have accessed the repo product directly in the template and obtained the products, but the result is a more complex template, and I find the mapping properties to be a preferable approach.

Listing 5-21. Defining a Property in the app.component.ts File in the ClientApp/src/app Folder

```
import { Component } from '@angular/core';
import { Repository } from "./models/repository";
import { Product } from "./models/product.model";

@Component({
    selector: 'app-root',
    templateUrl: './app.component.html',
    styleUrls: ['./app.component.css']
})
export class AppComponent {

    constructor(private repo: Repository) { }

    get product(): Product {
        return this.repo.product;
    }

    get products(): Product[] {
        return this.repo.products;
    }
}
```

Updating the Component's Template

To display the data obtained from the web service, replace the contents of the app.component.html file with those shown in Listing 5-22.

Listing 5-22. Displaying Data in the app.component.html File in the ClientApp/src/app Folder

```
<div class="p-2">
    <table class="table table-sm table-striped">
        <tbody>
            <tr>
                <th>Name</th><th>Category</th><th>Price</th>
                <th>Supplier</th><th>Ratings</th>
            </tr>
```

```
            <tr *ngFor="let product of products">
                <td>{{product.name}}</td>
                <td>{{product.category}}</td>
                <td>{{product.price}}</td>
                <td>{{product.supplier?.name || 'None'}}</td>
                <td>{{product.ratings?.length || 0}}</td>
            </tr>
        </tbody>
    </table>
</div>
```

The important part of the template is an Angular *directive*, which is used to change the HTML that is presented to the user based on the data in the model. Here is the element that this directive has been applied to, with the directive itself shown in bold:

```
...
<tr *ngFor="let product of products">
...
```

This is an example of a structural directive, which alters the structure or content of an HTML element. In this case, the directive, which is called ngFor, is responsible for repeating the HTML element it is applied to for each object in an array. The directive's expression specifies the array and tells Angular to assign each object in the collection returned by the component's products property in turn to a variable called product that can be used in data bindings in the element's content, like this:

```
...
<td>{{product.name}}</td>
...
```

The effect is similar to a Razor @foreach expression, but the ngFor expression is applied as an attribute of the HTML element that will be duplicated.

Some of the data binding expressions in Listing 5-22 use the || operator, which produces useful results even when there is no data available to display. This does loosely the same thing as the C# ?? operator but has some wrinkles, as explained in the "Understanding JavaScript Truth" sidebar.

UNDERSTANDING JAVASCRIPT TRUTH

JavaScript has an unusual approach to evaluating expressions as true or false, which you need to understand to create effective Angular data-binding expressions. All expressions can be *truthy* or *falsy*, which means they will evaluate as either true or false. This can lead to some unexpected results. The following expressions are always falsy and will always evaluate to false in an Angular data binding expression:

- The false (boolean) value

- The 0 (number) value

- The empty string ("")

- null

- undefined

- NaN (a special number value)

All other values are truthy and will evaluate to true, which can be confusing. For example, "false" (a string whose content is the word false) is truthy.

In Listing 5-22, one of the data binding expressions relies on the fact that the product.supplier.name property may be null, which will be falsy, in which case placeholder content should be shown.

```
...
<td>{{product.supplier?.name || 'None'}}</td>
...
```

The || operator performs an OR comparison to coalesce null values. If the value of the product. supplier.name value isn't falsy, then it will be used as the result of the data binding expression. If it is falsy, typically because it is null, then the None string literal value will be used as the expression result.

The result is that a tr element is created, along with the td elements it contains, for each of the objects obtained from the web service, which you can see by navigating to https://localhost:5001, as shown in Figure 5-8.

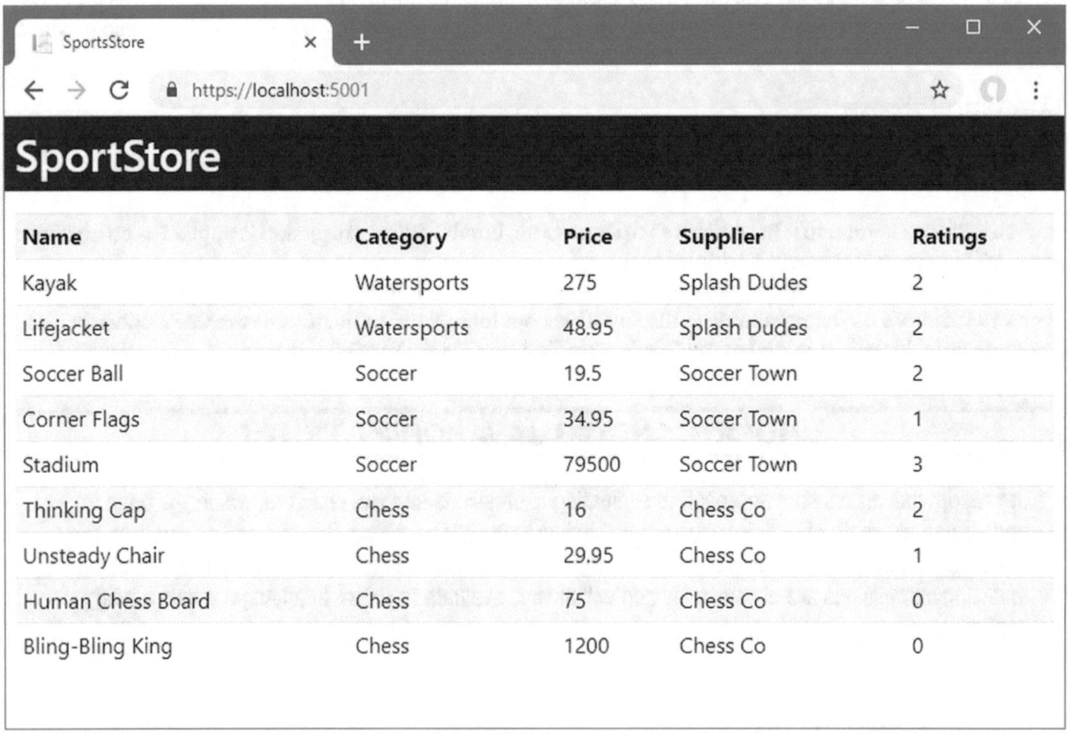

Figure 5-8. *Displaying multiple objects*

Filtering the Data

The web service responds to GET requests sent to the /api/products URL by sending all of the Product objects that have been stored in the database. That's fine for an example application that has nine items, but most real applications store enough data that it doesn't make sense to send it all to the client for every request.

To finish this chapter, I am going to add support for allowing the client to provide the web service with instructions for filtering the data it receives. I am going to define three different ways for the client to select Product objects: filtering by category, searching by name, or searching by description. The client will be able to specify a category by adding a query string to the base URL, like this:

/api/products**?category=soccer**

This URL will return only those Product objects whose Category property equals soccer.

For the second filter, the client will be able to perform a search by adding a search term to the query string, like this:

/api/products?category=soccer**&search=stadium**

This URL will return only those Product objects that are in the soccer category and whose Name or Description property contains stadium.

Applying Filtering in the Web Service

Not all of the filters will be applied to every request, which means that the web service must carefully build up the query for Entity Framework Core to execute. To add support for the three data filters, add the code shown in Listing 5-23 to the GetProducts method in the ProductValues controller.

Listing 5-23. Filtering Data in the ProductValuesController.cs File in the ServerApp/Controllers Folder

```
...
[HttpGet]
public IEnumerable<Product> GetProducts(string category, string search,
        bool related = false) {
    IQueryable<Product> query = context.Products;

    if (!string.IsNullOrWhiteSpace(category)) {
        string catLower = category.ToLower();
        query = query.Where(p => p.Category.ToLower().Contains(catLower));
    }
    if (!string.IsNullOrWhiteSpace(search)) {
        string searchLower = search.ToLower();
        query = query.Where(p => p.Name.ToLower().Contains(searchLower)
            || p.Description.ToLower().Contains(searchLower));
    }

    if (related) {
        query = query.Include(p => p.Supplier).Include(p => p.Ratings);
        List<Product> data = query.ToList();
```

```
        data.ForEach(p => {
            if (p.Supplier != null) {
                p.Supplier.Products = null;
            }
            if (p.Ratings != null) {
                p.Ratings.ForEach(r => r.Product = null);
            }
        });
        return data;
    } else {
        return query;
    }
}
...
```

The IQueryable<T> interface is especially useful for filtering data because it allows the query to be constructed step-by-step and will be executed only when the results are enumerated. In the listing, I inspect the parameter values and use them to build up the query using LINQ.

To test the ability to filter data, restart the ASP.NET Core MVC application and use a browser to request https://localhost:5001/api/products?category=soccer. This URL requests the Product objects in the Soccer category and will produce the following result:

```
...
[{"productId":3,"name":"Soccer Ball","category":"Soccer",
  "description":"FIFA-approved size and weight","price":19.50},
{ "productId":4,"name":"Corner Flags","category":"Soccer",
  "description":"Give your pitch a professional touch","price":34.95},
{ "productId":5,"name":"Stadium","category":"Soccer",
  "description":"Flat-packed 35,000-seat stadium","price":79500.00}]
...
```

You can also search for data. Use the browser to request https://localhost:5001/api/products?category=soccer&search=flat, and you will receive the products in the Soccer category whose name or description contains flat. There is only one matching product.

```
...
[{"productId":5,"name":"Stadium","category":"Soccer",
  "description":"Flat-packed 35,000-seat stadium","price":79500.00}]
...
```

Applying Filtering in the Angular Application

A corresponding set of changes are required in the Angular repository to support data filtering. First, add a TypeScript file called configClasses.repository.ts to the models folder and use it to define the class shown in Listing 5-24.

Listing 5-24. The Content of the configClasses.repository.ts File in the ClientApp/src/app/models Folder

```
export class Filter {
    category?: string;
    search?: string;
    related: boolean = false;

    reset() {
        this.category = this.search = null;
        this.related = false;
    }
}
```

This class will be used to specify the filtering that will be applied to product data. To update the repository to use this class and implement the filtering, make the changes shown in Listing 5-25.

Listing 5-25. Filtering Data in the repository.ts File in the ClientApp/src/app/models Folder

```
import { Product } from "./product.model";
import { Injectable } from "@angular/core";
import { HttpClient } from "@angular/common/http";
import { Filter } from "./configClasses.repository";

const productsUrl = "/api/products";

@Injectable()
export class Repository {
    product: Product;
    products: Product[];
    filter: Filter = new Filter();

    constructor(private http: HttpClient) {
        this.filter.category = "soccer";
        this.filter.related = true;
        this.getProducts();
    }

    getProduct(id: number) {
        this.http.get<Product>(`${productsUrl}/${id}`)
            .subscribe(p => this.product = p);
    }

    getProducts() {
        let url = `${productsUrl}?related=${this.filter.related}`;
        if (this.filter.category) {
            url += `&category=${this.filter.category}`;
        }
        if (this.filter.search) {
            url += `&search=${this.filter.search}`;
        }
```

```
        this.http.get<Product[]>(url).subscribe(prods => this.products = prods);
    }
}
```

The Repository class defines a `filter` property that provides access to a `Filter` object and that is used in the `getProducts` method to compose the URL for the HTTP request. For testing, the constructor has also been updated to use the filter so that the web service will be asked to select the `Product` objects that are in the `Soccer` category. When you save the changes to the TypeScript file and navigate to `https://localhost:5001`, the browser will show the filtered data, as illustrated in Figure 5-9.

Name	Category	Price	Supplier	Ratings
Soccer Ball	Soccer	19.5	Soccer Town	2
Corner Flags	Soccer	34.95	Soccer Town	1
Stadium	Soccer	79500	Soccer Town	3

Figure 5-9. Filtering data in the Angular application

Understanding the Structure of the Web Service

The web service isn't complete, but its basic structure has been defined, allowing the client to send a request for single and multiple product objects. The structure of the MVC part of the application will be familiar to most ASP.NET Core MVC developers because it follows the approach used for round-trip applications, with the exception that the action methods return data that is serialized into JSON, as shown in Figure 5-10.

Figure 5-10. The structure of the ASP.NET Core MVC web service

The Angular application is more complex than the ASP.NET Core MVC application. In particular, the way that Angular responds immediately to changes in the data that is displayed through its data bindings means that there is a separation between the methods by which data is requested and the properties that are used to make that data available to the rest of the application, as shown in Figure 5-11.

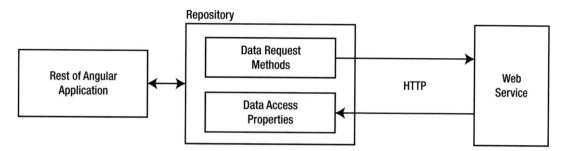

Figure 5-11. *The structure of the repository in the Angular application*

This indirection will start to make sense in Chapter 7, where I explain how the structure of an Angular application allows features to cooperate with one another and how the data model becomes the heart of the application.

Summary

In this chapter, I replaced the static JSON data in the Razor view with an HTTP web service that follows the basic principles of REST. I created a new MVC controller for handling data requests and explained the interactions between related data and the JSON serializer. I created a repository in the Angular application and used it to demonstrate how Angular provides support for making asynchronous HTTP requests and explained how the responses are representing using observables. In the next chapter, I continue to work on the web service providing the features that are required to create, modify, and delete data objects.

CHAPTER 6

Completing the Web Service

In Chapter 5, I created the web service and added support for handling HTTP GET requests. In this chapter, I complete the implementation by adding support for the POST, PUT, PATCH, and DELETE methods, which allows the client to create, update, and delete data.

The web service features in this chapter are unsecured, which means that any client can access the data and make changes. I show you how to add authentication and authorization to the web service in Chapter 12.

Preparing for This Chapter

This chapter uses the SportsStore project that I created in Chapter 3 and modified in the chapters since. Open a new PowerShell command prompt, navigate to the `SportsStore/ServerApp` folder, and run the command shown in Listing 6-1 to start the ASP.NET Core runtime and the Angular development tools. If you need to reset the database, run the `dotnet ef database drop --force` command in the `ServerApp` folder before running the command in Listing 6-1.

Listing 6-1. Starting the Development Tools

```
dotnet watch run
```

Open a new browser window and navigate to `https://localhost:5001`; you will see the content shown in Figure 6-1.

■ **Tip**   You can download the complete project for every chapter without charge from the source code repository, `https://github.com/Apress/esntl-angular-for-asp.net-core-mvc-3`. Run `npm install` in the `ClientApp` folder to install the packages required for Angular development and then start the development tools as instructed.

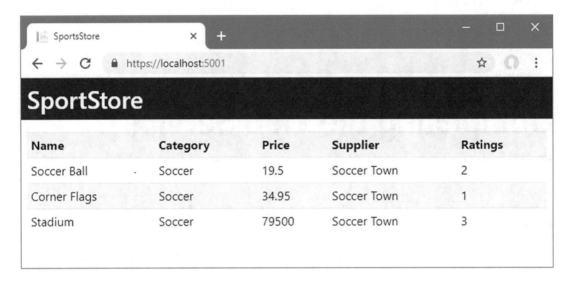

Figure 6-1. *Running the example application*

Implementing the POST Method

The HTTP POST method is used to store new data objects in the database. Chapter 5 showed that getting Angular, ASP.NET Core MVC, and Entity Framework Core to work together requires some care, especially when it comes to related data, and implementing POST requests has its share of pitfalls. In the sections that follow, I show you how to add support for creating data while avoiding the most common problems.

Understanding the API Enhancements

Adding support for the POST method will expand the API provided by the web service, as shown in Table 6-1.

Table 6-1. *The Web Service API with POST Support for Storing New Objects*

Method	URL	Description
GET	/api/products/<id>	Retrieves a single Product object
GET	/api/products	Retrieves multiple Product objects
POST	/api/products	Stores a new Product object
POST	/api/suppliers	Stores a new Product object

The additions in Table 6-1 provide URLs for both the Product and Supplier classes in the data model. It can be tempting to allow clients to supply new related data in a request so that a Product object is received along with a new Supplier object and both are stored in the database. This is an approach that works well at first but quickly becomes complex and ultimately produces a client that requires deep knowledge of how the web service works internally, and a web service that requires constant tinkering responds badly to changes elsewhere in the application.

A more robust approach is to handle the creation of each type of data separately. This requires more work initially but produces a better result that more easily responds to changes.

AVOIDING KEY VALUES IN URLS

Notice that the URLs in Table 6-1 do not include an ID, such as /api/products/100, for example, to tell the web service to store a new Product object with a ProductId value of 100, mirroring the URL format for querying single objects with the GET method.

Storing application data as relational data creates restrictions on the values that can be used for a Product object's ProductId property because the value is used as a primary key in the database. ProductId values must be numeric, and they must not exceed the maximum value of the SQL data type that has been assigned to store ProductId values in the database table. Most critically, values must be unique. The client must know about all of these restrictions and be updated if they change, and the activity of clients must be coordinated in some way to avoid selecting duplicate values. All of this is possible, but it is much simpler to leave the database server to generate the values automatically when it stores data, which is how Entity Framework Core configures the database by default. This ensures that only valid values will be used and avoids any need to deal with multiple clients trying to store data using the same key at the same time.

Creating the Data Binding Classes

I am going to define a separate class that will be used by the MVC model binder to get details for the Product object that should be created from a POST request. Create a Models/BindingTargets folder and add to it a C# class file called ProductData.cs with the code shown in Listing 6-2.

Listing 6-2. The Contents of the ProductData.cs File in the ServerApp/Models/BindingTargets Folder

```
using System.ComponentModel.DataAnnotations;

namespace ServerApp.Models.BindingTargets {

    public class ProductData {

        [Required]
        public string Name { get; set; }

        [Required]
        public string Category { get; set; }

        [Required]
        public string Description { get; set; }

        [Range(1, int.MaxValue, ErrorMessage = "Price must be at least 1")]
        public decimal Price { get; set; }

        public long Supplier { get; set; }
```

```
    public Product Product => new Product {
        Name = Name, Category = Category,
        Description = Description, Price = Price,
        Supplier = Supplier == 0 ? null : new Supplier { SupplierId = Supplier }
    };
}
}
```

In the next section, I will use the ProductData class as the parameter for the action method that will receive POST requests. This will allow me to receive JSON data from the client that looks like this:

```
{ "name": "X-Ray Scuba Mask", "category": "Watersports",
  "description": "See what the fish are hiding", "price": 49.99,
  "supplier": 1 }
```

The Product property defined by the ProductData class creates a Product object and a Supplier object that I will use to perform the database operation, as shown in the next section.

USING DATA BINDING CLASSES

You don't have to use a separate class like the one in Listing 6-2, but there comes a point where using the original data model class, which is Product in this case, becomes too complex to manage.

I could get the data I require using the Product class, but it would be complicated trying to get the right result from the MVC model binder while avoiding problems with Entity Framework Core and the JSON serializer.

To start, I don't want the client to provide a ProductId value or to include a Supplier object as related data, preferring instead to receive details of the Supplier that a Product should be associated with by specifying its key. To allow the client to send the data as I want, I would have to add a property to the Product class. But this isn't straightforward; I can't add a property called Supplier, for example, because it is already used as a navigation property. I could add a property called SupplierId, but that would be detected by Entity Framework Core and used to update the database schema to prevent Product objects from being stored without a relationship with a Supplier. And the value of this property would be set by Entity Framework Core when it reads data and then included in the responses for GET requests by the JSON serializer. If I use a different property name, Entity Framework Core will add a new column to the Products table in the database.

The validation attributes used by the MVC model binder, which includes the Required and Range attributes used in Listing 6-2, are also used by Entity Framework Core to apply constraints to the database schema. Applying these attributes to the Product class will change the schema the next time that a database migration is created and applied, causing unexpected effects and even data loss in some cases.

All of these problems can be solved using attributes. The JSON serializer supports an attribute that tells it to ignore a property. Entity Framework Core supports an attribute that tells it not to create a new column in the database table. The MVC framework supports attributes that prevent the model binder from populating a property from the request data and for specifying a buddy class to provide the validation metadata so that it isn't detected by Entity Framework Core.

But the result is that the Product class is festooned in attributes that are trying to manage the interactions of the serializer, the model binder, and the data layer. As the application gets more complex, managing the model classes and their behavior gets difficult. Adding a class specifically for data binding lets me partition up the functionality so that I can get the data I want from the client in a reasonable format without worrying about causing unexpected side effects.

A similar class is required to handle data when creating Supplier objects. Add a C# class file called SupplierData.cs to the Models/BindingTargets folder with the statements shown in Listing 6-3.

Listing 6-3. The Contents of the SupplierData.cs File in the ServerApp/Models/BindingTargets Folder

```
using System.ComponentModel.DataAnnotations;

namespace ServerApp.Models.BindingTargets {

    public class SupplierData {

        [Required]
        public string Name { get; set; }

        [Required]
        public string City { get; set; }

        [Required]
        [StringLength(2, MinimumLength = 2)]
        public string State { get; set; }

        public Supplier Supplier => new Supplier {
            Name = Name, City = City, State = State
        };
    }
}
```

Implementing the Web Service Action Methods

The implementation of the action method to handle POST requests is simpler than the GET actions from Chapter 5. To add support for creating objects, add the method shown in Listing 6-4 to the ProductValues controller.

Listing 6-4. Adding an Action in the ProductValuesController.cs File in the ServerApp/Controllers Folder

```
using Microsoft.AspNetCore.Mvc;
using ServerApp.Models;
using Microsoft.EntityFrameworkCore;
using System.Linq;
using System.Collections.Generic;
using ServerApp.Models.BindingTargets;
```

```
namespace ServerApp.Controllers {

    [Route("api/products")]
    [ApiController]
    public class ProductValuesController : Controller {
        private DataContext context;

        public ProductValuesController(DataContext ctx) {
            context = ctx;
        }

        // ..other action methods omitted for brevity...

        [HttpPost]
        public IActionResult CreateProduct([FromBody] ProductData pdata) {
            if (ModelState.IsValid) {
                Product p = pdata.Product;
                if (p.Supplier != null && p.Supplier.SupplierId != 0) {
                    context.Attach(p.Supplier);
                }
                context.Add(p);
                context.SaveChanges();
                return Ok(p.ProductId);
            } else {
                return BadRequest(ModelState);
            }
        }
    }
}
```

The CreateProduct method has a ProductData parameter, which will be populated by the MVC model binder with the data sent by the client. This parameter is decorated with the FromBody attribute, which tells the model binder to get data values from the request body, without which the JSON data sent by the client will be ignored.

The result of the CreateProduct method is an IActionResult method, which provides flexibility for returning an error if the data sent by the client doesn't pass the validation checks applied using the Required and Range attributes. If the data doesn't perform validation, then a 400 Bad Request response is sent to the client, along with JSON data containing a list of the validation errors.

```
...
return BadRequest(ModelState);
...
```

If the data does pass validation, then I get the Product object by calling the ProductData.Product property. To work out whether the Product will be related to a Supplier, I check the value of the Product.Suppler. SupplierId property and, if it is defined and isn't zero, I call the database context object's Attach method, like this:

```
...
if (p.Supplier != null && p.Supplier.SupplierId != 0) {
    context.Attach(p.Supplier);
}
...
```

By default, Entity Framework Core will create related objects automatically, which means that it will try to create a new `Supplier` object as well as a new `Product` object. This is because Entity Framework Core doesn't know anything about the `Product` and `Supplier` objects and just assumes that both are new and must be stored in the database. This presents a problem because the database won't allow `Supplier` objects to be created when the `SupplierId` value is specified because there should already be a `Supplier` with that `SupplierId` value. The `Attach` method makes Entity Framework Core aware of an object and tells it that only subsequent changes to it should be written to the database.

■ **Tip** Notice that the `Supplier` object has only a `SupplierId` value. Since the purpose of the POST operation is to create a `Product` object, only the data required for the new row in the `Products` table is required. That means that Entity Framework Core only needs to know the value of the `SupplierId` property so that it can create the foreign key relationship and will ignore the rest of the `Supplier` properties, which means that there is no need for the client to send values for those properties to the web service.

The database context's `Add` method tells Entity Framework Core that the `Product` object should be stored in the database, and the operation is performed when the `SaveChanges` method is called.

```
...
context.Add(p);
context.SaveChanges();
...
```

When the data is stored, the database will generate a value for the `ProductId` property and will automatically update the `Product` object with that value. To provide the client with the value, I pass it to the `Ok` method so that it can be included in the 200 OK response.

```
...
return Ok(p.ProductId);
...
```

Creating the Web Service Controller for Supplier Objects

The MVC framework is flexible enough to support multiple data types and URLs in a single web service controller, but defining one controller for each data type produces code that is easier to understand and manage. Add a new C# class file called `SupplierValuesController.cs` to the `ServerApp/Controllers` folder and add the code shown in Listing 6-5.

Listing 6-5. The Contents of the SupplierValuesController.cs File in the ServerApp/Controllers Folder

```
using Microsoft.AspNetCore.Mvc;
using ServerApp.Models;
using ServerApp.Models.BindingTargets;
using System.Collections.Generic;
```

```
namespace ServerApp.Controllers {

    [Route("api/suppliers")]
    public class SupplierValuesController : Controller {
        private DataContext context;

        public SupplierValuesController(DataContext ctx) {
            context = ctx;
        }

        [HttpGet]
        public IEnumerable<Supplier> GetSuppliers() {
            return context.Suppliers;
        }

        [HttpPost]
        public IActionResult CreateSupplier([FromBody]SupplierData sdata) {
            if (ModelState.IsValid) {
                Supplier s = sdata.Supplier;
                context.Add(s);
                context.SaveChanges();
                return Ok(s.SupplierId);
            } else {
                return BadRequest(ModelState);
            }
        }
    }
}
```

This controller uses the Route attribute so that it can handle requests sent to the /api/suppliers URL. There are action methods for GET and POST requests, following the same pattern for querying and creating Supplier objects.

Stop the ASP.NET Core runtime using Control+C and use the command prompt to run the command shown in Listing 6-6 in the ServerApp folder to restart the runtime and incorporate the new class in the build process.

Listing 6-6. Starting the ASP.NET Core Runtime

```
dotnet watch run
```

Once the ASP.NET Core runtime has restarted, you can explore the changes to the web service by navigating to https://localhost:5001/swagger, which displays the tools installed and configured in Chapter 5. The new controller and actions are automatically detected and are shown in the list of operations in Figure 6-2.

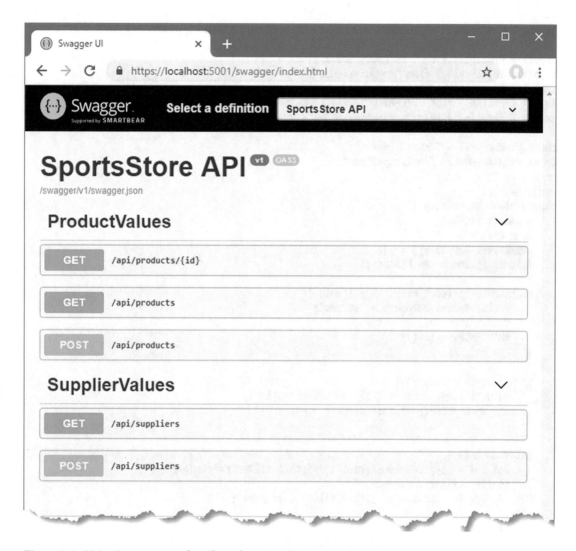

Figure 6-2. *Using Swagger to explore the web service changes*

Clicking the GET and POST buttons allows HTTP requests to be sent to the server. Sending the POST requests can be awkward because the data structures required are complex, but Swagger is a good way to check that the changes you make to your web services have the effect you intended.

Creating Data Objects in the Angular Application

To add support for creating new Product and Supplier objects in the Angular application, add the method shown in Listing 6-7 to the Repository class so that it can send POST requests to the web service.

Listing 6-7. Sending POST Requests in the repository.ts File in the ClientApp/src/app Folder

```
import { Product } from "./product.model";
import { Injectable } from "@angular/core";
import { HttpClient } from "@angular/common/http";
import { Filter } from "./configClasses.repository";
import { Supplier } from "./supplier.model";

const productsUrl = "/api/products";
const suppliersUrl = "/api/suppliers";

@Injectable()
export class Repository {
    product: Product;
    products: Product[];
    suppliers: Supplier[] = [];
    filter: Filter = new Filter();

    constructor(private http: HttpClient) {
        //this.filter.category = "soccer";
        this.filter.related = true;
        this.getProducts();
    }

    getProduct(id: number) {
        this.http.get<Product>(`${productsUrl}/${id}`)
            .subscribe(p => this.product = p);
    }

    getProducts() {
        let url = `${productsUrl}?related=${this.filter.related}`;
        if (this.filter.category) {
            url += `&category=${this.filter.category}`;
        }
        if (this.filter.search) {
            url += `&search=${this.filter.search}`;
        }
        this.http.get<Product[]>(url).subscribe(prods => this.products = prods);
    }

    getSuppliers() {
      this.http.get<Supplier[]>(suppliersUrl)
          .subscribe(sups => this.suppliers = sups);
    }

    createProduct(prod: Product) {
        let data = {
            name: prod.name, category: prod.category,
            description: prod.description, price: prod.price,
            supplier: prod.supplier ? prod.supplier.supplierId : 0
        };
```

```
        this.http.post<number>(productsUrl, data)
            .subscribe(id => {
                prod.productId = id;
                this.products.push(prod);
            });
    }

    createProductAndSupplier(prod: Product, supp: Supplier) {
        let data = {
            name: supp.name, city: supp.city, state: supp.state
        };

        this.http.post<number>(suppliersUrl, data)
          .subscribe(id => {
                supp.supplierId = id;
                prod.supplier = supp;
                this.suppliers.push(supp);
                if (prod != null) {
                    this.createProduct(prod);
                }
          });
    }
}
```

The createProduct method accepts a Product object, uses it to create an object in the format that the web service requires, and sends it using a POST request by calling the HttpClient.post method.

The generic type argument is used to specify the data type returned by the POST request, which is number because the server sends back the ID assigned to the new object. The request result is received through the subscribe method on the Observable returned from the post method and used to update the Product object, which is then added to the local array of Product objects.

The createProductAndSupplier method builds on the createProduct method to create a Supplier and then create a related Product.

Adding Support for Creating an Object in the Component

The next step is to define methods in the Angular component that can be called when the user wants to create a new product or supplier, as shown in Listing 6-8.

Listing 6-8. Adding Methods in the app.component.ts File in the ClientApp/src/app Folder

```
import { Component } from '@angular/core';
import { Repository } from "./models/repository";
import { Product } from "./models/product.model";
import { Supplier } from "./models/supplier.model";

@Component({
    selector: 'app-root',
    templateUrl: './app.component.html',
    styleUrls: ['./app.component.css']
})
```

```
export class AppComponent {

    constructor(private repo: Repository) { }

    get product(): Product {
        return this.repo.product;
    }

    get products(): Product[] {
        return this.repo.products;
    }

    createProduct() {
        this.repo.createProduct(new Product(0, "X-Ray Scuba Mask", "Watersports",
            "See what the fish are hiding", 49.99, this.repo.products[0].supplier));
    }

    createProductAndSupplier() {
        let s = new Supplier(0, "Rocket Shoe Corp", "Boston", "MA");
        let p = new Product(0, "Rocket-Powered Shoes", "Running",
            "Set a new record", 100, s);
        this.repo.createProductAndSupplier(p, s);
    }
}
```

The createProduct method creates a new Product object and asks the repository to send it to the web service. The Supplier that will be associated with the Product is taken from the first element in the products array, just so that the web service can be tested. The createProductAndSupplier creates both Product and Supplier objects and passes them to the corresponding repository method.

Updating the Component Template

The final step is to add a new element to the HTML template in the Angular application that will allow the user to trigger the creation of a new object by calling the createProduct in the component, as shown in Listing 6-9.

Listing 6-9. Adding Elements in the app.component.html File in the ClientApp/src/app Folder

```
<div class="p-2">
  <table class="table table-sm table-striped">
      <tbody>
          <tr>
              <th>Name</th><th>Category</th><th>Price</th>
              <th>Supplier</th><th>Ratings</th>
          </tr>
          <tr *ngFor="let product of products">
              <td>{{product.name}}</td>
              <td>{{product.category}}</td>
              <td>{{product.price}}</td>
```

```
            <td>{{product.supplier?.name || 'None'}}</td>
            <td>{{product.ratings?.length || 0}}</td>
        </tr>
    </tbody>
</table>
  <button class="btn btn-primary m-1" (click)="createProduct()">
      Create Product
  </button>
  <button class="btn btn-primary m-1" (click)="createProductAndSupplier()">
      Create Product and Supplier
  </button>
</div>
```

The button elements have been configured using the Angular *event binding* feature, which responds to events generated by an HTML element by evaluating an expression. The highlighted part of this element is the event binding:

```
...
<button class="btn btn-primary m-1" (click)="createProduct()">
...
```

The parentheses (the (and) characters) denote an event binding and surround the name of the event, which is click. The click event is triggered when the user clicks the button, at which point Angular evaluates the expression and invokes the component's createProduct method, defined in Listing 6-8. Event binding expressions can only access methods and properties defined by the component. The result is that clicking the buttons will create new products.

Navigate to https://localhost:5001 and click the Create Product button, and a new item will appear in the table, associated with the existing Splash Dudes supplier. Click the Create Product And Supplier button, and a new item will appear, associated with a new Rocker Shoe Corp supplier. Figure 6-3 shows the effect of both buttons. If you click the buttons repeatedly, multiple objects will be created, but each will have different ProductId or SupplierId property value, which will be assigned by the database server.

■ **Note**   The structure of the Angular application separates the process of creating new objects from displaying them. The object that is returned by the web service is added to the data model and automatically displayed by Angular through the ngFor directive, which adds a new row to the table. You may find this approach convoluted, but it simplifies the process of creating application features because any change to the data model is automatically displayed to the user.

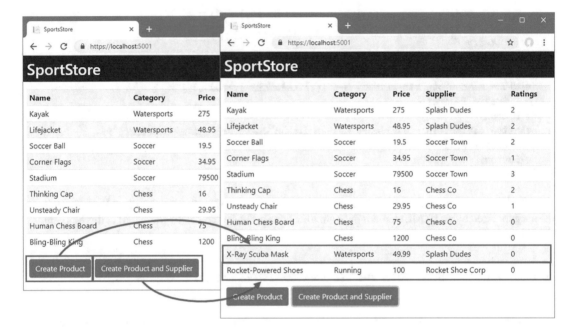

Figure 6-3. *Creating new products*

Implementing the PUT Method

The HTTP PUT method is used to replace an existing data object with a new one and requires an approach similar to the one required by the POST method in the previous section. Supporting the PUT method leads to the expansion of the web service API, as described in Table 6-2. For all of the new URLs, the object that is being updated will be identified using the id segment of the request URL.

■ **Tip** When using the PUT method, the client must provide values for all of the new object's properties. If you want to perform more selective updates, then see the section on implementing the PATCH method.

Table 6-2. *The Web Service API with PUT Support for Updating Objects*

Method	URL	Description
GET	/api/products/<id>	Retrieves a single Product object
GET	/api/products	Retrieves multiple Product objects
POST	/api/products	Stores a new Product object
POST	/api/suppliers	Stores a new Supplier object
PUT	/api/products/<id>	Replaces an existing Product object
PUT	/api/suppliers/<id>	Replaces an existing Supplier object

Implementing the Web Service Action Methods

To add support for updating Product data, add the action method shown in Listing 6-10 to the ProductValues controller.

Listing 6-10. Adding an Action in the ProductValuesController.cs File in the ServerApp/Controllers Folder

```
using Microsoft.AspNetCore.Mvc;
using ServerApp.Models;
using Microsoft.EntityFrameworkCore;
using System.Linq;
using System.Collections.Generic;
using ServerApp.Models.BindingTargets;

namespace ServerApp.Controllers {

    [Route("api/products")]
    [ApiController]
    public class ProductValuesController : Controller {
        private DataContext context;

        public ProductValuesController(DataContext ctx) {
            context = ctx;
        }

        // ...other methods omitted for brevity...

        [HttpPut("{id}")]
        public IActionResult ReplaceProduct(long id, [FromBody] ProductData pdata) {
            if (ModelState.IsValid) {
                Product p = pdata.Product;
                p.ProductId = id;
                if (p.Supplier != null && p.Supplier.SupplierId != 0) {
                    context.Attach(p.Supplier);
                }
                context.Update(p);
                context.SaveChanges();
                return Ok();
            } else {
                return BadRequest(ModelState);
            }
        }
    }
}
```

The MVC model binder will create the ProductData object from the request data, which is then used to create a Product, whose ProductId property is set from the id parameter so that Entity Framework Core knows which existing object is to be updated.

The data context object's Attach method is used to prevent Entity Framework Core from trying to store a new the Supplier object, while the Update method is used to register the Product object with Entity Framework Core so that it will replace the existing data.

The database is updated by calling the SaveChanges method, and the Ok method is used to return a 200 OK response to the client. If the request data doesn't pass validation, a 400 Bad Request response will be sent, and no update will be performed.

Similar code is required to replace Supplier objects. Add the action method shown in Listing 6-11 to the SupplierValues controller.

Listing 6-11. Adding an Action in the SupplierValuesController.cs File in the ServerApp/Controllers Folder

```
using Microsoft.AspNetCore.Mvc;
using ServerApp.Models;
using ServerApp.Models.BindingTargets;
using System.Collections.Generic;

namespace ServerApp.Controllers {

    [Route("api/suppliers")]
    [ApiController]
    public class SupplierValuesController : Controller {
        private DataContext context;

        public SupplierValuesController(DataContext ctx) {
            context = ctx;
        }

        // ...other methods omitted for brevity...

        [HttpPut("{id}")]
        public IActionResult ReplaceSupplier(long id,
                [FromBody] SupplierData sdata) {
            if (ModelState.IsValid) {
                Supplier s = sdata.Supplier;
                s.SupplierId = id;
                context.Update(s);
                context.SaveChanges();
                return Ok();
            } else {
                return BadRequest(ModelState);
            }
        }
    }
}
```

No special measures are required to replace Supplier objects, and the context object's Update method is used to tell Entity Framework Core to replace a Supplier that is obtained from the SupplierData parameter.

Replacing Products in the Angular Application

By now the process of taking advantage of new web service features will be familiar, even if not all of the details about how Angular works are clear. First, add new methods to the Angular Repository class that will accept Product or Supplier objects and send a PUT request to the web service, as shown in Listing 6-12.

Listing 6-12. Adding Methods in the repository.ts File in the ClientApp/src/app Folder

```
import { Product } from "./product.model";
import { Injectable } from "@angular/core";
import { HttpClient } from "@angular/common/http";
import { Filter } from "./configClasses.repository";
import { Supplier } from "./supplier.model";

const productsUrl = "/api/products";
const suppliersUrl = "/api/suppliers";

@Injectable()
export class Repository {
    product: Product;
    products: Product[];
    suppliers: Supplier[] = [];
    filter: Filter = new Filter();

    constructor(private http: HttpClient) {
        this.filter.related = true;
        this.getProducts();
    }

    // ...other methods omitted for brevity...

    replaceProduct(prod: Product) {
        let data = {
            name: prod.name, category: prod.category,
            description: prod.description, price: prod.price,
            supplier: prod.supplier ? prod.supplier.supplierId : 0
        };
        this.http.put(`${productsUrl}/${prod.productId}`, data)
            .subscribe(() => this.getProducts());
    }

    replaceSupplier(supp: Supplier) {
        let data = {
            name: supp.name, city: supp.city, state: supp.state
        };
        this.http.put(`${suppliersUrl}/${supp.supplierId}`, data)
            .subscribe(() => this.getProducts());
    }
}
```

I send the HTTP PUT request by calling the HttpClient.put method and use the subscribe method to refresh the Product data. This is an inefficient approach, but it demonstrates that you can handle the response from one HTTP request by starting another request.

Adding Support for Replacing Objects in the Component

The next step is to add methods to the Angular component that can be invoked using event bindings in the component's template, as shown in Listing 6-13.

Listing 6-13. Adding Methods in the app.component.ts File in the ClientApp/src/app Folder

```
import { Component } from '@angular/core';
import { Repository } from "./models/repository";
import { Product } from "./models/product.model";
import { Supplier } from "./models/supplier.model";

@Component({
    selector: 'app-root',
    templateUrl: './app.component.html',
    styleUrls: ['./app.component.css']
})
export class AppComponent {

    constructor(private repo: Repository) { }

    // ...other methods omitted for brevity...

    replaceProduct() {
        let p = this.repo.products[0];
        p.name = "Modified Product";
        p.category = "Modified Category";
        this.repo.replaceProduct(p);
    }

    replaceSupplier() {
        let s = new Supplier(3, "Modified Supplier", "New York", "NY");
        this.repo.replaceSupplier(s);
    }
}
```

The new methods, `replaceProduct` and `replaceSupplier`, create replacement objects and use the repository to send them to the web service. Add the elements shown in Listing 6-14 to the component's template so that the new component methods can be invoked.

Listing 6-14. Adding Elements in the app.component.html File in the ClientApp/src/app Folder

```
<div class="p-2">
    <table class="table table-sm table-striped">
        <tbody>
            <tr>
                <th>Name</th><th>Category</th><th>Price</th>
                <th>Supplier</th><th>Ratings</th>
            </tr>
```

```
                <tr *ngFor="let product of products">
                    <td>{{product.name}}</td>
                    <td>{{product.category}}</td>
                    <td>{{product.price}}</td>
                    <td>{{product.supplier?.name || 'None'}}</td>
                    <td>{{product.ratings?.length || 0}}</td>
                </tr>
            </tbody>
        </table>
        <button class="btn btn-primary m-1" (click)="createProduct()">
            Create Product
        </button>
        <button class="btn btn-primary m-1" (click)="createProductAndSupplier()">
            Create Product and Supplier
        </button>
        <button class="btn btn-primary m-1" (click)="replaceProduct()">
            Replace Product
        </button>
        <button class="btn btn-primary m-1" (click)="replaceSupplier()">
            Replace Supplier
        </button>
</div>
```

The new button elements use the click event binding with expressions that invoke the component methods. Allow the ASP.NET Core runtime to restart, use a browser to navigate to https://localhost:5001, and click the Replace Product and Replace Supplier buttons, the effects of which are shown in Figure 6-4.

Figure 6-4. *Replacing objects*

When you click the Replace Product button, the first Product in the table is replaced. When you click the Replace Supplier button, the Supplier related to the Chess products is replaced.

Implementing the PATCH Method

For simple data types, edit operations can be handled by replacing the existing object using the PUT method. Even if you need to change only a single property value in the Product class, for example, it isn't too much trouble to use a PUT method and include the values for all of the other Product properties, too.

But not all data types are as easy to work with, either because they define many more properties or because the client doesn't have access to all of them for security reasons. The solution is to use a PATCH request, which sends just the changes to the web service rather than a complete replacement object. Supporting the PATCH method leads to the expansion of the web service API, as described in Table 6-3.

■ **Tip** You can be selective about the data types for which you implement the PATCH method. For the SportsStore application, I am going to provide support only for Product objects, which means that changes to Supplier objects can be performed only using PUT requests.

Table 6-3. *The Web Service API with PUT Support for Updating Objects*

Method	URL	Description
GET	/api/products/<id>	Retrieves a single Product object
GET	/api/products	Retrieves multiple Product objects
POST	/api/products	Stores a new Product object
POST	/api/suppliers	Stores a new Supplier object
PUT	/api/products/<id>	Replaces an existing Product object
PUT	/api/suppliers/<id>	Replaces an existing Supplier object
PATCH	/api/products/<id>	Updates a Product object

Understanding JSON Patch

ASP.NET Core MVC has support for working with the JSON Patch standard, which allows changes to be specified in a uniform way. The JSON Patch standard allows for a complex set of changes to be described, but for the SportsStore application, I need to deal with only two kinds of change for the Product object: altering the value of a property and removing a property. Changing property values will allow the client to selectively edit existing data, while removing a property will allow the client to break the relationship between a Product and its Supplier.

I am not going to get into the details of the JSON Patch standard, which you can read at https://tools. ietf.org/html/rfc6902, but the client is going to send the web service JSON data like this in its HTTP PATCH requests:

```
[
  { "op": "replace", "path": "name", "value": "Green Kayak"},
  { "op": "replace", "path": "price", "value": 200},
  { "op": "replace", "path": "supplier", "value": null}
]
```

A JSON Patch document is expressed as an array of operations. Each operation has an op property, which specifies the type of operation, and a path property, which specifies where the operation will be applied.

For the SportsStore application—and, in fact, for most applications—only the replace operation is required, which is used to change the value of a property. This JSON Patch document sets new values for the name, price, and supplier properties. (The effect of setting the supplier property to null will be to break the relationship with a supplier.) The properties defined by the Product class not included in the JSON Patch document will not be modified.

Enhancing the Product Binding Target

I need to enhance the model binding target for Product objects to get JSON Patch documents working seamlessly with ASP.NET Core MVC and Entity Framework Core to ensure that only the values affected by a PATCH request will be modified. To that end, make the changes shown in Listing 6-15 to the ProductData class.

Listing 6-15. Adding an Object in the ProductData.cs File in the ServerApp/Models/BindingTargets Folder

```
using System.ComponentModel.DataAnnotations;

namespace ServerApp.Models.BindingTargets {

    public class ProductData {

        [Required]
        public string Name {
            get => Product.Name; set => Product.Name = value;
        }

        [Required]
        public string Category {
            get => Product.Category; set => Product.Category = value;
        }

        [Required]
        public string Description {
            get => Product.Description; set => Product.Description = value;
        }

        [Range(1, int.MaxValue, ErrorMessage = "Price must be at least 1")]
        public decimal Price {
            get => Product.Price; set => Product.Price = value;
        }

        public long? Supplier {
            get => Product.Supplier?.SupplierId ?? null;
            set {
                if (!value.HasValue) {
                    Product.Supplier = null;
                } else {
                    if (Product.Supplier == null) {
                        Product.Supplier = new Supplier();
                    }
```

```
                    Product.Supplier.SupplierId = value.Value;
                }
            }
        }

        public Product Product { get; set; } = new Product();
    }
}
```

These changes map the properties defined by the ProductData class onto a Product object. This allows me to take advantage of the Entity Framework Core change-tracking feature on the Product object, which ensures that only values that are changed by the operations in the JSON Patch document are updated in the database.

Implementing the Web Service Action Method

To add support for handling PATCH requests for Product objects, add the action method shown in Listing 6-16 to the ProductValues controller.

Listing 6-16. Adding an Action in the ProductValuesController.cs File in the ServerApp/Controllers Folder

```
using Microsoft.AspNetCore.Mvc;
using ServerApp.Models;
using Microsoft.EntityFrameworkCore;
using System.Linq;
using System.Collections.Generic;
using ServerApp.Models.BindingTargets;
using Microsoft.AspNetCore.JsonPatch;
using System.Text.Json;
using System.Reflection;
using System.ComponentModel;

namespace ServerApp.Controllers {

    [Route("api/products")]
    [ApiController]
    public class ProductValuesController : Controller {
        private DataContext context;

        public ProductValuesController(DataContext ctx) {
            context = ctx;
        }

        // ...other methods omitted for brevity...

        [HttpPatch("{id}")]
        public IActionResult UpdateProduct(long id,
                [FromBody]JsonPatchDocument<ProductData> patch) {
```

```
        Product product = context.Products
                            .Include(p => p.Supplier)
                            .First(p => p.ProductId == id);
        ProductData pdata = new ProductData { Product = product };

        patch.ApplyTo(pdata, ModelState);

        if (ModelState.IsValid && TryValidateModel(pdata)) {

            if (product.Supplier != null && product.Supplier.SupplierId != 0) {
                context.Attach(product.Supplier);
            }
            context.SaveChanges();
            return Ok();
        } else {
            return BadRequest(ModelState);
        }
    }

    }
}
```

The UpdateProduct method is decorated with the HttpPatch attribute and defines a long parameter that will identify the Product that is being modified and a JsonPatchDocument<ProductData> parameter that represents the JSON Patch document (this parameter must be decorated with the FromBody attribute). The JsonPatchDocument that describes the operation is defined in the Microsoft.AspNetCore.JsonPatch namespace.

To get the current data from the database, I retrieve the Product object identified by the id parameter and use it to create a ProductData object.

```
...
Product product = context.Products
                    .Include(p => p.Supplier)
                    .First(p => p.ProductId == id);
ProductData pdata = new ProductData { Product = product };
...
```

Entity Framework Core performs change tracking on the objects it creates, which means that only modifications to the Product objects will be written to the database. The next step is to apply the operations in the JSON Patch document to the ProductData object, which will pass on those changes to the Product object.

```
...
patch.ApplyTo(pdata, ModelState);
...
```

The ApplyTo method updates the controller's model state to record any errors in the JSON Patch document, such as an operation on a property that isn't defined by the ProductData class. Before storing the changes in the database, I check the ModelState.IsValid property and explicitly validate the ProductData object to make sure that the changes have not created an invalid outcome.

```
...
if (ModelState.IsValid && TryValidateModel(pdata)) {
...
```

If there are no validation errors, the changes are written to the database by calling the context object's SaveChanges method, and the modified Product object is returned to the client. To enable support for parsing JSON patch requests, add the statement shown in Listing 6-17 to the Startup class.

Listing 6-17. Enabling JSON Patch Parsing in the Startup.cs File in the ServerApp Folder

```
...
public void ConfigureServices(IServiceCollection services) {

    string connectionString =
        Configuration["ConnectionStrings:DefaultConnection"];
    services.AddDbContext<DataContext>(options =>
        options.UseSqlServer(connectionString));

    services.AddControllersWithViews()
        .AddJsonOptions(opts => {
            opts.JsonSerializerOptions.IgnoreNullValues = true;
    }).AddNewtonsoftJson();

    services.AddRazorPages();

    services.AddSwaggerGen(options => {
        options.SwaggerDoc("v1",
            new OpenApiInfo { Title = "SportsStore API", Version = "v1" });
    });
}
...
```

The AddNewtonsoftJson enables the JSON parser that was used in earlier versions of ASP.NET Core and which is still required for JSON PATCH support. To install the package that provides the JSON features, open a new command prompt and run the command shown in Listing 6-18 in the ServerApp folder.

Listing 6-18. Installing the JSON Package

```
dotnet add package Microsoft.AspNetCore.Mvc.NewtonsoftJson --version 3.0.0
```

Updating Objects in the Angular Application

To add support for sending PATCH requests to the web service, add the method shown in Listing 6-19 to the Repository class in the Angular application.

Listing 6-19. Adding a Method in the repository.ts File in the ClientApp/src/app/models Folder

```
import { Product } from "./product.model";
import { Injectable } from "@angular/core";
import { HttpClient } from "@angular/common/http";
```

```
import { Filter } from "./configClasses.repository";
import { Supplier } from "./supplier.model";

const productsUrl = "/api/products";
const suppliersUrl = "/api/suppliers";

@Injectable()
export class Repository {
    product: Product;
    products: Product[];
    suppliers: Supplier[] = [];
    filter: Filter = new Filter();

    constructor(private http: HttpClient) {
        this.filter.related = true;
        this.getProducts();
    }

    // ...other methods omitted for brevity...

    updateProduct(id: number, changes: Map<string, any>) {
        let patch = [];
        changes.forEach((value, key) =>
            patch.push({ op: "replace", path: key, value: value }));
        this.http.patch(`${productsUrl}/${id}`, patch)
            .subscribe(() => this.getProducts());
    }
}
```

The updateProduct method receives a number parameter that identifies the Product to be modified and a Map object whose keys are the names of the properties that have changed. A simple JSON Patch document is created using the replace operation for each of the entries in the Map, which is then sent to the web service using an HTTP PATCH request. The subscribe method is used to reload the data from the web service.

Adding Support for Updating Objects in the Component

The next step is to add a method to the Angular component that can be invoked using event bindings in the component's template and that will respond by calling the new method in the repository, as shown in Listing 6-20.

Listing 6-20. Adding a Method in the app.component.ts File in the ClientApp/src/app Folder

```
import { Component } from '@angular/core';
import { Repository } from "./models/repository";
import { Product } from "./models/product.model";
import { Supplier } from "./models/supplier.model";
```

```
@Component({
    selector: 'app-root',
    templateUrl: './app.component.html',
    styleUrls: ['./app.component.css']
})
export class AppComponent {

    constructor(private repo: Repository) { }

    // ...other methods omitted for brevity...

    updateProduct() {
        let changes = new Map<string, any>();
        changes.set("name", "Green Kayak");
        changes.set("supplier", null);
        this.repo.updateProduct(1, changes);
    }
}
```

The new method, updateproduct, changes the name property and sets the supplier property to null. Add the elements shown in Listing 6-21 to the component's template so that the new component method can be invoked.

Listing 6-21. Adding an Element in the app.component.html File in the ClientApp/src/app Folder

```
<div class="p-2">
    <table class="table table-sm table-striped">
        <tbody>
            <tr>
                <th>Name</th><th>Category</th><th>Price</th>
                <th>Supplier</th><th>Ratings</th>
            </tr>
            <tr *ngFor="let product of products">
                <td>{{product.name}}</td>
                <td>{{product.category}}</td>
                <td>{{product.price}}</td>
                <td>{{product.supplier?.name || 'None'}}</td>
                <td>{{product.ratings?.length || 0}}</td>
            </tr>
        </tbody>
    </table>
    <button class="btn btn-primary m-1" (click)="createProduct()">
        Create Product
    </button>
    <button class="btn btn-primary m-1" (click)="createProductAndSupplier()">
        Create Product and Supplier
    </button>
    <button class="btn btn-primary m-1" (click)="replaceProduct()">
        Replace Product
    </button>
```

```
<button class="btn btn-primary m-1" (click)="replaceSupplier()">
    Replace Supplier
</button>
<button class="btn btn-primary m-1" (click)="updateProduct()">
    Update Product
</button>
</div>
```

The new button element uses the click event binding with an expression that invokes the component's updateProduct method. Allow the ASP.NET Core runtime to restart, use a browser to navigate to https://localhost:5001, and click the Update Product button, the effect of which is shown in Figure 6-5.

Figure 6-5. *Updating objects*

■ **Tip**   The code for the update operation is just to check that the feature is working. If you want to repeat the update, then stop the ASP.NET Core runtime, run the dotnet ef database drop --force command in the ServerApp folder, and then start the ASP.NET Core runtime again. The database will be re-created as part of the startup sequence, and you will see the original, unmodified data in the Angular app.

Implementing the DELETE Method

The last HTTP method that the web service must support is DELETE, which is used to remove data. Supporting the DELETE method leads to the expansion of the web service API, as described in Table 6-4. The object to delete will be identified by the last segment in the request URL.

Table 6-4. *The Web Service API with PUT Support for Updating Objects*

Method	URL	Description
GET	/api/products/<id>	Retrieves a single Product object
GET	/api/products	Retrieves multiple Product objects
POST	/api/products	Stores a new Product object
POST	/api/suppliers	Stores a new Supplier object
PUT	/api/products/<id>	Replaces an existing Product object
PUT	/api/suppliers/<id>	Replaces an existing Supplier object
PATCH	/api/products/<id>	Updates a Product object
DELETE	/api/products/<id>	Deletes a Product object
DELETE	/api/suppliers/<id>	Deletes a Supplier object

Configuring the Database

Databases won't allow data to be deleted if doing so creates an inconsistency. For the SportsStore application, an inconsistency would be to delete a Product but leave its related Rating objects in the database, resulting in table rows that have a foreign key relationship to nonexistent data. Avoiding inconsistencies means either removing related data or updating it so that it refers to another object.

The easiest way to avoid inconsistencies is to have the database handle related data for you automatically. To change the configuration of the database, add the method shown in Listing 6-22 to the database context class.

Listing 6-22. Configuring Delete Operations in the DataContext.cs File in the ServerApp/Models Folder

```
using Microsoft.EntityFrameworkCore;

namespace ServerApp.Models {

    public class DataContext : DbContext {

        public DataContext(DbContextOptions<DataContext> opts)
            : base(opts) { }

        public DbSet<Product> Products { get; set; }
        public DbSet<Supplier> Suppliers { get; set; }
        public DbSet<Rating> Ratings { get; set; }

        protected override void OnModelCreating(ModelBuilder modelBuilder) {
            modelBuilder.Entity<Product>().HasMany<Rating>(p => p.Ratings)
                .WithOne(r => r.Product).OnDelete(DeleteBehavior.Cascade);
```

```
        modelBuilder.Entity<Product>().HasOne<Supplier>(p => p.Supplier)
            .WithMany(s => s.Products).OnDelete(DeleteBehavior.SetNull);
    }
  }
}
```

When you create a database migration, Entity Framework Core builds up the schema that will be applied to the database by looking at the data model classes and following a set of conventions for deciding how to store instances of those classes and how to represent relationships between them. For the most part, this process is invisible to the ASP.NET Core developer, who just uses the context class to store and retrieve data as .NET objects.

The DbContext class, from which context classes are derived, provides the OnModelCreating method, which can be used to override the conventions used to create the database schema. The OnModelCreating method receives a ModelBuilder object, which is used to configure the schema using a feature known as the Entity Framework Core *Fluent API*, through which it is possible to describe the schema programmatically.

In Listing 6-22, I used the Fluent API to describe the relationship between the Product and Rating classes, like this:

```
...
modelBuilder.Entity<Product>().HasMany<Rating>(p => p.Ratings)
    .WithOne(r => r.Product).OnDelete(DeleteBehavior.Cascade);
...
```

The Entity method tells Entity Framework Core which data model class I want to configure, and the HasMany and WithOne methods are used to describe both sides of the one-to-many relationship between the Product and Rating classes. These three methods simply describe the relationship that Entity Framework Core had already determined by following its usual conventions, and it is only the OnDelete method that introduces a new change. This method is used to specify how the database should act when an object is deleted using one of the three values of the DeleteBehavior enumeration described in Table 6-5.

Table 6-5. *The Values Defined by the DeleteBehavior Enumeration*

Name	Description
Restrict	This value prevents an object from being deleted unless there is no related data.
Cascade	This value automatically deletes related data when an object is deleted.
SetNull	This value sets the foreign key column in the related data to NULL when an object is deleted.

The Restrict value is the one that Entity Framework Core used by default when I created the database migration in Chapter 5. In Listing 6-22, I specified the Cascade behavior for the relationship between Product and Rating objects and to specify the SetNull behavior for the relationship between the Product and Supplier objects. This means that deleting Product data will automatically delete the related Rating data, while deleting a Supplier will leave the related Product data in the database but cause the Supplier property for those objects to be set to NULL.

To create a migration that will apply the new behaviors to the database schema, stop the ASP.NET Core runtime and run the command shown in Listing 6-23 in the ServerApp folder. This migration will change the delete behavior in the database and will be applied automatically when the application is started.

Listing 6-23. Creating a New Database Migration

```
dotnet ef migrations add ChangeDeleteBehavior
```

Implementing the Web Service Action Method

Performing the delete operation is simple once the database configuration has been changed. To add support for deleting Product objects, add the method shown in Listing 6-24 to the ProductValues controller.

Listing 6-24. Adding a Method in the ProductValuesController.cs File in the ServerApp/Controllers Folder

```
using Microsoft.AspNetCore.Mvc;
using ServerApp.Models;
using Microsoft.EntityFrameworkCore;
using System.Linq;
using System.Collections.Generic;
using ServerApp.Models.BindingTargets;
using Microsoft.AspNetCore.JsonPatch;
using System.Text.Json;
using System.Reflection;
using System.ComponentModel;

namespace ServerApp.Controllers {

    [Route("api/products")]
    [ApiController]
    public class ProductValuesController : Controller {
        private DataContext context;

        public ProductValuesController(DataContext ctx) {
            context = ctx;
        }

        // ...other methods omitted for brevity...

        [HttpDelete("{id}")]
        public void DeleteProduct(long id) {
            context.Products.Remove(new Product { ProductId = id });
            context.SaveChanges();
        }
    }
}
```

The DeleteProduct method creates a new Product object that has the ID value provided by the client and passes it to the database context's Remove method. This gives Entity Framework Core enough information to perform the delete operation when the SaveChanges method is called.

The same technique can be used to delete Supplier objects, even though the behavior of the database will be different. To add support for removing Supplier data from the database, add the action shown in Listing 6-25 to the SupplierValues controller.

Listing 6-25. Deleting Data in the SupplierValuesController.cs File in the ServerApp/Controllers Folder

```
using Microsoft.AspNetCore.Mvc;
using ServerApp.Models;
using ServerApp.Models.BindingTargets;
using System.Collections.Generic;
```

```
namespace ServerApp.Controllers {

    [Route("api/suppliers")]
    [ApiController]
    public class SupplierValuesController : Controller {
        private DataContext context;

        public SupplierValuesController(DataContext ctx) {
            context = ctx;
        }

        // ...other methods omitted for brevity...

        [HttpDelete("{id}")]
        public void DeleteSupplier(long id) {
            context.Remove(new Supplier { SupplierId = id });
            context.SaveChanges();
        }
    }
}
```

Deleting Objects in the Angular Application

To add support for sending DELETE requests to the web service, add the methods shown in Listing 6-26 to the Repository class in the Angular application.

Listing 6-26. Adding a Method in the repository.ts File in the ClientApp/src/app/models Folder

```
import { Product } from "./product.model";
import { Injectable } from "@angular/core";
import { HttpClient } from "@angular/common/http";
import { Filter } from "./configClasses.repository";
import { Supplier } from "./supplier.model";

const productsUrl = "/api/products";
const suppliersUrl = "/api/suppliers";

@Injectable()
export class Repository {
    product: Product;
    products: Product[];
    suppliers: Supplier[] = [];
    filter: Filter = new Filter();

    constructor(private http: HttpClient) {
        this.filter.related = true;
        this.getProducts();
    }
```

```
// ...other methods omitted for brevity...

    deleteProduct(id: number) {
        this.http.delete(`${productsUrl}/${id}`)
            .subscribe(() => this.getProducts());
    }

    deleteSupplier(id: number) {
        this.http.delete(`${suppliersUrl}/${id}`)
            .subscribe(() => {
                this.getProducts();
                this.getSuppliers();
            });
    }
}
```

The HTTP requests are sent using the HttpClient class, and both methods refresh the application's data when the request completes.

Adding Support for Deleting Objects in the Component

The next step is to add methods to the component that will act as a bridge between the buttons that the user will click and the repository, as shown in Listing 6-27.

Listing 6-27. Adding Methods in the app.component.ts File in the ClientApp/src/app Folder

```
import { Component } from '@angular/core';
import { Repository } from "./models/repository";
import { Product } from "./models/product.model";
import { Supplier } from "./models/supplier.model";

@Component({
    selector: 'app-root',
    templateUrl: './app.component.html',
    styleUrls: ['./app.component.css']
})
export class AppComponent {

    constructor(private repo: Repository) { }

    // ...other methods omitted for brevity...

    deleteProduct() {
        this.repo.deleteProduct(1);
    }

    deleteSupplier() {
        this.repo.deleteSupplier(2);
    }
}
```

To use these methods, add the elements shown in Listing 6-28 to the component's template. These button elements use the Angular event binding to invoke the deleteProduct or deleteSupplier method when they are clicked.

Listing 6-28. Adding Elements in the app.component.html File in the ClientApp/src/app Folder

```
<div class="p-2">
    <table class="table table-sm table-striped">
        <tbody>
            <tr>
                <th>Name</th><th>Category</th><th>Price</th>
                <th>Supplier</th><th>Ratings</th>
            </tr>
            <tr *ngFor="let product of products">
                <td>{{product.name}}</td>
                <td>{{product.category}}</td>
                <td>{{product.price}}</td>
                <td>{{product.supplier?.name || 'None'}}</td>
                <td>{{product.ratings?.length || 0}}</td>
            </tr>
        </tbody>
    </table>
    <button class="btn btn-primary m-1" (click)="createProduct()">
        Create Product
    </button>
    <button class="btn btn-primary m-1" (click)="createProductAndSupplier()">
        Create Product and Supplier
    </button>
    <button class="btn btn-primary m-1" (click)="replaceProduct()">
        Replace Product
    </button>
    <button class="btn btn-primary m-1" (click)="replaceSupplier()">
        Replace Supplier
    </button>
    <button class="btn btn-primary m-1" (click)="updateProduct()">
        Update Product
    </button>
    <button class="btn btn-primary m-1" (click)="deleteProduct()">
        Delete Product
    </button>
    <button class="btn btn-primary m-1" (click)="deleteSupplier()">
        Delete Supplier
    </button>
</div>
```

Use a command prompt to run the command shown in Listing 6-29 in the ServerApp folder to restart the ASP.NET Core runtime, which will apply the new migration.

Listing 6-29. Starting the ASP.NET Core Runtime

```
dotnet watch run
```

Once the runtime has started, use a browser to navigate to `https://localhost:5001`. Clicking the Delete Product button will delete the `Product` object whose `ProductId` value is 1 (the Kayak product), and clicking the Delete Supplier button will delete the `Supplier` object whose `SupplierId` value is 2 (the Soccer Town supplier), as shown in Figure 6-6.

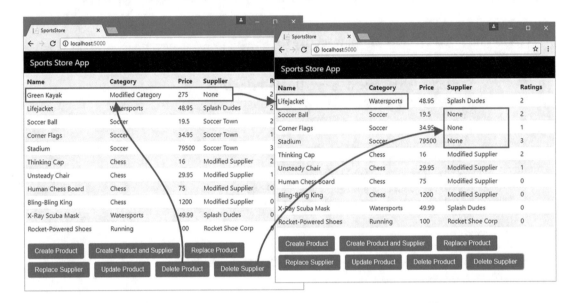

Figure 6-6. *Deleting products and suppliers*

■ **Tip** The code for the delete operation is just to check that the feature is working. If you want to repeat the deletions, then stop the ASP.NET Core MVC runtime, run the `dotnet ef database drop --force` command in the `ServerApp` folder, and then use the command in Listing 6-29 to start the ASP.NET Core runtime. The database will be re-created as the runtime starts, and the Angular client will display the original, unmodified data.

Summary

In this chapter, I showed you how to add support to the web service for the HTTP methods that allow the client to modify the application data. I showed you how to use the POST method to store new objects, the PUT and PATCH methods to replace or modify existing data, and the DELETE method to remove data. In the next chapter, I show you how to structure an Angular application, building functionality around the data model and the HTTP web service.

CHAPTER 7

■ ■ ■

Structuring an Angular Application

One of the biggest causes of confusion is the way that an Angular application is structured. The building blocks of an Angular application seem, at first glance, to be direct counterparts to those in an ASP.NET Core MVC application. But you will end up with a client-side application that doesn't work or becomes impossible to modify if you treat the Angular building blocks in the same way as their ASP.NET counterparts.

In this chapter, I explain the two key features that shape the structure of an Angular application and demonstrate how they are used to allow features to work together. The first Angular feature is the live data model, which is the beating heart of an Angular application and reflects data changes in the content that is displayed to the user. The second feature is URL routing, which is used to decide which content the user sees. The ASP.NET Core MVC part of the application also uses a data model and URL routing, but as you will see, there are important differences in both how they work and how they are used. Table 7-1 puts these features in context.

Table 7-1. *Putting Angular Application Structure in Context*

Question	Answer
What is it?	Angular applications are built by composing small features. The structure of the application lets these features work together to deliver complex functionality to the user.
Why is it useful?	These features make it easier to write and maintain Angular applications.
How is it used?	Features can cooperate using the data model or using the Angular URL routing system.
Are there any pitfalls or limitations?	The idea of collaborating using the data model can be confusing if you are new to Angular development and can require a lot of iterative development until you get everything working the way you want.
Are there any alternatives?	You can build monolithic Angular applications. These don't require as much planning or structural development but are harder to enhance and maintain.

Preparing for This Chapter

This chapter uses the SportsStore project that I created in Chapter 3 and modified in the chapters since. To remove the database so that the application will use fresh seed data, open a new command prompt, navigate to the ServerApp folder, and run the command shown in Listing 7-1.

Listing 7-1. Resetting the Database

```
dotnet ef database drop --force
```

Run the command shown in Listing 7-2 to start the ASP.NET Core runtime and the Angular development tools.

Listing 7-2. Starting the Development Tools

```
dotnet watch run
```

Open a new browser window and navigate to `https://localhost:5001`; you will see the content shown in Figure 7-1.

■ **Tip** You can download the complete project for every chapter without charge from the source code repository, `https://github.com/Apress/esntl-angular-for-asp.net-core-mvc-3`. Run `npm install` in the `ClientApp` folder to install the packages required for Angular development and then start the development tools as instructed.

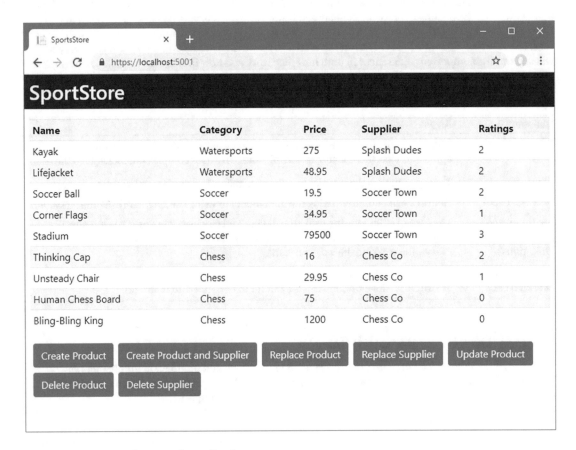

Figure 7-1. Running the example application

Using the Data Model for Component Cooperation

Components are the building blocks for an Angular application. Each component is a TypeScript class that provides the methods and properties required to support an HTML template that contains directives and data bindings. Every feature in an Angular application usually has its own component, which can be combined to create more functionality. The key to getting components to work together is the application's data model.

In Chapters 5 and 6, the Angular `Repository` class that provides access to the application data has two sets of features. The first set of `Repository` features consists of three properties that provide access to the application's data: the `product` property provides access to a single `Product` object, the `products` property provides access to a collection of `Product` objects, and the `suppliers` property provides access to a collection of `Supplier` objects. The second set of `Repository` features is the set of methods that send HTTP requests to the web service and use the results to update the `product`, `products`, and `suppliers` properties.

This two-part design makes it easier for components to cooperate without being tightly coupled, producing a flexible way to build applications. This isn't the only way that components can cooperate, but it is the simplest and takes advantage of the way that Angular automatically responds to data changes. In the sections that follow, I create some new Angular components and use them to demonstrate how they can cooperate through the data model.

Creating the Display Component

To keep this example simple, the first component will only display data from the data model, which it will obtain through the `products` property defined by the `Repository` class.

Creating the Component Class

Create a `ClientApp/src/app/structure` folder and add to it a TypeScript file called `productTable.component.ts`. The convention is to use descriptive file names in Angular projects, and this name tells you that this is the TypeScript class for a component called `productTable`, which gives you a hint of what the component is for. Once you have created the file, add the code shown in Listing 7-3.

Listing 7-3. The Contents of the productTable.component.ts File in the ClientApp/src/app/structure Folder

```
import { Component } from '@angular/core';
import { Repository } from "../models/repository";
import { Product } from "../models/product.model";

@Component({
    selector: "product-table",
    templateUrl: "./productTable.component.html"
})
export class ProductTableComponent {

    constructor(private repo: Repository) { }

    get products(): Product[] {
        return this.repo.products;
    }
}
```

Most components start like the one shown in the listing and grow as features are added to the application. Since this is the first new component that I have added to the SportsStore project, I will go through each statement and explain its purpose.

Understanding the Import Statements

The first three statements use the `import` keyword to declare dependencies on the types that the component relies on.

```
...
import { Component } from '@angular/core';
import { Repository } from "../models/repository";
import { Product } from "../models/product.model";
...
```

In any component, the `import` statements will be a mix of Angular classes, which are found in modules whose names start with `@angular`, and custom classes that are specific to the application, which are specified using a relative file path. In this case, the component depends on `Component` in the `@angular/core` module, which is used to tell Angular when a class is a component, and on the `Repository` and `Product` files, which are defined in the `models` folder.

■ **Tip** The paths used in `import` statements exclude file extensions. That means that if you want to declare a dependency on the `Product` class, for example, you use the path `"../models/product.model"` and not `"../models/product.model.ts"` or `"../models.product.model.js"`.

Understanding the Class

Components are TypeScript classes that provide the methods and properties required to support a template. The convention is to include the term `Component` in the class name, which is why the class in Listing 7-3 is called `ProductTableComponent`. You don't have to follow this convention, but it helps to keep the files in a project organized.

```
...
export class ProductTableComponent {

    constructor(private repo: Repository) { }

    get products(): Product[] {
        return this.repo.products;
    }
}
...
```

The `constructor` is used to declare a dependency on the `Repository` class, which will be resolved using the dependency injection feature when a new instance of the component is created. The other feature in the component class is a read-only property called `products`, which returns the value of the `products` property defined by the `Repository` class. The directives and bindings in an HTML template can only access the methods and properties defined by its component. This means that most components start out just providing access to the data in the model and start defining more complex logic as the application develops.

Understanding the Decorator

The @Component decorator is what brings the component to life and provides Angular with the information it needs to apply the component in the application.

```
...
@Component({
    selector: "product-table",
    templateUrl: "productTable.component.html"
})
export class ProductTableComponent {
...
```

The configuration properties of the @Component decorator tell Angular how the component should be used. The selector property tells Angular that it should apply the component when it encounters a product-table element in an HTML template. (You will see how I create this element shortly.) The templateUrl property specifies the component's HTML template file, which provides the content that will be displayed by the component.

Creating the HTML Template

A component's template provides the HTML content that will be displayed to the user, as well as the directives and data bindings that will present dynamic content to the user. Create an HTML file called productTable.component.html in the ClientApp/src/app/structure folder and add the content shown in Listing 7-4. (It is important that the name of the template file exactly matches the value of the templateUrl property in the component's decorator.)

If you are using Visual Studio, right-click the structure folder, select Add ➤ New Item from the popup menu, and use the HTML Page template to add the new file. If you are using Visual Studio Code, then right-click the structure folder and select New File from the popup menu.

Listing 7-4. The productTable.component.html File in the ClientApp/src/app/structure Folder

```
<table class="table table-striped">
    <tbody>
        <tr><th>Name</th><th>Category</th><th>Price</th></tr>
        <tr *ngFor="let product of products">
            <td>{{product.name}}</td>
            <td>{{product.category}}</td>
            <td>{{product.price}}</td>
        </tr>
    </tbody>
</table>
```

This template uses features seen in earlier chapters. The ngFor directive is used to read the value of the component's products property and generate a tr element for each Product in the array that returns. Each object is assigned to a temporary variable called product, which is then used in data bindings to set the content of td elements. The result is a table that contains a row for each Product in the repository, showing the value of the name, category, and price properties.

Creating the Filter Component

The next component will present the user with a selection of buttons that will be used to filter the Product objects in the repository. Add a TypeScript file called categoryFilter.component.ts in the ClientApp/src/ app/structure folder and add the code shown in Listing 7-5.

Listing 7-5. The Contents of the categoryFilter.component.ts File in the ClientApp/src/app/ structure Folder

```
import { Component } from '@angular/core';
import { Repository } from "../models/repository";

@Component({
    selector: "category-filter",
    templateUrl: "categoryFilter.component.html"
})
export class CategoryFilterComponent {
    public chessCategory = "chess";

    constructor(private repo: Repository) { }

    setCategory(category: string) {
        this.repo.filter.category = category;
        this.repo.getProducts();
    }
}
```

This file defines the CategoryFilterComponent class, to which the @Component decorator has been applied. The decorator tells Angular to use this component when it encounters a category-filter HTML element and to use a template file called categoryFilter.component.html. The component class defines a constructor that allows it to receive a Repository object through dependency injection. The setCategory method accepts a category, which is used to configure the Repository object's filter and refresh the application's data.

Creating the HTML Template

To create the template for the filter component, add a file called categoryFilter.component.html to the ClientApp/src/app/structure folder and add the markup shown in Listing 7-6.

Listing 7-6. The categoryFilter.component.html File in the ClientApp/src/app/structure Folder

```
<div>
    <button class="btn btn-primary m-1" (click)="setCategory('soccer')">
        Soccer
    </button>
    <button class="btn btn-primary m-1" (click)="setCategory(chessCategory)">
        Chess
    </button>
    <button class="btn btn-primary m-1" (click)="setCategory('Water' + 'Sports')">
        Watersports
    </button>
    <button class="btn btn-primary m-1" (click)="setCategory(null)">All</button>
</div>
```

The event binding feature tells Angular to evaluate an expression when an event is triggered. The event bindings in this template are for the click event, and the expressions invoke the component's setCategory method. Notice the different ways that the argument to the setCategory method is specified by the event bindings. The first binding specifies the category in the expression.

```
...
<button class="btn btn-primary" (click)="setCategory('soccer')">
...
```

The value soccer is a literal string and must be quoted. JavaScript supports both double and single quotes (the " and ' characters), and I have used double quotes to denote the expression and single quotes for the literal value.

No quotes are required in the second event binding, which specifies a property defined by the component as the argument.

```
...
<button class="btn btn-primary" (click)="setCategory(chessCategory)">
...
```

This binding will use the value of the chessCategory property as the value to the setCategory method. The third binding shows that Angular will evaluate the expression, allowing operations to be performed in expressions.

```
...
<button class="btn btn-primary"  (click)="setCategory('Water' + 'Sports')">
...
```

When this button is clicked, Angular will evaluate the expression, which concatenates two literal string values and passes the result to the setCategory method.

Applying the New Components

Angular must be configured to use new components, which is in contrast to the convention-over-configuration philosophy of ASP.NET Core MVC. In most applications, a new Angular module is created for each major area of functionality in the application, such as the model module, but to keep things simple, register the new components in the Angular application's root module, as shown in Listing 7-7.

Listing 7-7. Registering Components in the app.module.ts File in the ClientApp/src/app Folder

```
import { BrowserModule } from '@angular/platform-browser';
import { NgModule } from '@angular/core';
import { AppRoutingModule } from './app-routing.module';
import { AppComponent } from './app.component';
import { ModelModule } from "./models/model.module";
import { ProductTableComponent } from "./structure/productTable.component"
import { CategoryFilterComponent } from "./structure/categoryFilter.component"

@NgModule({
    declarations: [AppComponent, ProductTableComponent, CategoryFilterComponent],
    imports: [BrowserModule, AppRoutingModule, ModelModule],
```

```
    providers: [],
    bootstrap: [AppComponent]
})
export class AppModule { }
```

The component classes are registered in the declarations property of the NgModule decorator, which makes Angular aware they exist and can be applied to HTML elements.

The next step is to add the HTML elements that are specified by the new component's selector properties. Replace the contents of the app.component.html file, which is the template for the component specified by the root component's bootstrap property in Listing 7-7, with the elements shown in Listing 7-8.

Listing 7-8. Replacing the Contents of the app.component.html File in the ClientApp/src/app Folder

```
<category-filter></category-filter>
<product-table></product-table>
```

These elements replace the content that was previously displayed by the user. When the application starts, Angular will process the template, discover the category-filter and product-table elements, and look at the list of components that have been registered to see which ones should be applied. The result is shown in Figure 7-2, although you may need to reload the browser for the changes to take effect.

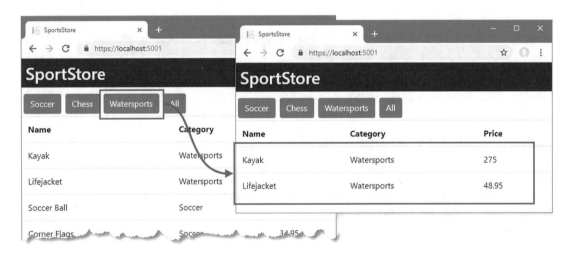

Figure 7-2. *Adding components to the Angular application*

Clicking one of the buttons changes the filter that is applied to the data. The figure shows the effect of clicking the Watersports button, which has the effect of selecting only those products in the Watersports category.

Understanding the Application Structure

The two new components have no direct knowledge of one another, but the actions performed using one component (clicking a button) are reflected in the other (filtering data). This works because the components take advantage of the two parts of the data repository that I described at the start of this section, as illustrated in Figure 7-3.

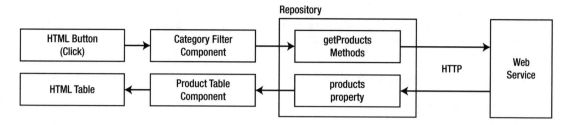

Figure 7-3. *Understanding collaborating components*

When the user clicks a button, the event binding invokes the category filter component's `setCategory` method, which updates the repository filter and reloads the data. At this point, the category filter component's job is done.

The repository sends the HTTP request to the ASP.NET Core MVC web service and receives the filtered `Product` data, which is assigned to the `products` property. This is the property used in the `ngFor` directive's expression in the product table component's template, and Angular updates the content that is displayed by that template to reflect the change.

Adding Another Component

The two new components may leave you with the impression that some components only read data from the model, while others only make changes. In fact, components are more flexible and can be used to create complex sets of relationships, while still relying on the data model to aid coordination. To see how this works, create a file called `productDetail.component.ts` in the `ClientApp/src/app/structure` folder and add the code shown in Listing 7-9.

Listing 7-9. The Contents of the productDetail.component.ts File in the ClientApp/src/app/ structure Folder

```
import { Component } from '@angular/core';
import { Repository } from "../models/repository";
import { Product } from "../models/product.model";

@Component({
    selector: "product-detail",
    templateUrl: "productDetail.component.html"
})
export class ProductDetailComponent {

    constructor(private repo: Repository) { }

    get product(): Product {
        return this.repo.product;
    }
}
```

The `ProductDetailComponent` class has a constructor that receives a `Repository` object, which will be provided through the dependency injection feature, and a `product` property that returns the value of the property with the same name in the `Repository`.

The @Component decorator tells Angular to apply this component when it encounters the product-detail element and provides the location of the component's template. To create the template, add a file called productDetail.component.html in the ClientApp/src/app/structure folder and add the HTML elements shown in Listing 7-10.

Listing 7-10. The productDetail.component.html File in the ClientApp/src/app/structure Folder

```
<table class="table table-striped">
    <tbody>
        <tr><th colspan="2" class="bg-info">Product</th></tr>
        <tr><th>Name</th><td>{{product?.name || 'No Data'}}</td></tr>
        <tr><th>Category</th><td>{{product?.category || 'No Data'}}</td></tr>
        <tr>
            <th>Description</th>
            <td>{{product?.description || 'No Data'}}</td>
        </tr>
        <tr><th>Price</th><td>{{product?.price  || 'No Data'}}</td></tr>
        <tr><th colspan="2" class="bg-info">Supplier</th></tr>
        <tr><th>Name</th><td>{{product?.supplier?.name}}</td></tr>
        <tr><th>City</th><td>{{product?.supplier?.city}}</td></tr>
        <tr><th>State</th><td>{{product?.supplier?.state}}</td></tr>
    </tbody>
</table>
```

To register the component so that it can be used by Angular, change the configuration of the root module, as shown in Listing 7-11.

Listing 7-11. Registering a Component in the app.module.ts File in the ClientApp/src/app Folder

```
import { BrowserModule } from '@angular/platform-browser';
import { NgModule } from '@angular/core';
import { AppRoutingModule } from './app-routing.module';
import { AppComponent } from './app.component';
import { ModelModule } from "./models/model.module";
import { ProductTableComponent } from "./structure/productTable.component"
import { CategoryFilterComponent } from "./structure/categoryFilter.component"
import { ProductDetailComponent } from "./structure/productDetail.component";

@NgModule({
    declarations: [AppComponent, ProductTableComponent, CategoryFilterComponent,
        ProductDetailComponent],
    imports: [BrowserModule, AppRoutingModule, ModelModule],
    providers: [],
    bootstrap: [AppComponent]
})
export class AppModule { }
```

The import statement provides access to the ProductDetailComponent class, which is added to the NgModule decorator's declarations property. Now that the component can be used, edit the root component's template to add the element that will apply the new component, as shown in Listing 7-12.

Listing 7-12. Adding an Element in the app.component.html File in the ClientApp/src/app Folder

```html
<div class="container">
    <div class="row">
        <div class="col">
            <category-filter></category-filter>
            <product-table></product-table>
        </div>
        <div class="col">
            <product-detail></product-detail>
        </div>
    </div>
</div>
```

The listing also adds some structure to the HTML document, using Bootstrap CSS classes to position the new component side-by-side with the existing ones.

Selecting a Product

The new component will display the details of a single product when it is selected, which means that the next step is to provide the user with the means to make that selection. First, add the elements shown in Listing 7-13 to the template for the product table.

Listing 7-13. Elements in the productTable.component.html File in the ClientApp/src/app/ structure Folder

```html
<table class="table table-striped">
    <tbody>
        <tr><th>Name</th><th>Category</th><th>Price</th><th></th></tr>
        <tr *ngFor="let product of products">
            <td>{{product.name}}</td>
            <td>{{product.category}}</td>
            <td>{{product.price}}</td>
            <td>
                <button class="btn btn-primary btn-sm"
                        (click)="selectProduct(product.productId)">
                    Details
                </button>
            </td>
        </tr>
    </tbody>
</table>
```

The new elements add a column to the table containing a Details button for each row produced by the ngFor directive. The click event binding will invoke a method called selectProduct when the button is clicked, providing the ID value of the corresponding product. To define the method that the event binding invokes, add the code shown in Listing 7-14 to the product table component.

Listing 7-14. Adding a Method in the productTable.component.ts File in the ClientApp/src/app/ structure Folder

```
import { Component } from '@angular/core';
import { Repository } from "../models/repository";
import { Product } from "../models/product.model";

@Component({
    selector: "product-table",
    templateUrl: "productTable.component.html"
})
export class ProductTableComponent {

    constructor(private repo: Repository) { }

    get products(): Product[] {
        return this.repo.products;
    }

    selectProduct(id: number) {
        this.repo.getProduct(id);
    }
}
```

The selectProduct method calls the repository object's getProduct method, which will cause it to send a request to the web service. When you save the changes, you will see the new content, and clicking one of the Details buttons will lead to the detailed view being populated with data, as shown in Figure 7-4.

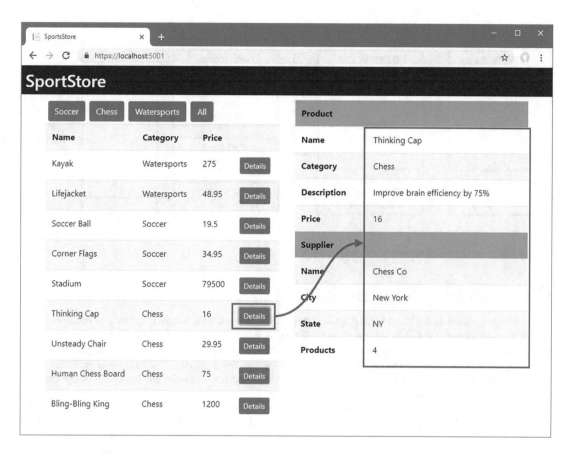

Figure 7-4. *Displaying detailed data*

Understanding the Revised Application Structure

The three new components rely on the data model, either as the target for the operations they perform for the user or as the source of the data they display. None of the components depends directly on any of other, and any of them can be changed without requiring corresponding changes in the other components. And, as the addition of the third component has shown, components can be both consumers of the data in the model and the source of changes to that data, as illustrated by Figure 7-5.

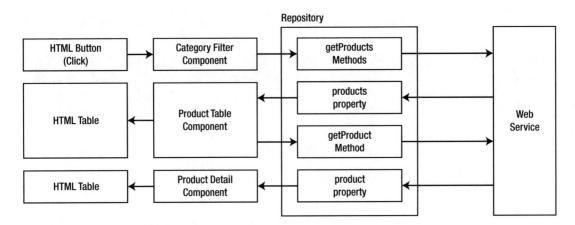

Figure 7-5. *The revised structure of the Angular application*

Understanding Angular Routing

Using the data model as the heart of an Angular application makes it easy to add and integrate components that add new features. For all but the simplest applications, however, you will soon reach the point where you want to display different components to the user at different times. For the SportsStore application, for example, it doesn't make sense to display the product table and the product detail components at the same time. Instead, the application should display the table until the user clicks a Details button, at which time the detailed view should be shown.

In an Angular application, this is done using URL routing, which provides another way for components to cooperate. As an ASP.NET Core MVC developer, you may already be familiar with the idea of URL routing, in which the segments of a URL are used to select a controller and action method to handle an HTTP request. In Angular applications, the segments in the URL are used to decide which components should be displayed to the user. This feature relies on the fact that browsers will allow small changes to the URL without sending a new request to the server, a process that becomes clearer with an example. In the sections that follow, I add support for URL routing to the SportsStore application and use it to display either the product table or the detailed view.

Creating the Routing Configuration

When the project was created in Chapter 3, one of the command-line arguments enabled the Angular routing feature, which means that the packages and basic configuration for routing were set up during the creation process.

Angular routing requires a base element in the head section of the HTML document that contains the script elements for the bundle files. I added this element to the Razor layout in Chapter 3, like this:

```
...
<head>
    <base href="/">
    <meta charset="utf-8" />
    <meta name="viewport" content="width=device-width, initial-scale=1.0" />
    <title>SportsStore</title>
    <link rel="stylesheet" href="~/lib/bootstrap/dist/css/bootstrap.css" />
</head>
...
```

The value of the href element tells Angular the starting URL to which routing features should respond. A value of / is used when the Angular application is delivered using the default URL. If the application is accessed through a specific URL segment, such as https://localhost:5001/myapp, then the base element's href attribute must be changed, to /myapp in this case.

The project was created with an app-routing.module.ts file in the ClientApp/src/app folder, and this file is used to define the routes supported by the Angular application. To configure the routes for the example application, add the statements shown in Listing 7-15.

Listing 7-15. Adding Routes in the app-routing.module.ts File in the ClientApp/src/app Folder

```
import { NgModule } from '@angular/core';
import { Routes, RouterModule } from '@angular/router';
import { ProductTableComponent } from "./structure/productTable.component"
import { ProductDetailComponent } from "./structure/productDetail.component";

const routes: Routes = [
    { path: "table", component: ProductTableComponent },
    { path: "detail", component: ProductDetailComponent },
    { path: "", component: ProductTableComponent }
];

@NgModule({
  imports: [RouterModule.forRoot(routes)],
  exports: [RouterModule]
})
export class AppRoutingModule { }
```

As with ASP.NET Core MVC, there are a lot of options available for URL routing in Angular, and this is a simple configuration. The first step is to define the set of URL segments and the components that they will display, which are combined with the value of the href attribute of the base element from the HTML document. The routes are prepared for use using the RouterModule.forRoot method, which produces a result that can be used in an Angular component's imports property.

```
...
@NgModule({
  imports: [RouterModule.forRoot(routes)],
  exports: [RouterModule]
})
export class AppRoutingModule { }
...
```

Just as with ASP.NET Core MVC, Angular routes are evaluated in the order in which they are defined, which means that the most specific routes must be defined first. The segments that the route will match are defined using the path property, and the component that will be displayed is specified by the component property. There are three routes in the listing, and they produce the mappings described in Table 7-2.

■ **Tip** You won't be able to navigate to the URLs shown in the table by entering them into the browser manually. I explain why and how this is resolved later in the chapter.

Table 7-2. *The URL Routes and Components*

URL	Description
https://localhost:5001	This URL is matched by the last route in the listing and displays the product table component.
https://localhost:5001/table	This URL is matched by the route whose path is table and displays the product table component.
https://localhost:5001/detail	This URL is matched by the route whose path is detail and displays the product detail component.

Applying the Routing Configuration

Angular uses a special HTML element, router-outlet, to display the components selected by the routing configuration. This element is used in the root component's template, replacing the existing content, as shown in Listing 7-16.

Listing 7-16. Replacing the Contents of the app.component.html File in the ClientApp/src/app Folder

```
<router-outlet></router-outlet>
```

When the changes to the Angular files are saved and the application has been recompiled, you will see just the product table, as shown in Figure 7-6. This is because the route from Listing 7-16 whose path is the empty string ("") has matched the URL displayed by the browser, and the routing system has selected the product table component to show in the router-outlet element.

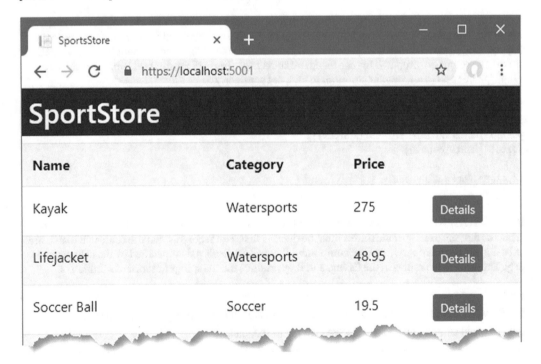

Figure 7-6. *A component selected by the routing system*

Navigating Using Routes

Clicking the Details buttons has no visible effect at the moment because the event binding applied to the button elements just triggers an HTTP request to the web service. To navigate to the URL that will display the product details component, add the code shown in Listing 7-17 to the `ProductTableComponent` class.

Listing 7-17. Navigating in the productTable.component.ts File in the ClientApp/src/app/structure Folder

```
import { Component } from '@angular/core';
import { Repository } from "../models/repository";
import { Product } from "../models/product.model";
import { Router } from "@angular/router";

@Component({
    selector: "product-table",
    templateUrl: "productTable.component.html"
})
export class ProductTableComponent {

    constructor(private repo: Repository,
                private router: Router) { }

    get products(): Product[] {
        return this.repo.products;
    }

    selectProduct(id: number) {
        this.repo.getProduct(id);
        this.router.navigateByUrl("/detail");
    }
}
```

The `Router` class, which is defined in the `@angular/router` module, provides support for navigating to a URL through its `navigateByUrl` method. The constructor for `ProductTableComponent` accepts a `Router` object, which will be provided by dependency injection, and uses it in the `selectProduct` method to move to the `/detail` URL, which will display the product detail component.

Once the application has been compiled and the browser has reloaded, click one of the Details buttons. The product detail component will replace the table, showing the details of the selected product. Notice that the URL displayed by the browser changes, as shown in Figure 7-7.

Figure 7-7. *Using the URL routing feature*

Navigating Using a Directive

The Router.navigateByUrl method isn't the only way to navigate using the routing system. Angular also provides a directive that can be applied to an element, which allows a URL to be specified in a template without needing a corresponding method in the component. To allow the user to navigate back from the detailed component to the table, add the elements shown in Listing 7-18.

Listing 7-18. Navigating in the productDetail.component.html File in the ClientApp/src/app/ structure Folder

```
<table class="table table-striped">
    <tbody>
        <tr><th colspan="2" class="bg-info">Product</th></tr>
        <tr><th>Name</th><td>{{product?.name || 'No Data'}}</td></tr>
        <tr><th>Category</th><td>{{product?.category || 'No Data'}}</td></tr>
        <tr>
            <th>Description</th>
            <td>{{product?.description || 'No Data'}}</td>
        </tr>
        <tr><th>Price</th><td>{{product?.price  || 'No Data'}}</td></tr>
        <tr><th colspan="2" class="bg-info">Supplier</th></tr>
        <tr><th>Name</th><td>{{product?.supplier?.name}}</td></tr>
        <tr><th>City</th><td>{{product?.supplier?.city}}</td></tr>
        <tr><th>State</th><td>{{product?.supplier?.state}}</td></tr>
    </tbody>
</table>
<div class="text-center">
    <button class="btn btn-primary" routerLink="/table">Back</button>
</div>
```

The routerLink attribute applies a directive that tells Angular to navigate to the /table URL when the button is clicked. Save the changes, use the browser to navigate to https://localhost:5001, and use the Details and Back buttons to navigate between the components, as shown in Figure 7-8.

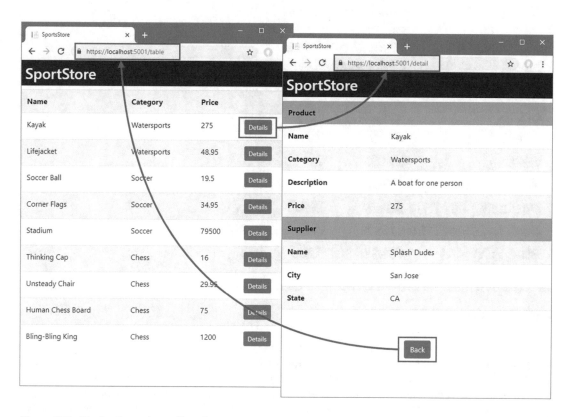

Figure 7-8. *Navigating using a directive*

Improving Navigation

The routing system is being used to handle navigation in the SportsStore application, but it has some rough edges that will confuse users. In the sections that follow, I describe the problems and explain how to solve them.

Allowing Direct Navigation

If you try to manually navigate to one of the URLs in the routing configuration, such as https://localhost:5001/table, by entering it into the browser's URL bar, you will receive an odd response, as shown in Figure 7-9.

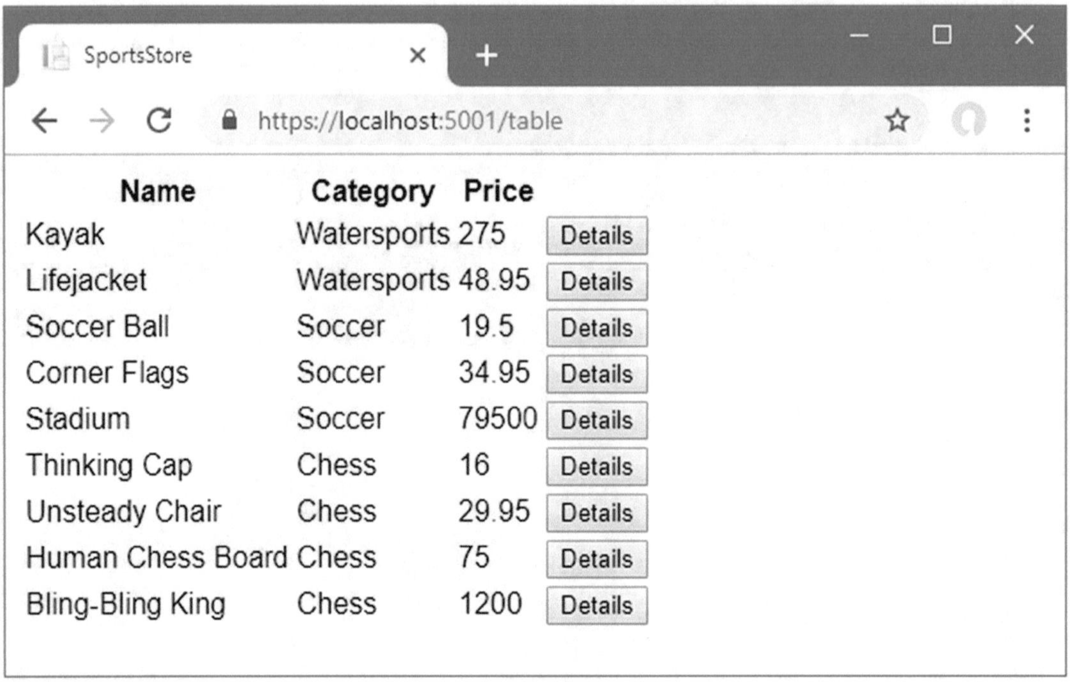

Figure 7-9. *Requesting a URL directly*

There is a difference between navigation to a URL within the Angular application and a URL entered by the user. No HTTP request is sent when the application performs navigation, and the application continues running. When the user enters a URL, an HTTP request is always sent. This is a sensible approach because it prevents JavaScript applications from hijacking the browser and preventing the user from navigating away.

The problem that is created is that the HTTP request targets a URL for which there is no corresponding MVC controller. The ASP.NET Core routing configuration forwards requests that don't match a controller to the Angular development server, which returns the `index.html` file in the `ClientApp/src` folder. This file doesn't contain a link for the Bootstrap CSS stylesheet nor does it contain the header elements from the Razor layout. When the Angular starts, it responds to the URL that has been selected, but the browser doesn't have all of the resources it requires to display the application correctly.

Catching the requests for URLs that are supported by the Angular routing system requires a corresponding entry in the ASP.NET Core routes, as shown in Listing 7-19. This is a problem that is specific to the development phase of the project, where the Angular development server is responsible for generating the bundle files but the rest of the content comes from ASP.NET Core. When the application is prepared for deployment in Chapter 13, the Angular development server won't be used, and the routing configuration will be simplified.

Listing 7-19. Adding a Route in the Startup.cs File in the ServerApp Folder

```
...
public void Configure(IApplicationBuilder app, IWebHostEnvironment env,
        IServiceProvider services) {

    if (env.IsDevelopment()) {
        app.UseDeveloperExceptionPage();
```

```
    } else {
        app.UseExceptionHandler("/Home/Error");
        app.UseHsts();
    }

    app.UseHttpsRedirection();
    app.UseStaticFiles();
    app.UseRouting();
    app.UseAuthorization();

    app.UseEndpoints(endpoints => {
        endpoints.MapControllerRoute(
            name: "default",
            pattern: "{controller=Home}/{action=Index}/{id?}");

        endpoints.MapControllerRoute(
            name: "angular_fallback",
            pattern: "{target:regex(table|detail)}/{*catchall}",
            defaults: new { controller = "Home", action = "Index" });

        endpoints.MapRazorPages();
    });

    app.UseSwagger();
    app.UseSwaggerUI(options => {
        options.SwaggerEndpoint("/swagger/v1/swagger.json",
            "SportsStore API");
    });

    app.UseSpa(spa => {
        string strategy = Configuration
            .GetValue<string>("DevTools:ConnectionStrategy");
        if (strategy == "proxy") {
            spa.UseProxyToSpaDevelopmentServer("http://127.0.0.1:4200");
        } else if (strategy == "managed") {
            spa.Options.SourcePath = "../ClientApp";
            spa.UseAngularCliServer("start");
        }
    });

    SeedData.SeedDatabase(services.GetRequiredService<DataContext>());
}
...
```

The new route matches the /table and /detail URLs and sends them to the Index action on the Home controller. This ensures that the Razor view—and its associated layout—is used to respond when the user navigates directly to one of the URLs supported by the Angular application, as shown in Figure 7-10.

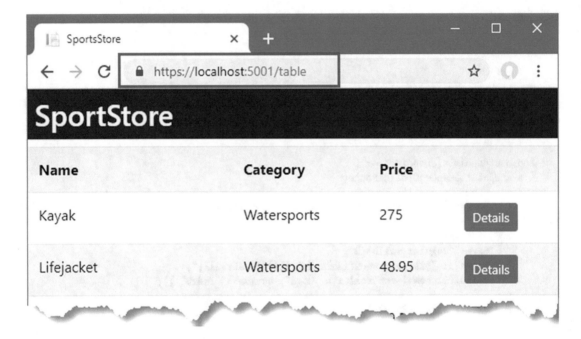

Figure 7-10. *The effect of direct navigation*

Using a Segment Variable

Allowing the user to navigate directly to one of the Angular application's URLs is a step forward but not perfect. You can see the problem by requesting `https://localhost:5001/detail`. The Angular application will display the detailed view component, but the placeholder data will never be replaced with real data, as shown in Figure 7-11.

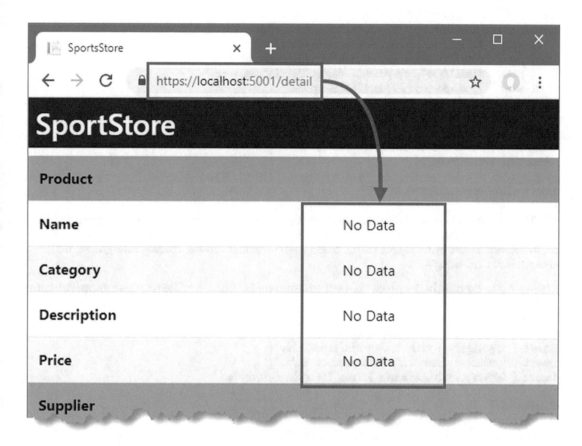

Figure 7-11. *Navigating directly to the detailed view URL*

When the user clicks a Details button triggering navigation within the Angular application, the template's component asks the repository to get the product data and then navigates to the URL that displays the detailed view. But when the user navigates directly to a URL, the repository is never asked to get the product data, so the component has nothing to display. Solving this problem means extending the product detail component so it can request its own data and include details of the product to be displayed to be included in the URL.

The first step is to change the routing configuration to add a segment variable, which will allow the route to match a range of URLs. Angular routing segments are similar to those in ASP.NET Core MVC, although the syntax is different. To add a segment to the Angular route for the product details component, add the route shown in Listing 7-20.

Listing 7-20. Adding a Route in the app-routing.module.ts File in the ClientApp/src/app Folder

```
import { NgModule } from '@angular/core';
import { Routes, RouterModule } from '@angular/router';
import { ProductTableComponent } from "./structure/productTable.component"
import { ProductDetailComponent } from "./structure/productDetail.component";
```

```
const routes: Routes = [
    { path: "table", component: ProductTableComponent },
    { path: "detail", component: ProductDetailComponent },
    { path: "detail/:id", component: ProductDetailComponent },
    { path: "", component: ProductTableComponent }
];

@NgModule({
  imports: [RouterModule.forRoot(routes)],
  exports: [RouterModule]
})
export class AppRoutingModule { }
```

The segment variable is denoted using a colon (the : character), so the new route in the listing will match a URL like /table/1, and the value of the last segment will be assigned to a segment variable called id. To access the value of the segment variable and use it to request data from the repository, make the changes shown in Listing 7-21.

Listing 7-21. Routing in the productDetail.component.ts File in the ClientApp/src/app/structure Folder

```
import { Component } from '@angular/core';
import { Repository } from "../models/repository";
import { Product } from "../models/product.model";
import { Router, ActivatedRoute } from "@angular/router";

@Component({
    selector: "product-detail",
    templateUrl: "productDetail.component.html"
})
export class ProductDetailComponent {

    constructor(private repo: Repository,
                router: Router,
                activeRoute: ActivatedRoute) {

        let id = Number.parseInt(activeRoute.snapshot.params["id"]);
        if (id) {
            this.repo.getProduct(id);
        } else {
            router.navigateByUrl("/");
        }
    }

    get product(): Product {
        return this.repo.product;
    }
}
```

The current route is available through the `ActivatedRoute` class, which is defined in the `@angular/router` module. In the listing, the component receives an `ActivatedRoute` object, which will be provided by dependency injection, and uses its `snapshot.params` property to get the value of the `id` segment variable. If the variable has a value and it can be parsed into an integer, then details of the product are requested through the repository. If there is no value for the `id` segment or it cannot be parsed, then the `Router` object is used to navigate to the `/` URL, which will display the product table.

The final adjustment is to change the way that the user navigates from the table to the detailed view for a product. At the moment, clicking a Details button invokes a method that triggers the HTTP request and then navigates to the detailed view, but that is no longer needed. To take advantage of the self-contained nature of the product details component, change the Details button elements in the product table component's template, as shown in Listing 7-22.

Listing 7-22. Navigating in the productTable.component.html File in the ClientApp/src/app/structure Folder

```html
<table class="table table-striped">
    <tbody>
        <tr><th>Name</th><th>Category</th><th>Price</th><th></th></tr>
        <tr *ngFor="let product of products">
            <td>{{product.name}}</td>
            <td>{{product.category}}</td>
            <td>{{product.price}}</td>
            <td>
                <button class="btn btn-primary btn-sm"
                        [routerLink]="['/detail', product.productId]">
                    Details
                </button>
            </td>
        </tr>
    </tbody>
</table>
```

The `routerLink` directive is applied differently when you need to include a variable in the navigation URL. The name of the attribute is enclosed in square brackets (the [and] characters), and the value is an array of values that will be combined to create the navigation URL. The individual values can be string literal values, such as `'/detail'`, or variables, such as `product.productId`. When the user clicks the element, Angular will evaluate each element in the array, combine the results, and navigate to the URL. In the listing, this means that clicking a `button` element will navigate to a URL such as `/detail/2`.

Click a Details button in the product table once the changes have been saved and the application has been reloaded. The routing system will navigate to a URL with a segment variable that provides the product detail component with the information it needs to request the data from the repository, shown in Figure 7-12.

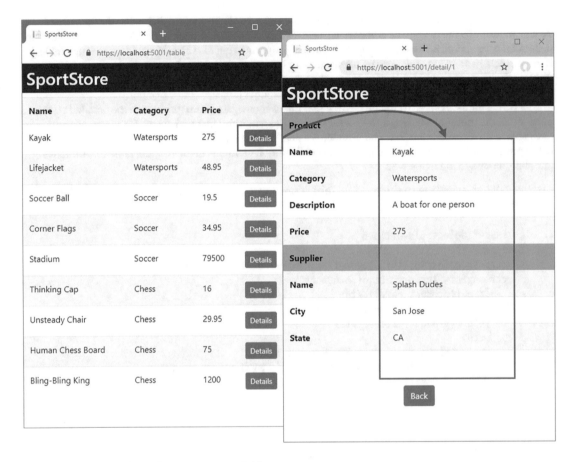

Figure 7-12. *Navigating using a segment variable*

This change allows the user to view details by entering a URL directly. If you enter `https://localhost:5001/details/2`, for example, you will see the details for the item whose ID is 2. Remember, however, that an HTTP request is sent to the server and the Angular application is restarted, which means any context data that is not contained in the URL will be lost.

Understanding the Application Structure

The URL routing feature provides an alternative way for Angular components to cooperate without being tightly coupled. Clicking a Details button in the SportsStore application lets the table component tell the detail component which product should be displayed, but neither component has knowledge of the other or depends on the code they define. Introducing URL routing has changed the structure of the application, as illustrated in Figure 7-13.

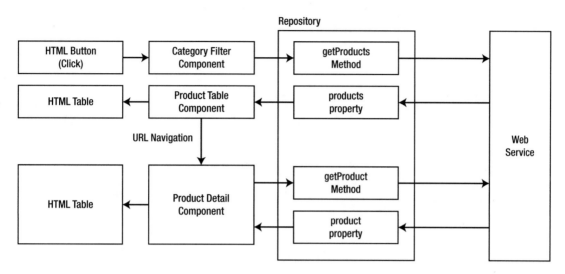

Figure 7-13. *The effect of URL routing on the application structure*

Being able to choose how components coordinate allows for more flexibility during development. In this case, using URL routing allows the user to navigate directly to a detail view and also means that other components in the application can trigger a detailed display without needing to explicitly load the data.

Summary

In this chapter, I explained how Angular applications are structured around the data model, and I explained the URL navigation feature. The data model provides the shared state for the application, allowing Angular components to work consistently together. The URL feature selects the components that will be displayed to the user, allowing features to be used without overwhelming the user with content. In the next chapter, I use the techniques described in this chapter to start working on the end-user features for the SportsStore application.

CHAPTER 8

■ ■ ■

Creating the Store

The publicly accessible part of the SportsStore application will allow customers to view the products that are on sale, add items to a cart, go through a checkout process, and provide ratings for the products they have purchased. All of these features are standard for most online stores, but as you might expect by now, there are some tricks and techniques required to get Angular and ASP.NET Core MVC to work together to create a good user experience. In this chapter, I create the structure of the Angular application's store feature and start adding features. Table 8-1 puts the store features in context.

Table 8-1. *Putting End-User Features in Context*

Question	Answer
What are they?	The end-user functionality provides the publicly accessible features of the application.
Why are they useful?	For most applications, the end-user functionality is the most important part of the project and is the reason that development was started. Other features, such as those required to administer the application, tend to receive less attention and effort.
How are they used?	The end user will use their browser to navigate to a URL that presents them with the Angular application, which displays the publicly accessible features. The HTML document that tells the browser to load the Angular application is produced by ASP.NET Core MVC, which is also responsible for delivering the data to the Angular application through the web service controllers.
Are there any pitfalls or limitations?	It is important to start with the structure of the application so that you have a sense of the Angular components that are required, how they will collaborate, and what data is required from the web service. Without this foundation, the Angular part of the project can become complex and difficult to manage.
Are there any alternatives?	No. If you are using Angular and ASP.NET Core MVC in the same project, there will be some type of end user.

Preparing for This Chapter

This chapter uses the SportsStore project that I created in Chapter 3 and modified in the chapters since. To remove the database so that the application will use fresh seed data, open a new command prompt, navigate to the ServerApp folder, and run the command shown in Listing 8-1.

© Adam Freeman 2019
A. Freeman, *Essential Angular for ASP.NET Core MVC 3*,
https://doi.org/10.1007/978-1-4842-5284-0_8

Listing 8-1. Resetting the Database

```
dotnet ef database drop --force
```

Run the command shown in Listing 8-2 to start the ASP.NET Core runtime and the Angular development tools.

Listing 8-2. Starting the Development Tools

```
dotnet watch run
```

Open a new browser window and navigate to https://localhost:5001; you will see the content shown in Figure 8-1.

■ **Tip** You can download the complete project for every chapter without charge from the source code repository, https://github.com/Apress/esntl-angular-for-asp.net-core-mvc-3. Run npm install in the ClientApp folder to install the packages required for Angular development and then start the development tools as instructed.

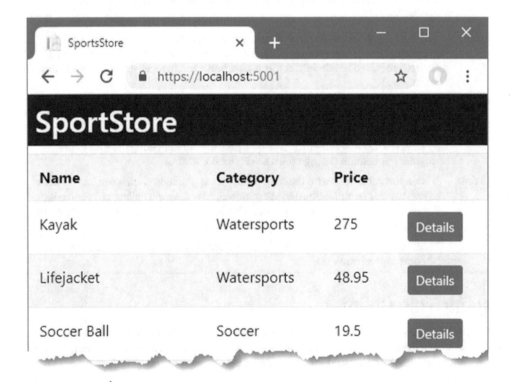

Figure 8-1. Running the example application

Starting the Product Selection Feature

The starting point for the store feature is presenting the user with details of the products for sale. Earlier chapters included some of the functionality required for this feature, but there are some important additions that will allow the user to filter the content, page through the data, and perform other common tasks.

To provide some context, Figure 8-2 shows the structure that I will be working toward. The layout for product selection will present the user with a list of products, which can be selected to add them to a shopping cart. The user will be able to navigate through the products by selecting a category filter and by moving between pages of products. This is a conventional layout for presenting products and will be familiar if you have followed the SportsStore example in my other books.

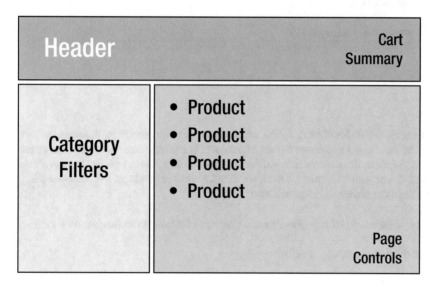

Figure 8-2. *The intended product selection structure*

In the sections that follow, I show you how to create this layout using Angular and how to enhance the ASP.NET Core MVC part of the application.

Blocking Out the Feature Components

When working on a new feature, I find it useful to start by creating components that display placeholder content so that I can define the basic structure shown in Figure 8-2. Once the placeholders are done, I can return to each component and implement the functionality that will be presented to the user.

Creating the Product List Component

Create the `ClientApp/src/app/store` folder. This is where the Angular classes and HTML templates for the product selection feature will live. Create a TypeScript file called `productList.component.ts` in the `store` folder and add the code shown in Listing 8-3.

Listing 8-3. The Contents of the productList.component.ts File in the ClientApp/src/app/store Folder

```
import { Component } from "@angular/core";
import { Repository } from "../models/repository";
import { Product } from "../models/product.model";

@Component({
    selector: "store-product-list",
    templateUrl: "productList.component.html"
})
export class ProductListComponent {

    constructor(private repo: Repository) { }

    get products(): Product[] {
        return this.repo.products;
    }
}
```

This component will be responsible for displaying the list of products to the user. Even though I am just blocking out the content at the moment, I know that the set of products in the repository is needed, so I have declared a Repository dependency in the constructor and defined a get-only products property that returns the data. To provide the component with a template, create an HTML file called productList.component. html in the store folder and add the element shown in Listing 8-4.

Listing 8-4. The Contents of the productList.component.html File in the ClientApp/src/app/store Folder

```
<h4 class="border border-dark bg-primary p-2">
    Placeholder: Product List
</h4>
```

I will replace this HTML content with more useful elements once the structure of the application has been completed, but this is enough with which to get started.

Creating the Pagination Component

The pagination component will make long lists of products more manageable by allowing the user to navigate through smaller pages. Add a TypeScript file called pagination.component.ts in the store folder and add the code shown in Listing 8-5.

Listing 8-5. The Contents of the pagination.component.ts File in the ClientApp/src/app/store Folder

```
import { Component } from "@angular/core";

@Component({
    selector: "store-pagination",
    templateUrl: "pagination.component.html"
})
export class PaginationComponent {

}
```

To provide the component with its template, create an HTML file called `pagination.component.html` in the `store` folder and add the element shown in Listing 8-6.

Listing 8-6. The Contents of the pagination.component.html File in the ClientApp/src/app/store Folder

```
<h4 class="border border-dark bg-info p-2">
    Placeholder: Page Controls
</h4>
```

Creating the Category Filter Component

The category filter component will allow the user to select a single category to display. Add a TypeScript file called `categoryFilter.component.ts` to the `store` folder with the code shown in Listing 8-7.

Listing 8-7. The Contents of the categoryFilter.component.ts File in the ClientApp/src/app/store Folder

```
import { Component } from "@angular/core";
import { Repository } from "../models/repository";

@Component({
    selector: "store-categoryfilter",
    templateUrl: "categoryFilter.component.html"
})
export class CategoryFilterComponent {

    constructor(private repo: Repository) { }

}
```

This component follows the pattern of defining a constructor that declares a `Repository` dependency, which will be resolved using the dependency injection feature and provide access to the filter feature defined in Chapter 5. To provide the component with its template, create an HTML file called `categoryFilter.component.html` in the `store` folder and add the element shown in Listing 8-8.

Listing 8-8. The Contents of the categoryFilter.component.html File in the ClientApp/src/app/store Folder

```
<h4 class="border border-dark bg-secondary p-2 h-100">
    Placeholder: Category Filter
</h4>
```

Creating the Cart Summary Component

The cart summary component will display an overview of the user's shopping cart. Create a TypeScript file called `cartSummary.component.ts` in the `store` folder and add the code shown in Listing 8-9.

Listing 8-9. The Contents of the cartSummary.component.ts File in the ClientApp/src/app/store Folder

```
import { Component } from "@angular/core";

@Component({
    selector: "store-cartsummary",
    templateUrl: "cartSummary.component.html"
})
export class CartSummaryComponent {

}
```

Unlike most of the other components created in this chapter, the cart summary component won't need access to the data repository. To provide the component with the template specified by the `templateUrl` property in the @Component decorator, create an HTML file called `cartSummary.component.html` in the `store` folder and add the element shown in Listing 8-10.

Listing 8-10. The Contents of the cartSummary.component.html File in the ClientApp/src/app/store Folder

```
<div>Placeholder: Cart Summary</div>
```

Creating the Ratings Component

The ratings component will display the ratings for a product. Create a TypeScript file called `ratings.component.ts` in the `store` folder and add the code shown in Listing 8-11.

Listing 8-11. The Contents of the ratings.component.ts File in the ClientApp/src/app/store Folder

```
import { Component } from "@angular/core";
import { Product } from "../models/product.model";

@Component({
    selector: "store-ratings",
    templateUrl: "ratings.component.html"
})
export class RatingsComponent {

}
```

This component doesn't need the repository to do its job, so it doesn't define a constructor. To provide the component with the template specified by the `templateUrl` property in the @Component decorator, create an HTML file called `ratings.component.html` in the `store` folder and add the elements shown in Listing 8-12.

Listing 8-12. The Contents of the ratings.component.html File in the ClientApp/src/app/store Folder

```
<h5>Placeholder: Ratings</h5>
```

Creating the Structural Component

The final component required for this chapter will provide the layout for the others. Angular doesn't have support for creating stand-alone HTML templates, which means that a component is required even when only the HTML structure is required. Add a TypeScript file called productSelection.component.ts to the store folder with the code shown in Listing 8-13.

Listing 8-13. The Contents of the productSelection.component.ts File in the ClientApp/src/app/store Folder

```
import { Component } from "@angular/core";

@Component({
    selector: "store-products",
    templateUrl: "productSelection.component.html"
})
export class ProductSelectionComponent {

}
```

To provide the component with its template, which is what will provide the layout structure, create an HTML file called productSelection.component.html in the store folder and add the elements shown in Listing 8-14.

Listing 8-14. The productSelection.component.html File in the ClientApp/src/app/store Folder

```
<div class="container-fluid">
    <div class="row">
        <div class="col bg-dark text-white">
            <div class="navbar-brand">SPORTS STORE</div>
            <div class="float-right navbar-text">
                <store-cartsummary></store-cartsummary>
            </div>
        </div>
    </div>
</div>
<div class="row no-gutters">
    <div class="col-3">
        <store-categoryfilter></store-categoryfilter>
    </div>
    <div class="col">
        <store-product-list></store-product-list>
        <store-pagination></store-pagination>
    </div>
</div>
```

This template uses the Bootstrap classes to create a grid layout, which makes it easy to position content without getting bogged down in the complexities of CSS. The ratings component isn't included in the layout, but I'll integrate into the application later in the chapter.

Creating and Registering the Store Feature Module

To create a feature module for the product selection feature, create a TypeScript file called `store.module.ts` in the store folder and add the code shown in Listing 8-15.

Listing 8-15. The Contents of the store.module.ts File in the ClientApp/src/app/store Folder

```
import { NgModule } from "@angular/core";
import { BrowserModule } from '@angular/platform-browser';
import { CartSummaryComponent } from "./cartSummary.component";
import { CategoryFilterComponent } from "./categoryFilter.component";
import { PaginationComponent } from "./pagination.component";
import { ProductListComponent } from "./productList.component";
import { RatingsComponent } from "./ratings.component";
import { ProductSelectionComponent } from "./productSelection.component";

@NgModule({
    declarations: [CartSummaryComponent, CategoryFilterComponent,
        PaginationComponent, ProductListComponent, RatingsComponent,
        ProductSelectionComponent],
    imports: [BrowserModule],
    exports: [ProductSelectionComponent]
})
export class StoreModule { }
```

The declarations property of the StoreModule feature module is used to register the components created in this section so they can be used by the Angular application. The exports property tells Angular which components can be used outside the feature module and has been used to specify the ProductSelectionComponent, which will be responsible for managing the others. (By default, the components specified by the declarations property can be referred to only in templates defined in the same feature module.)

The imports property tells Angular which other modules this module depends on. In this case, this is the BrowserModule, which provides the standard directives and data bindings required for an Angular application running in a browser.

To tell Angular about the store feature module, register it with the root module, as shown in Listing 8-16.

Listing 8-16. Registering a Feature Module in the app.module.ts File in the ClientApp/src/app Folder

```
import { BrowserModule } from '@angular/platform-browser';
import { NgModule } from '@angular/core';
import { AppRoutingModule } from './app-routing.module';
import { AppComponent } from './app.component';
import { ModelModule } from "./models/model.module";
// import { ProductTableComponent } from "./structure/productTable.component"
// import { CategoryFilterComponent } from "./structure/categoryFilter.component"
// import { ProductDetailComponent } from "./structure/productDetail.component";
import { FormsModule } from '@angular/forms';
import { StoreModule } from "./store/store.module";

@NgModule({
    declarations: [AppComponent],
    imports: [BrowserModule, AppRoutingModule, ModelModule,FormsModule, StoreModule],
```

```
    providers: [],
    bootstrap: [AppComponent]
})
export class AppModule { }
```

Unlike ASP.NET Core MVC, Angular doesn't discover its building blocks automatically, so every module or component that you rely on must be registered either directly with the root module or in a feature module, which must then be registered with the root module.

Configuring the Angular URL Routes

The routing configuration for the Angular application is still set up for the components from Chapter 7. To update the configuration for the components in this chapter, replace the routes with the ones shown in Listing 8-17.

Listing 8-17. Configuring the Routes in the app-routing.module.ts File in the ClientApp/src/app Folder

```
import { NgModule } from '@angular/core';
import { Routes, RouterModule } from '@angular/router';
// import { ProductTableComponent } from "./structure/productTable.component"
// import { ProductDetailComponent } from "./structure/productDetail.component";
import { ProductSelectionComponent } from "./store/productSelection.component";

const routes: Routes = [
    // { path: "table", component: ProductTableComponent },
    // { path: "detail", component: ProductDetailComponent },
    // { path: "detail/:id", component: ProductDetailComponent },
    // { path: "", component: ProductTableComponent }
    { path: "store", component: ProductSelectionComponent },
    { path: "", redirectTo: "/store", pathMatch: "full" }];

@NgModule({
  imports: [RouterModule.forRoot(routes)],
  exports: [RouterModule]
})
export class AppRoutingModule { }
```

There are two routes in this configuration, which will show the ProductSelectionComponent for the /store URL and redirect to /store for the default URL. To ensure that the new URL works correctly when it is requested directly, I updated the routing configuration in the ASP.NET Core part of the project, as shown in Listing 8-18.

Listing 8-18. Changing Routes in the Startup.cs File in the ServerApp Folder

```
...
app.UseEndpoints(endpoints => {
    endpoints.MapControllerRoute(
        name: "default",
        pattern: "{controller=Home}/{action=Index}/{id?}");
```

```
    endpoints.MapControllerRoute(
        name: "angular_fallback",
        pattern: "{target:regex(store)}/{*catchall}",
        defaults: new  { controller = "Home", action = "Index"});

    endpoints.MapRazorPages();
});
...
```

Removing the Layout Header

The shard Razor layout used by ASP.NET Core MVC duplicates the SportsStore header contained in the template for the product selection component. I want Angular to be responsible for the header so that I can create a component that summarizes the cart's content, so I commented out the duplicate element, as shown in Listing 8-19.

Listing 8-19. Commenting Out a Header in the _Layout.cshtml File in the ServerApp/Views/Shared Folder

```
<!DOCTYPE html>
<html lang="en">
<head>
    <base href="/">
    <meta charset="utf-8" />
    <meta name="viewport" content="width=device-width, initial-scale=1.0" />
    <title>SportsStore</title>
    <link rel="stylesheet" href="~/lib/bootstrap/dist/css/bootstrap.css" />
</head>
<body>
    <!-- <h2 class="bg-dark text-white p-2">SportStore</h2> -->
    @RenderBody()
    @RenderSection("Scripts", required: false)
</body>
</html>
```

Once you have saved the changes and the browser has reloaded, you will see the content shown in Figure 8-3. (You may have to manually navigate to `https://localhost:5001` or reload the browser to see the changes.) It doesn't look like much, but it provides the basic structure of the product selection feature and provides a structure into which I can add individual features.

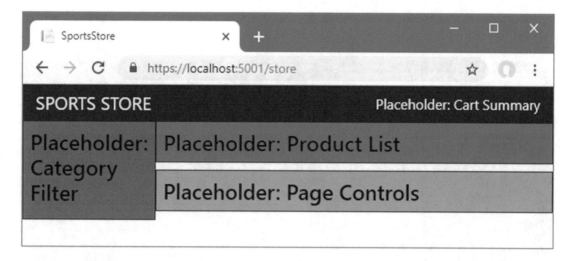

Figure 8-3. *Creating the structure for the product selection feature*

Displaying the Product List

Showing a list of available products is relatively easy because this is one of the features used in Chapter 5 to create the web service. The product list component has a `products` property that provides access to the `Product` objects in the repository. Edit the component's template as shown in Listing 8-20 to display the `Product` objects provided by the `Repository` and the component.

Listing 8-20. Displaying Data in the productList.component.html File in the ClientApp/src/app/store Folder

```html
<div *ngIf="products?.length > 0; else nodata" class="">
    <div *ngFor="let product of products" class="card m-1 p-1 bg-light">
        <h4>
            {{ product.name }}
            <span class="float-right badge badge-pill badge-primary">
                {{ product.price  | currency:"USD":"symbol" }}
            </span>
        </h4>
        <div class="card-text">
            {{ product.description }}
            <button class="float-right btn btn-sm btn-success"
                    (click)="addToCart(product)">
                Add to Cart
            </button>
        </div>
    </div>
</div>

<ng-template #nodata>
    <h4 class="m-2">Waiting for data...</h4>
</ng-template>
```

Save the change to the template and reload the Angular application to see the list of products illustrated in Figure 8-4.

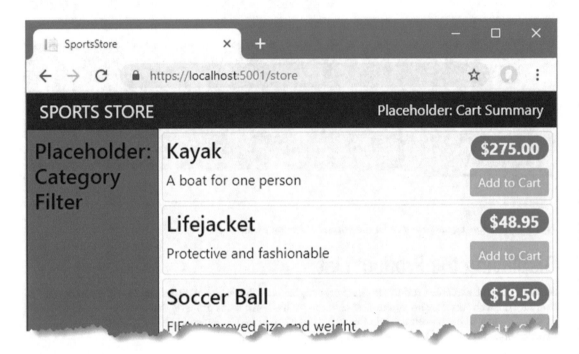

Figure 8-4. *Displaying a list of products*

Understanding the Product List Template Features

This template uses some of the Angular features seen in previous chapters but introduces some new ones, too. In the sections that follow, I describe each of the template features used in Listing 8-20.

Understanding the ngIf Directive

The first Angular feature used in the template is the ngIf directive, which comes in two parts, like this:

```
<div *ngIf="products?.length > 0; else nodata">
    <!-- content to be displayed if expression evaluates as true -->
</div>

<ng-template #nodata>
    <!-- content to be displayed if expression evaluates as false -->
</ng-template>
```

If the ngIf directive's expression evaluates to true, then the element it has been applied to and its content are inserted into the HTML shown to the user. If the expression is false, then the element is removed. Like other Angular directives, ngIf reevaluates its expression when there is a data change, which allows elements to be created or deleted dynamically. In this case, the expression checks to see that there are Product objects to display, and if there are, the div element to which the ngIf directive has been applied will be added to the HTML document.

178

This listing uses an optional feature of the ngIf directive. The directive's expression is followed by a semicolon (the ; character) and the else keyword, followed by a name. The name corresponds to the ng-template element, which will be added to the HTML document when the ngIf directive's expression is false. In this case, the effect is that a Waiting for Data message will be displayed when there is no Product data to display.

STRUCTURAL DIRECTIVES REQUIRE AN ASTERISK

Some Angular directives are applied with an asterisk before their names, such as *ngIf and *ngFor, and you will receive an error if you omit it. Directives that add or remove content contained in the element they are applied to are known as *structural directives*, and they can be used in two ways: the full syntax and the concise syntax.

The asterisk tells Angular that you want to use the concise syntax, which is easier to work with and is what I use throughout this book. The full syntax is required only when you can't apply the directive directly to an element, which I demonstrate in Chapter 11. It can be difficult to remember which directives require an asterisk when you first start working with Angular, but it quickly becomes second nature.

Understanding the ngFor Directive

The ngFor directive generates the same content for each object in a sequence, such as an array. The directive assigns each object to a temporary variable, whose name is defined in the expression and which can be used for data bindings (and other directives) inside the directive's element. In this case, the ngFor directive is applied to the set of objects returned by the component's products property and assigns each object in turn to a variable called product, like this:

```
...
<div *ngFor="let product of products" class="card m-1 p-1 bg-light">
...
```

Directives and data bindings applied to elements contained within the div element that the ngFor directive has been applied to can access the current object by using the product variable, like this:

```
...
<h4>
    {{ product.name }}
    <span class="float-right badge badge-pill badge-primary">
        {{product.price  | currency:"USD":"symbol" }}
    </span>
</h4>
...
```

In Listing 8-20, the ngFor directive generates content for each Product object, and the content and data bindings that are produced provide the user with the name, price, and description of each product that is available.

Understanding the Currency Pipe

Angular pipes are responsible for formatting data values so they can be presented to the user. Angular includes some pipes that perform common formatting tasks, as described in Table 8-2.

Table 8-2. *The Built-in Angular Pipes*

Name	Description
number	This pipe is used to specify the number of integer and fraction digits shown for a number value.
currency	This pipe is used to format a number value as a currency amount.
percent	This pipe is used to format a number value as a percentage.
uppercase	This pipe is used to convert a string value to uppercase characters.
lowercase	This pipe is used to convert a string value to lowercase characters.
json	This pipe is used to serialize an object to JSON data.
slice	This pipe is used to select elements from an array.

I used the currency pipe in Listing 8-20 to format the price of a product as a currency value, like this:

```
...
{{ product.price  | currency:"USD":"symbol" }}
...
```

Pipes are applied to a data value using the vertical bar (the | character), followed by the name of the pipe and its configuration settings. Each built-in pipe has its own options, and the ones used in this case specify the U.S. dollar as the currency and select the currency symbol rather than the currency code, so that $ is displayed rather than USD.

Understanding the Click Handler

The final template feature used in Listing 8-20 is the event binding, which is used to handle the click event on the button element and allows the user to add a product to the shopping cart.

```
...
<button class="float-right btn btn-sm btn-success"
        (click)="addToCart(product)">
    Add to Cart
</button>
...
```

The binding tells Angular to invoke a method called addToCart, using the value of the product variable created by the ngFor directive as an argument. The addToCart method doesn't exist yet, but I will create it in Chapter 9 when I create the shopping cart functionality. Until then, clicking the button element will produce an error in the browser's JavaScript console.

Creating the Category Filter

The challenge in implementing the category filter is getting the complete set of categories. The requests made by the Repository class to the web service to get Product objects may return only a subset of the available data, which means that deriving the categories from that data may return an incomplete list.

As a consequence, I need additional information that describes the complete set of data that is available, even if not all of the data is being sent to the client. In the sections that follow, I enhance the ASP. NET Core MVC web service to provide a description of the data available and demonstrate how to consume that data in the Angular application.

Enhancing the ASP.NET Core MVC Application

To provide the client with category information, add a new method to the ProductValues controller and update the GetProducts method, as shown in Listing 8-21.

Listing 8-21. Adding an Action in the ProductValuesController.cs File in the ServerApp/Controllers Folder

```
using Microsoft.AspNetCore.Mvc;
using ServerApp.Models;
using Microsoft.EntityFrameworkCore;
using System.Linq;
using System.Collections.Generic;
using ServerApp.Models.BindingTargets;
using Microsoft.AspNetCore.JsonPatch;
using System.Text.Json;
using System.Reflection;
using System.ComponentModel;

namespace ServerApp.Controllers {

    [Route("api/products")]
    [ApiController]
    public class ProductValuesController : Controller {
        private DataContext context;

        public ProductValuesController(DataContext ctx) {
            context = ctx;
        }

        // ...other methods omitted for brevity...

        [HttpGet]
        public IActionResult GetProducts(string category, string search,
                bool related = false, bool metadata = false) {
            IQueryable<Product> query = context.Products;

            if (!string.IsNullOrWhiteSpace(category)) {
                string catLower = category.ToLower();
                query = query.Where(p => p.Category.ToLower().Contains(catLower));
            }
```

```
            if (!string.IsNullOrWhiteSpace(search)) {
                string searchLower = search.ToLower();
                query = query.Where(p => p.Name.ToLower().Contains(searchLower)
                    || p.Description.ToLower().Contains(searchLower));
            }

            if (related) {
                query = query.Include(p => p.Supplier).Include(p => p.Ratings);
                List<Product> data = query.ToList();
                data.ForEach(p => {
                    if (p.Supplier != null) {
                        p.Supplier.Products = null;
                    }
                    if (p.Ratings != null) {
                        p.Ratings.ForEach(r => r.Product = null);
                    }
                });
                return metadata ? CreateMetadata(data) : Ok(data);
            } else {
                return metadata ? CreateMetadata(query) : Ok(query);
            }
        }

        private IActionResult CreateMetadata(IEnumerable<Product> products) {
            return Ok(new {
                data = products,
                categories = context.Products.Select(p => p.Category)
                    .Distinct().OrderBy(c => c)
            });
        }

        // ...other methods omitted for brevity...
    }
}
```

This listing adds an optional parameter called metadata to the GetProducts method. When this parameter is true, then the CreateMetadata method is used to generate a result with data and categories properties, which allows the product data and the category data to be combined in a single response. The data property is set to the sequence of Product objects that the client has requested, and the categories property is set using a LINQ query that produces an ordered set of distinct category names.

Receiving Category Data in the Angular Data Repository

To allow the Angular application to receive the category data, make the changes shown in Listing 8-22 to the Repository class.

Listing 8-22. Receiving Category Data in the repository.ts File in the ClientApp/src/app/models Folder

```
import { Product } from "./product.model";
import { Injectable } from "@angular/core";
import { HttpClient } from "@angular/common/http";
```

```
import { Filter } from "./configClasses.repository";
import { Supplier } from "./supplier.model";

const productsUrl = "/api/products";
const suppliersUrl = "/api/suppliers";

type productsMetadata = {
    data: Product[],
    categories: string[];
}

@Injectable()
export class Repository {
    product: Product;
    products: Product[];
    suppliers: Supplier[] = [];
    filter: Filter = new Filter();
    categories: string[] = [];

    constructor(private http: HttpClient) {
        //this.filter.category = "soccer";
        this.filter.related = true;
        this.getProducts();
    }

    getProduct(id: number) {
        this.http.get<Product>(`${productsUrl}/${id}`)
            .subscribe(p => this.product = p);
    }

    getProducts() {
        let url = `${productsUrl}?related=${this.filter.related}`;
        if (this.filter.category) {
            url += `&category=${this.filter.category}`;
        }
        if (this.filter.search) {
            url += `&search=${this.filter.search}`;
        }
        url += "&metadata=true";

        this.http.get<productsMetadata>(url)
            .subscribe(md => {
                this.products = md.data;
                this.categories = md.categories;
            });
    }

    // ...other methods omitted for brevity...
}
```

Although it would be possible to be selective about getting the category data, I have chosen to receive a new set of categories every time the application refreshes its product data by calling the getProducts method, ensuring that any changes to the data stored in the database will be reflected in the client.

The set of category names returned by the web service is made available through the Repository class's categories property, which is initialized to an empty array until the data from the web service is assigned to it.

A type alias is used to describe the data that will be received from the web service, like this:

```
...
type productsMetadata = {
    data: Product[],
    categories: string[];
}
...
```

This is a useful way to describe a data type to TypeScript and can be used in a generic type argument, like this:

```
...
this.http.get<productsMetadata>(url)
    .subscribe(md => {
        this.products = md.data;
        this.categories = md.categories;
});
...
```

Defining a Navigation Service

I want to manage category selection through URL navigation. There are lots of ways to connect components and the URL routing feature together, and the approach I am going to take for this application is to define a simple shared service that will define methods that components can invoke to change the application's state, such as selecting a category, and trigger a navigation change. To create the service, add a file named navigation.service.ts to the ClientApp/src/app/models folder with the code shown in Listing 8-23.

Listing 8-23. The Contents of the navigation.service.ts File in the ClientApp/src/app/models Folder

```
import { Injectable } from "@angular/core";
import { Router, ActivatedRoute, NavigationEnd } from "@angular/router";
import { Repository } from '../models/repository';
import { filter } from "rxjs/operators";

@Injectable()
export class NavigationService {

    constructor(private repository: Repository, private router: Router,
            private active: ActivatedRoute) {
        router.events
            .pipe(filter(event => event instanceof NavigationEnd))
            .subscribe(ev => this.handleNavigationChange());
    }
```

```
    private handleNavigationChange() {
        let active = this.active.firstChild.snapshot;
        if (active.url.length > 0 && active.url[0].path === "store") {
            let category = active.params["category"];
            this.repository.filter.category = category || "";
            this.repository.getProducts();
        }
    }

    get categories(): string[] {
        return this.repository.categories;
    }

    get currentCategory(): string {
        return this.repository.filter.category || "";
    }

    set currentCategory(newCategory: string) {
        this.router.navigateByUrl(`/store/${(newCategory || "").toLowerCase()}`);
    }
}
```

The NavigationService class defines categories and currentCategory properties that return the state data from the repository. Setting the currentCategory property triggers a navigation change.

When responding to navigation changes in a service, a different approach is required from the approach I used for a component in Chapter 7. The service uses the Router.events property to subscribe to notification events and then uses the ActivatedRoute.firstChild property to get information about the new route. Responding to navigation changes triggered by the same service may seem like an odd approach, but it means that the application will respond consistently when the user navigates directly to a URL.

Angular emits a routing event when the application first starts, which means that the HTTP request triggered by the Repository constructor can be removed, as shown in Listing 8-24.

Listing 8-24. Commenting a Statement in the repository.ts File in the ClientApp/src/app/model Folder

```
...
constructor(private http: HttpClient) {
    this.filter.related = true;
    //this.getProducts();
}
...
```

Registering the Service

To enable the service, register the NavigationService class with the module for the data model, as shown in Listing 8-25.

Listing 8-25. Registering a Service in the model.module.ts File in the ClientApp/src/app/models Folder

```
import { NgModule } from "@angular/core";
import { Repository } from "./repository";
import { HttpClientModule } from '@angular/common/http';
import { NavigationService } from "./navigation.service";

@NgModule({
    imports: [HttpClientModule],
    providers: [Repository, NavigationService]
})
export class ModelModule {}
```

Updating the Angular Routing Configuration

To add support for the URL format that contains the selected category, add the route shown in Listing 8-26 to the application's routing module.

Listing 8-26. Adding a Route in the app-routing.module.ts File in the ClientApp/src/app Folder

```
import { NgModule } from '@angular/core';
import { Routes, RouterModule } from '@angular/router';
import { ProductSelectionComponent } from "./store/productSelection.component";

const routes: Routes = [
    { path: "store/:category", component: ProductSelectionComponent },
    { path: "store", component: ProductSelectionComponent },
    { path: "", redirectTo: "/store", pathMatch: "full" }
];

@NgModule({
  imports: [RouterModule.forRoot(routes)],
  exports: [RouterModule]
})
export class AppRoutingModule { }
```

Updating the Filter Component and Template

All that remains is to present the user with a list of categories and use their selection to change the category, both of which are done through the service defined in the previous section. The first step is to update the component class so it declares a constructor dependency on the service, as shown in Listing 8-27.

Listing 8-27. Using a Service in the categoryFilter.component.ts File in the ClientApp/src/app/store Folder

```
import { Component } from "@angular/core";
import { NavigationService } from '../models/navigation.service';

@Component({
    selector: "store-categoryfilter",
    templateUrl: "categoryFilter.component.html"
```

```
})
export class CategoryFilterComponent {

    constructor(public service: NavigationService) { }
}
```

I usually define local properties and methods in a component that provides access to the service features in the template, but for this component I am going to access the service through the component property directly, just to show the different ways in which Angular can be used. To use the method and properties defined by the service, replace the content in the component's template with the elements shown in Listing 8-28.

Listing 8-28. Categories in the categoryFilter.component.html File in the ClientApp/src/app/store Folder

```
<div class="m-1">
    <button class="btn btn-outline-primary btn-block"
    [class.active]="service.currentCategory == ""
            (click)="service.currentCategory = "">
        All Categories
    </button>
    <button *ngFor="let category of service.categories"
            class="btn btn-outline-primary btn-block"
            [class.active]="service.currentCategory.toLowerCase()
                == category.toLowerCase()"
            (click)="service.currentCategory = category">
        {{category}}
    </button>
</div>
```

The template has two button elements. The first button element allows the user to select all of the categories and has a click event binding that calls the setCurrentCategory method with null as the argument.

The ngFor directive has been applied to the other element, with an expression that operates on the category names and produces a button for each of them. There is a click event binding that calls the setCurrentCategory method to select a category. There is also a new kind of binding, known as the *class binding*:

```
...
<button *ngFor="let category of service.categories"
        class="btn btn-outline-primary btn-block"
        [class.active]="service.currentCategory.toLowerCase()
            == category.toLowerCase()"
        (click)="service.currentCategory = category">
    {{category}}
</button>
...
```

The class binding is applied using square brackets (the [and] characters) containing the class keyword, followed by a period, followed by the name of a class, such as the Bootstrap active class, which applies a style to the element that shows it is selected. The element is added to the class when the expression evaluates as true and is removed when it is false. The expression is evaluated when the data model changes, which means that the button elements will be added and removed from the active class automatically as the selected category changes.

The category buttons will be displayed once the application has reloaded. Clicking the button filters the products so that only those in the selected category are displayed, as shown in Figure 8-5. The selected category is reflected in the URL so that the application will navigate to /store/chess when the Chess category is selected. The user can also navigate directly to a URL to select a category.

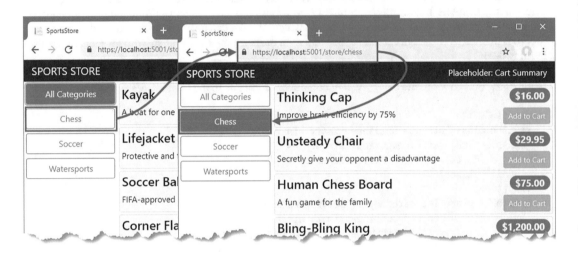

Figure 8-5. *Filtering categories*

Creating the Pagination Controls

Most applications have too much data to display in one go or even to send to the client in one go. The most common solution is to break the data into pages and allow the user to navigate between pages on demand.

Updating the Routing Configuration

To provide support for paging data, make the changes shown in Listing 8-29 to the Angular application's URL routing configuration.

Listing 8-29. Supporting Pagination in the app-routing.module.ts File in the ClientApp/src/app Folder

```
import { NgModule } from '@angular/core';
import { Routes, RouterModule } from '@angular/router';
import { ProductSelectionComponent } from "./store/productSelection.component";

const routes: Routes = [
    { path: "store/:category/:page", component: ProductSelectionComponent },
    { path: "store/:categoryOrPage", component: ProductSelectionComponent },
    { path: "store", component: ProductSelectionComponent },
    { path: "", redirectTo: "/store", pathMatch: "full" }
];
```

```
@NgModule({
  imports: [RouterModule.forRoot(routes)],
  exports: [RouterModule]
})
export class AppRoutingModule { }
```

The combined effect of these routes is that the URL can specify a category or a page number or both. This means that /store, /store/chess, /store/1, and /store/chess/1 are all supported.

Representing Pagination State

I am going to create multiple building blocks to implement the pagination controls. To help them cooperate, I am going to create a class that represents the current pagination state and provide access to it through the Repository class. Add the class shown in Listing 8-30 to the configClasses.repository.ts file.

Listing 8-30. Adding a Class in the configClasses.repository.ts File in the ClientApp/src/app/model Folder

```
export class Filter {
    category?: string;
    search?: string;
    related: boolean = false;

    reset() {
        this.category = this.search = null;
        this.related = false;
    }
}

export class Pagination {

    productsPerPage: number = 4;
    currentPage = 1;
}
```

The Pagination class defines properties that specify how many products will be displayed by each page and which page is currently selected. These are simple data values, but making them available through the Repository class will make it easy to write the building blocks that will provide the pagination feature and get them to work together. Make the changes shown in Listing 8-31 to the Repository class to create shared pagination state and to reset the selected page when the product data is refreshed by the getProducts method.

Listing 8-31. Exposing Page Data in the repository.ts File in the ClientApp/src/app/models Folder

```
import { Product } from "./product.model";
import { Injectable } from "@angular/core";
import { HttpClient } from "@angular/common/http";
import { Filter, Pagination } from "./configClasses.repository";
import { Supplier } from "./supplier.model";

const productsUrl = "/api/products";
const suppliersUrl = "/api/suppliers";
```

```
type productsMetadata = {
    data: Product[],
    categories: string[];
}

@Injectable()
export class Repository {
    product: Product;
    products: Product[];
    suppliers: Supplier[] = [];
    categories: string[] = [];
    filter: Filter = new Filter();
    paginationObject = new Pagination();

    constructor(private http: HttpClient) {
        this.filter.related = true;
    }

    // ...methods omitted for brevity...
}
```

Updating the Navigation Service and Routing Configuration

I am going to use the service I defined for dealing with category selection to handle page selection as well. Add the statements shown in Listing 8-32 to the NavigationService class.

Listing 8-32. Adding Features in the navigation.service.ts File in the ClientApp/src/app/models Folder

```
import { Injectable } from "@angular/core";
import { Router, ActivatedRoute, NavigationEnd } from "@angular/router";
import { Repository } from '../models/repository';
import { filter } from "rxjs/operators";

@Injectable()
export class NavigationService {

    constructor(private repository: Repository, private router: Router,
            private active: ActivatedRoute) {
        router.events
            .pipe(filter(event => event instanceof NavigationEnd))
            .subscribe(ev => this.handleNavigationChange());
    }

    private handleNavigationChange() {
        let active = this.active.firstChild.snapshot;
        if (active.url.length > 0 && active.url[0].path === "store") {
            if (active.params["categoryOrPage"] !== undefined) {
                let value = Number.parseInt(active.params["categoryOrPage"]);
                if (!Number.isNaN(value)) {
                    this.repository.filter.category = "";
```

```
                    this.repository.paginationObject.currentPage = value;
                } else {
                    this.repository.filter.category
                        = active.params["categoryOrPage"];
                    this.repository.paginationObject.currentPage = 1;
                }
            } else {
                let category = active.params["category"];
                this.repository.filter.category = category || "";
                this.repository.paginationObject.currentPage
                    = Number.parseInt(active.params["page"]) || 1
            }
            this.repository.getProducts();
        }
    }

    get categories(): string[] {
        return this.repository.categories;
    }

    get currentCategory(): string {
        return this.repository.filter.category;
    }

    set currentCategory(newCategory: string) {
        this.router.navigateByUrl(`/store/${(newCategory || "").toLowerCase()}`);
    }

    get currentPage(): number {
        return this.repository.paginationObject.currentPage;
    }

    set currentPage(newPage: number) {
        if (this.currentCategory === "") {
            this.router.navigateByUrl(`/store/${newPage}`);
        } else {
            this.router.navigateByUrl(`/store/${this.currentCategory}/${newPage}`);
        }
    }

    get productsPerPage(): number {
        return this.repository.paginationObject.productsPerPage;
    }

    get productCount(): number {
        return (this.repository.products || []).length;
    }
}
```

The changes in the handleNavigationChange method determine whether the URL specifies a category, a page, or both. The new properties expose the pagination state data.

Updating the Pagination Button Component

Now that the navigation service provides access to pagination data, I can update the component so that it can provide the support required for the page navigation buttons, as shown in Listing 8-33.

Listing 8-33. Adding Page Support in the pagination.component.ts File in the ClientApp/src/app/store Folder

```
import { Component } from "@angular/core";
import { NavigationService } from "../models/navigation.service";

@Component({
    selector: "store-pagination",
    templateUrl: "pagination.component.html"
})
export class PaginationComponent {

    constructor(public navigation: NavigationService) { }

    get pages(): number[] {
        if (this.navigation.productCount > 0) {
            return Array(Math.ceil(this.navigation.productCount
                    / this.navigation.productsPerPage))
                .fill(0).map((x, i) => i + 1);
        } else {
            return [];
        }
    }
}
```

The pages property uses the features added to the NavigationService class to generate a sequence of page numbers, which will provide the ngFor directive with the objects it needs to create and configure the buttons that will change the page. (The ngFor directive cannot be used to create a for loop and must always be provided with a sequence of objects to work with.)

Edit the component's template to generate the elements that will allow the user to change pages, as shown in Listing 8-34.

Listing 8-34. Adding Page Support in the pagination.component.html File in the ClientApp/src/app/store Folder

```
<div *ngIf="pages.length > 1" class="text-right my-2">
    <button *ngFor="let page of pages"
            class="btn btn-outline-primary mx-1"
            [class.active]="navigation.currentPage == page"
            (click)="navigation.currentPage = page">
        {{page}}
    </button>
</div>
```

All the features used in this template have been described in earlier examples. The ngIf directive is used to ensure that page buttons are displayed only if there are multiple pages of products available. The ngFor directive is used to generate button elements for each page, with the class binding showing the active page and the click event binding allowing the user to change pages. Save the changes and reload the browser, and you will see the page buttons displayed at the end of the product list, as shown in Figure 8-6.

The buttons are displayed only when there are more than four products to display, which means that they are not shown when a category filter is applied because there are not enough products to require pagination in any of the categories.

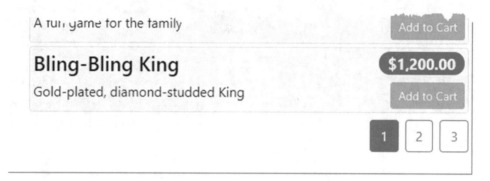

Figure 8-6. *The page navigation buttons*

Paging the Product Data

The page navigation buttons are in place, and clicking them triggers a navigation change but doesn't change the list of products displayed to the user. To complete the feature, update the product list component so that its products property takes into account the pagination data, as shown in Listing 8-35.

Listing 8-35. Paging Data in the productList.component.ts File in the ClientApp/src/app/store Folder

```
import { Component } from "@angular/core";
import { Repository } from "../models/repository";
import { Product } from "../models/product.model";

@Component({
    selector: "store-product-list",
    templateUrl: "productList.component.html"
})
export class ProductListComponent {

    constructor(private repo: Repository) { }

    get products(): Product[] {
        if (this.repo.products != null && this.repo.products.length > 0) {
            let pageIndex = (this.repo.paginationObject.currentPage - 1)
                * this.repo.paginationObject.productsPerPage;
            return this.repo.products.slice(pageIndex,
                pageIndex + this.repo.paginationObject.productsPerPage);
        }
    }
}
```

The implementation of the products getter uses the JavaScript array slice method to select a subset of the Product objects available in the repository. Save the change, and you will see that the list of products is paginated and changes when a new page is selected, as shown in Figure 8-7.

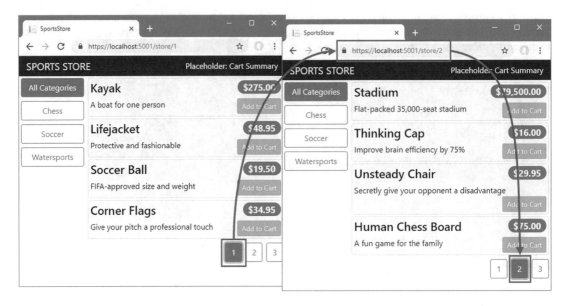

Figure 8-7. *Paginating products*

Displaying Ratings

Displaying ratings requires some different techniques, since multiple instances of the ratings component will be created, each of which will be responsible for displaying the rating of a single product. In the sections that follow, I add a package to the project that will provide the graphics required for the rating and show you how to create a component that handles a single data object.

Adding the Font Awesome Package

The Font Awesome package provides access to a large collection of icons that can be easily integrated into web applications. When using Angular to create stand-alone projects, packages are added to the project using NPM. For combined projects, a little more thought is required. If a package contains code that will be included in the bundle files produced by the Angular build tools, then NPM should be used. For packages that contain content that is processed directly by the browser, such as images or CSS stylesheets, such as Font Awesome, then the package should be added to the ASP.NET Core MVC project and referenced using an element in a Razor view or layout. Microsoft has had several changes in direction when it comes to dealing with client-side packages and has recently introduced the Library Manager tool for this purpose.

Open a new command prompt, navigate to the `ServerApp` folder, and run the commands shown in Listing 8-36 to use the Library Manager tool to install the Font Awesome package.

Listing 8-36. Adding a Client-Side Package Using Library Manager

```
dotnet tool install -g Microsoft.Web.LibraryManager.Cli

libman install font-awesome@5.9.0 -p cdnjs -d wwwroot/lib/font-awesome
```

These commands install the LibMan tool and use it to install version 5.9.0 of Font Awesome into the wwwroot/lib folder, using CNDJS as the source for the package. (You may receive an error from the libman command, telling you that a compatible version of the .NET Core SDK cannot be found. If this happens, then you need to download and install the SDK version specified in the error message. This won't affect the version of .NET Core that is used by the example project and is required only to run the libman command. The .NET Core SDKs can be downloaded from https://dotnet.microsoft.com/download).

To include Font Awesome in the content sent to the browser, add the element shown in Listing 8-37 to the Razor layout.

Listing 8-37. Adding an Element in the _Layout.cshtml File in the ServerApp/Views/Shared Folder

```
<!DOCTYPE html>
<html lang="en">
<head>
    <base href="/">
    <meta charset="utf-8" />
    <meta name="viewport" content="width=device-width, initial-scale=1.0" />
    <title>SportsStore</title>
    <link rel="stylesheet" href="~/lib/bootstrap/dist/css/bootstrap.css" />
    <link rel="stylesheet" href="~/lib/font-awesome/css/all.css" />
</head>
<body>
    @RenderBody()
    @RenderSection("Scripts", required: false)
</body>
</html>
```

Updating the Rating Component and Template

To display the ratings for a product, I am going to average the number of stars that have been awarded. The component will display five star icons, which will be shown in solid color or outline to indicate the overall rating. The component needs to provide its template with a sequence of five values that indicate whether a star should be solid or outline, as shown in Listing 8-38.

Listing 8-38. Generating Rating Data in the ratings.component.ts File in the ClientApp/src/app/store Folder

```
import { Component, Input } from "@angular/core";
import { Product } from "../models/product.model";

@Component({
    selector: "store-ratings",
    templateUrl: "ratings.component.html"
})
export class RatingsComponent {

    @Input()
    product: Product;
```

```
    get stars(): boolean[] {
        if (this.product != null && this.product.ratings != null) {
            let total = this.product.ratings.map(r => r.stars)
                .reduce((prev, curr) => prev + curr, 0);
            let count = Math.round(total / this.product.ratings.length);
            return Array(5).fill(false).map((value, index) => {
                return index < count;
            });
        } else {
            return [];
        }
    }
}
```

The component needs to know which Product object it is responsible for, and for this I have used an Angular *input property*. Input properties are decorated with the @Input decorator, which is defined in the @angular/core module, like this:

```
...
@Input()
product: Product;
...
```

Input properties allow components to receive data from the template in which they are applied. You'll see how this is used in the next section, but when Angular creates this component, it will set the value of the product property to the Product object for which rating information should be displayed.

The stars function uses the Product object to generate an array of boolean values that can be used with the ngFor directive. If a Product has an average of three stars, for example, then the stars property will return an array containing the values true, true, true, false, false. To display the star rating, add the elements shown in Listing 8-39 to the component's template.

Listing 8-39. Displaying Ratings in the ratings.component.html File in the ClientApp/src/app/store Folder

```
<span class="h6 ml-1">
    <i *ngFor="let s of stars"
        [class]="s ? 'fas fa-star' : 'far fa-star'"
        [style.color]="s ? 'goldenrod' : 'gray'">
    </i>
</span>
```

The i element is how Font Awesome icons are applied, with the classes to which the element is assigned determining which icon is shown.

The ngFor directive creates an i element for each of the five entries in the array returned by the stars property. To configure the i element, the listing uses two data bindings, which are the attributes whose names are in square brackets.

The class data binding evaluates an expression and uses the result to set the classes to which an element is a member. In the listing, this binding is used to choose between two different sets of classes that select Font Awesome icons.

```
...
[class]="s ? 'fas fa-star' : 'far fa-star'"
...
```

This is another example of the class data binding, except that it sets all of the classes that the element is assigned to using the result of its expression. In this case, the expression uses the JavaScript ternary operator to examine the value of the s variable and selects the fas and fa-star classes if it is true (which creates a solid star icon) and the far and fa-star classes if it is false (which creates an outline star icon). Notice that the classes in the expression are specified as string literals and that the fa-star class is required for both outcomes since this binding replaces all existing classes.

The color CSS property is used to set the color of the Font Awesome icons. The style data binding is used to set style properties and has been used in this listing to set the color property.

```
...
[style.color]="s ? 'goldenrod' : 'gray'">
...
```

The expression for this data binding uses the ternary operator to inspect the s variable and chooses goldenrod if it is true and gray if it is false.

Applying the Rating Component

The last step required to display the product ratings is to add the store-ratings element, which tells Angular to apply the ratings component. Add the element shown in Listing 8-40 to the product list component's template.

Listing 8-40. Adding an Element in the productList.component.html File in the ClientApp/src/app/model Folder

```
<div *ngIf="products?.length > 0; else nodata" class="">
    <div *ngFor="let product of products" class="card m-1 p-1 bg-light">
        <h4>
            {{ product.name }}
            <store-ratings [product]="product"></store-ratings>
            <span class="float-right badge badge-pill badge-primary">
                {{ product.price | currency:"USD":"symbol" }}
            </span>
        </h4>
        <div class="card-text">
            {{ product.description }}
            <button class="float-right btn btn-sm btn-success"
                    (click)="addToCart(product)">
                Add to Cart
            </button>
        </div>
    </div>
</div>

<ng-template #nodata>
    <h4 class="m-2">Waiting for data...</h4>
</ng-template>
```

The store-ratings element has been applied inside the content generated by the ngFor directive, which means that Angular will create an instance of the controller class for each product that is displayed to the user. To provide the ratings component with the Product object whose ratings will be displayed, a data binding is applied to the store-ratings element, like this:

```
...
<store-ratings [product]="product"></store-ratings>
...
```

The square brackets are used to denote the binding, enclosing the name of the input property defined in Listing 8-40. The value for the input property is set using the binding expression, which is the value of the product variable created by the ngFor directive.

Save the changes and let the application restart. You will see that the product list has been updated so that each product includes its rating data, as shown in Figure 8-8.

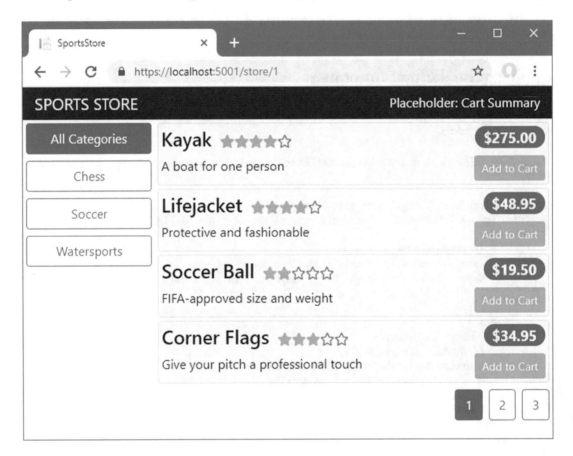

Figure 8-8. *Displaying ratings*

Summary

In this chapter, I started work on using the Angular application to present the product selection feature to the user. I created the components that will cooperate to provide features to the user and organized them with placeholder content to create the overall structure. I then added support for listing the products available, filtering the products by category, paging through products when there are too many to display, and showing the ratings awarded to each product. In the next chapter, I complete the SportsStore store.

CHAPTER 9

Completing the Angular Store

In this chapter, I complete the customer-facing features for the SportsStore application, allowing the user to add products to a shopping cart and checking out to place an order.

Preparing for This Chapter

This chapter uses the SportsStore project that I created in Chapter 3 and modified in the chapters since. To remove the database so that the application will use fresh seed data, open a new command prompt, navigate to the ServerApp folder, and run the command shown in Listing 9-1.

Listing 9-1. Resetting the Database

```
dotnet ef database drop --force
```

Run the command shown in Listing 9-2 to start the ASP.NET Core runtime and the Angular development tools.

Listing 9-2. Starting the Development Tools

```
dotnet watch run
```

Open a new browser window and navigate to `https://localhost:5001`; you will see the content shown in Figure 9-1.

█ Tip You can download the complete project for every chapter without charge from the source code repository, `https://github.com/Apress/esntl-angular-for-asp.net-core-mvc-3`. Run `npm install` in the `ClientApp` folder to install the packages required for Angular development and then start the development tools as instructed.

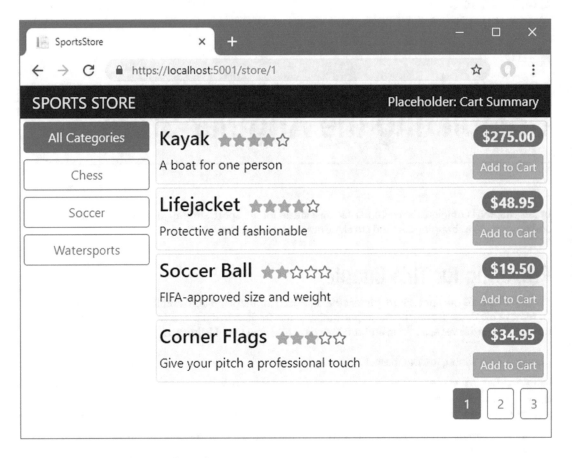

Figure 9-1. *Running the example application*

Creating the Shopping Cart

Most online stores allow users to gather the products they require into a shopping cart, which is then used to complete a purchase. In the sections that follow, I demonstrate how to create a shopping cart in the Angular application and how to store the contents of carts using ASP.NET Core MVC and Entity Framework Core.

Extending the Angular Data Model

The starting point is to define a new class that will represent the cart in the Angular application. Add a new TypeScript file called `cart.model.ts` in the `ClientApp/src/app/models` folder and use it to define the class shown in Listing 9-3.

Listing 9-3. The Contents of the cart.model.ts File in the ClientApp/src/app/models Folder

```typescript
import { Injectable } from "@angular/core";
import { Product } from "./product.model";

@Injectable()
export class Cart {
    selections: ProductSelection[] = [];
    itemCount: number = 0;
    totalPrice: number = 0;

    addProduct(product: Product) {
        let selection = this.selections
            .find(ps => ps.productId == product.productId);
        if (selection) {
            selection.quantity++;
        } else {
            this.selections.push(new ProductSelection(this,
                product.productId, product.name,
                product.price, 1));
        }
        this.update();
    }

    updateQuantity(productId: number, quantity: number) {
        if (quantity > 0) {
            let selection = this.selections.find(ps => ps.productId == productId);
            if (selection) {
                selection.quantity = quantity;
            }
        } else {
            let index = this.selections.findIndex(ps => ps.productId == productId);
            if (index != -1) {
                this.selections.splice(index, 1);
            }
            this.update();
        }
    }

    clear() {
        this.selections = [];
        this.update();
    }

    update() {
        this.itemCount = this.selections.map(ps => ps.quantity)
            .reduce((prev, curr) => prev + curr, 0);
        this.totalPrice = this.selections.map(ps => ps.price * ps.quantity)
            .reduce((prev, curr) => prev + curr, 0);
    }
}
```

```
export class ProductSelection {

    constructor(public cart: Cart,
        public productId?: number,
        public name?: string,
        public price?: number,
        private quantityValue?: number) { }

    get quantity() {
        return this.quantityValue;
    }

    set quantity(newQuantity: number) {
        this.quantityValue = newQuantity;
        this.cart.update();
    }
}
}
```

The Cart class represents the user's shopping cart, using the ProductSelection class to represent individual product choices. The Cart class provides methods that allow the product selections to be managed and provides properties those values report on the number of items in the cart and their total cost.

The update method must be called each time the product selection changes to recalculate the total cost and number of items in the cart. Remember that Angular evaluates data binding expressions repeatedly when there is an update and that it is a good idea to perform this kind of calculation only when required to avoid repeatedly inspecting the products in the cart.

Registering the Cart as a Service

I am going to register the Cart class as a service, which will allow other classes, including components, to declare a constructor dependency that will be resolved using dependency injection and will ensure that a single Cart object is shared throughout the application. To register the service, add the Cart class to the providers property of the model feature module, as shown in Listing 9-4.

Listing 9-4. Registering a Service in the model.module.ts File in the ClientApp/src/app/models Folder

```
import { NgModule } from "@angular/core";
import { Repository } from "./repository";
import { HttpClientModule } from '@angular/common/http';
import { NavigationService } from "./navigation.service";
import { Cart } from "./cart.model";

@NgModule({
    imports: [HttpClientModule],
    providers: [Repository, NavigationService, Cart]
})
export class ModelModule {}
```

Angular will create a Cart object and use it to satisfy constructor dependencies for the components that will provide the user-facing cart functionality.

Wiring Up the Buttons

The Add to Cart buttons that are displayed for each product in the list invoke a method in the template's component. This method doesn't yet exist but is required so that the user can select the products they want to buy. To allow the user to add products to the cart, make the changes shown in Listing 9-5 to the product list component.

Listing 9-5. Adding Cart Items in the productList.component.ts File in the ClientApp/src/app/store Folder

```
import { Component } from "@angular/core";
import { Repository } from "../models/repository";
import { Product } from "../models/product.model";
import { Cart } from '../models/cart.model';

@Component({
    selector: "store-product-list",
    templateUrl: "productList.component.html"
})
export class ProductListComponent {

    constructor(private repo: Repository, private cart: Cart) { }

    get products(): Product[] {
        if (this.repo.products != null && this.repo.products.length > 0) {
            let pageIndex = (this.repo.paginationObject.currentPage - 1)
                * this.repo.paginationObject.productsPerPage;
            return this.repo.products.slice(pageIndex,
                pageIndex + this.repo.paginationObject.productsPerPage);
        }
    }

    addToCart(product: Product) {
        this.cart.addProduct(product);
    }
}
```

The constructor receives a Cart object, whose addProduct method is called by the component's addToCart method.

Creating the Cart Summary Component

The first cart-related component will appear at the top of the product list and show the number of products that the user has in the cart and their total cost. Make the changes to the cartSummary.component.ts file in the store folder, as shown in Listing 9-6.

Listing 9-6. Adding Code in the cartSummary.component.ts File in the ClientApp/src/app/store Folder

```
import { Component } from "@angular/core";
import { Cart } from "../models/cart.model";

@Component({
    selector: "store-cartsummary",
    templateUrl: "cartSummary.component.html"
})
export class CartSummaryComponent {

    constructor(private cart: Cart) { }

    get itemCount(): number {
        return this.cart.itemCount;
    }

    get totalPrice(): number {
        return this.cart.totalPrice;
    }
}
```

The new constructor declares a dependency on the Cart class, which will be resolved using the service defined in Listing 9-3 and which is used to provide the values for the read-only itemCount and totalPrice properties. To display a summary of the cart to the user, replace the placeholder content in the component's template with the elements shown in Listing 9-7.

Listing 9-7. The cartSummary.component.html File in the ClientApp/src/app/store Folder

```
<div class="text-right p-1">
    <small *ngIf="itemCount > 0; else empty">
        {{ itemCount }} item(s), {{ totalPrice | currency:"USD":"symbol" }}
    </small>
    <button class="btn btn-sm ml-1"
            [disabled]="itemCount == 0"
            routerLink="/cart">
        <i class="text-white fa fa-shopping-cart"></i>
    </button>
</div>

<ng-template #empty>
    <small class="text-muted">
        (cart is empty)
    </small>
</ng-template>
```

This template uses features shown in earlier examples to present a summary of the cart to the user. The ngIf directive is used to change the content displayed to the user based on the number of items in the shopping cart. If there are no items, the empty template is displayed. If the cart contains items, then the number of items and total cost are shown instead.

There is a `button` element that uses a Font Awesome icon for a shopping cart and that is configured with a data binding on the `disabled` attribute like this:

```
...
<button class="btn btn-sm ml-1" [disabled]="itemCount == 0" routerLink="/cart">
...
```

This data binding disables the button when there are no items in the cart. The button element has also been configured with the `routerLink` attribute so that the application will navigate to the `/cart` URL when the button is clicked. This URL is not yet defined, but it will display a details list of the cart contents and allow the user to start the checkout process.

Save the changes and reload the application in the browser to see the cart summary. The summary will indicate that the cart is empty until you click the Add to Cart button for one or more products, after which the number of items in the cart and their cost will be displayed, as shown in Figure 9-2.

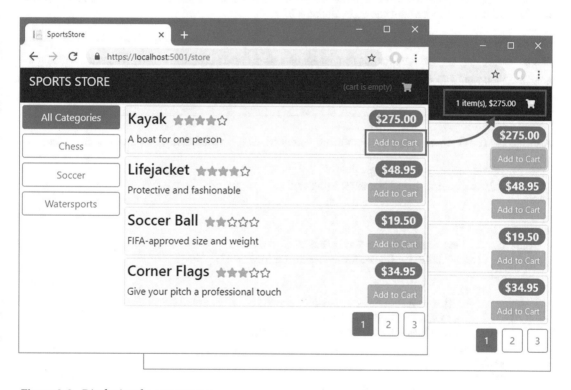

Figure 9-2. *Displaying the cart summary*

Displaying the Cart Detail

The next step is to create the component that will display a detailed view of the cart, allowing the user to make changes to the quantities of each product, to remove products from the cart, and to commence the checkout process. Create a TypeScript file called `cartDetail.component.ts` in the `store` folder and add the code shown in Listing 9-8.

Listing 9-8. The Contents of the cartDetail.component.ts File in the ClientApp/src/app/store Folder

```
import { Component } from "@angular/core";
import { Cart } from "../models/cart.model";

@Component({
    templateUrl: "cartDetail.component.html"
})
export class CartDetailComponent {

    constructor(public cart: Cart) { }
}
```

This component defines a constructor `Cart` parameter that is used to create a `cart` property that can be accessed by the template. To create the template, create an HTML file called `cartDetail.component.html` in the `store` folder with the content shown in Listing 9-9.

▪ **Tip**   Notice that the decorator for this component doesn't define a `selector` property. A selector is required only when you want Angular to apply the component to a specific HTML element in an HTML template and can be omitted if the component is going to be displayed only in a `router-outlet` element by the URL routing system.

Listing 9-9. The Contents of the cartDetail.component.html File in the ClientApp/src/app/store Folder

```html
<div class="bg-dark text-white p-2">
    <div class="navbar-brand">SPORTS STORE</div>
</div>

<div class="m-1">
    <h2 class="text-center">Your Cart</h2>
    <table class="table table-bordered table-striped p-1">
        <thead>
            <tr>
                <th>Quantity</th><th>Product</th>
                <th class="text-right">Price</th>
                <th class="text-right">Subtotal</th>
            </tr>
        </thead>
        <tbody>
            <tr *ngIf="cart.selections.length == 0">
                <td colspan="4" class="text-xs-center">
                    Your cart is empty
                </td>
            </tr>
            <tr *ngFor="let sel of cart.selections">
                <td>
                    <input type="number" class="form-control-sm"
                            style="width:5em" [(ngModel)]="sel.quantity" />
                </td>
```

```
                <td>{{sel.name}}</td>
                <td class="text-right">
                    {{sel.price | currency:"USD":"symbol":"2.2-2"}}
                </td>
                <td class="text-right">
                    {{(sel.quantity * sel.price) | currency:"USD":"symbol":"2.2-2" }}
                </td>
                <td class="text-center">
                    <button class="btn btn-sm btn-danger"
                            (click)="cart.updateQuantity(sel.productId, 0)">
                        Remove
                    </button>
                </td>
            </tr>
        </tbody>
        <tfoot>
            <tr>
                <td colspan="3" class="text-right">Total:</td>
                <td class="text-right">
                    {{cart.totalPrice | currency:"USD":"symbol":"2.2-2"}}
                </td>
            </tr>
        </tfoot>
    </table>
</div>
<div class="text-center">
    <button class="btn btn-primary m-1" routerLink="/store">Continue Shopping</button>
    <button class="btn btn-secondary m-1" routerLink="/checkout"
            [disabled]="cart.selections.length == 0">
        Checkout
    </button>
</div>
```

The HTML elements in the template list the contents of the cart, along with the subtotal for each item and the overall total. This is done using standard data bindings (denoted by the {{ and }} characters), built-in directives (ngFor and ngIf), and pipes (for formatting currency amounts). There is one new feature in this template, which allows the user to change the quantity of a product in the cart by changing the value in an input element, like this:

```
...
<input type="number" class="form-control-sm"
    style="width:5em" [(ngModel)]="sel.quantity" />
...
```

This is a two-way data binding, which means that a single binding can read a data value and modify it. Two-way data bindings are used with form elements and are denoted by square brackets and parentheses ([(and)]), which is known as the "banana in a box," where the parentheses is the banana and the square brackets are the box. Two-way data bindings are most frequently used with the ngModel directive, which knows how to set the value displayed by form elements and which events to listen to in order to detect a change. The expression used with the ngModel binding specifies the property whose value will be displayed by the form element and which will be updated when the user makes a change. In this case, the quantity property of the product selection is specified.

To make the component available for use in the application, register it in the store feature module, as shown in Listing 9-10.

Listing 9-10. Registering a Component in the store.module.ts File in the ClientApp/src/app/store Folder

```
import { NgModule } from "@angular/core";
import { BrowserModule } from '@angular/platform-browser';
import { CartSummaryComponent } from "./cartSummary.component";
import { CategoryFilterComponent } from "./categoryFilter.component";
import { PaginationComponent } from "./pagination.component";
import { ProductListComponent } from "./productList.component";
import { RatingsComponent } from "./ratings.component";
import { ProductSelectionComponent } from "./productSelection.component";
import { CartDetailComponent } from "./cartDetail.component";
import { FormsModule } from "@angular/forms";
import { RouterModule } from "@angular/router";

@NgModule({
    declarations: [CartSummaryComponent, CategoryFilterComponent,
        PaginationComponent, ProductListComponent, RatingsComponent,
        ProductSelectionComponent, CartDetailComponent],
    imports: [BrowserModule, FormsModule, RouterModule],
    exports: [ProductSelectionComponent]
})
export class StoreModule { }
```

In addition to adding the `CartDetailComponent` class to the `NgModule` decorator's declarations property, this listing also adds two of the Angular modules to the `imports` property.

The `RouterModule` is required because there are `button` elements in the template in Listing 9-9 to which the `routerLink` directive has been applied, and this doesn't work if the `RouterModule` has not been imported into the component's feature module. The `FormsModule` is required to enable the `ngModel` directive, which is used in the two-way data binding that allows the user to change product quantities.

To create the URL route that will display the cart detail, add the configuration entry to the routing configuration, as shown in Listing 9-11.

Listing 9-11. Adding a Route in the app-routing.module.ts File in the ClientApp/src/app Folder

```
import { NgModule } from '@angular/core';
import { Routes, RouterModule } from '@angular/router';
import { ProductSelectionComponent } from "./store/productSelection.component";
import { CartDetailComponent } from "./store/cartDetail.component";

const routes: Routes = [
    { path: "cart", component: CartDetailComponent },
    { path: "store/:category/:page", component: ProductSelectionComponent },
    { path: "store/:categoryOrPage", component: ProductSelectionComponent },
    { path: "store", component: ProductSelectionComponent },
    { path: "", redirectTo: "/store", pathMatch: "full" }
];
```

```
@NgModule({
  imports: [RouterModule.forRoot(routes)],
  exports: [RouterModule]
})
export class AppRoutingModule { }
```

To ensure the user can navigate directly to the /cart URL, update the fallback route used by the ASP. NET Core MVC part of the project, as shown in Listing 9-12.

Listing 9-12. Updating the Fallback Route in the Startup.cs File in the ServerApp Folder

```
...
app.UseEndpoints(endpoints => {
    endpoints.MapControllerRoute(
        name: "default",
        pattern: "{controller=Home}/{action=Index}/{id?}");

    endpoints.MapControllerRoute(
        name: "angular_fallback",
        pattern: "{target:regex(store|cart)}/{*catchall}",
        defaults: new  { controller = "Home", action = "Index"});

    endpoints.MapRazorPages();
});
...
```

Allow the application to reload and click one of the Add to Cart buttons to add a product to the cart. Click the cart icon at the top of the page to navigate to the /cart URL, which shows the detailed view of the cart, as shown in Figure 9-3.

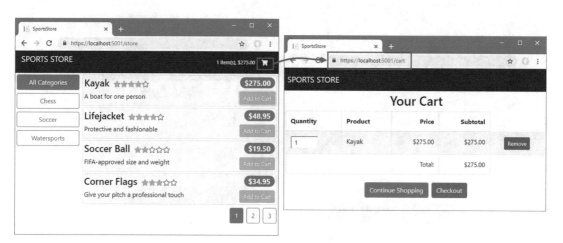

Figure 9-3. *Displaying the cart detail*

The two-way data binding allows the user to change the quantity for a product using the `input` element. If you change the value 1 in the input element to 5, for example, the subtotal and total will be updated to reflect the change, as shown in Figure 9-4.

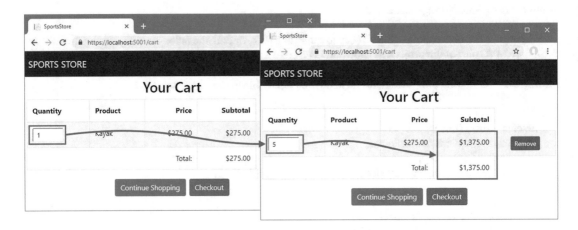

Figure 9-4. *Changing a product quantity*

Storing Carts

There is a hidden problem with the way that the cart works at the moment. To see the issue, add some products to the cart and then reload the browser window. The Angular application is reloaded, which means that the contents of the cart are lost, as shown in Figure 9-5.

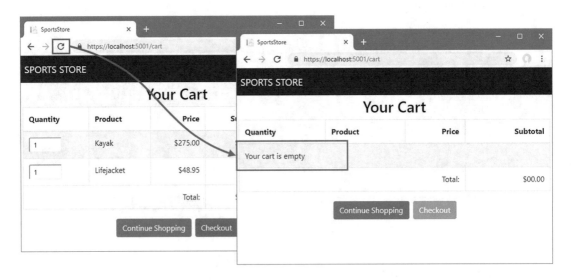

Figure 9-5. *The effect of reloading the browser window*

In the sections that follow, I demonstrate how to store the cart data using the ASP.NET Core MVC session data feature and explain how this can be used to prevent the problem shown in the figure.

Extending the ASP.NET Core MVC Data Model

The first step is to define a C# model class that will represent a cart. The mechanism that I will use to store the data can be used to store any string data, but using a C# class and the MVC model binding feature will ensure only cart data can be stored, preventing this feature from being abused to store any arbitrary data that a client sends. Add a new C# class file called CartProductSelection.cs to the ServerApp/Models folder and use it to define the class shown in Listing 9-13.

Listing 9-13. The Contents of the CartProductSelection.cs File in the ServerApp/Models Folder

```
namespace ServerApp.Models {

    public class ProductSelection {
        public long productId { get; set; }
        public string name { get; set; }
        public decimal price { get; set; }
        public int quantity { get; set; }
    }
}
```

This class will allow the MVC model binder to process the data sent by the client and represent each product that the user has added to the cart.

■ **Tip** Notice that the property names start with lowercase letters in Listing 9-13. This makes it easier to parse the JSON session data correctly when working directly with JSON strings, which is how the Angular application will send cart data to the server for storage.

Creating the Cart Storage Web Service

The next step is to create an HTTP web service that will allow the client to send cart data to ASP.NET Core MVC to be stored. The web service will store the data using the ASP.NET Core MVC session data feature, which will automatically manage the life of the data. Not all cart data will result in completed purchases, and using session data will ensure that abandoned cart data will automatically expire and, as you will see, make it simple to provide the client with its client data when the user reloads the browser.

Installing the NuGet Packages

To install the packages required for this feature, open a new command prompt, navigate to the ServerApp folder, and run the commands shown in Listing 9-14.

Listing 9-14. Installing Packages

```
dotnet add package Microsoft.Extensions.Caching.SqlServer --version 3.0.0
dotnet tool uninstall --global dotnet-sql-cache
dotnet tool install --global dotnet-sql-cache --version 3.0.0
```

Preparing the Database

The next step is to prepare the database so that it can be used to store session data. Run the command shown in Listing 9-15 in the ServerApp folder.

■ **Note** ASP.NET Core MVC can store its session data in a number of different ways, including using an in-memory store. I have chosen SQL Server for this example because it simplifies the infrastructure required to deploy the application. The in-memory option means that each ASP.NET Core MVC server has its own session data and can require additional work to ensure that requests from a single client are always handled by the same server. Using a database allows the ASP.NET Core MVC to share session data and means that any server can handle any request.

Listing 9-15. Creating the Session Database Table

```
dotnet sql-cache create "Server=(localdb)\MSSQLLocalDB;Database=EssentialApp" "dbo"
"SessionData"
```

The dotnet sql-cache command sets up the schema and required arguments for the connection string, the schema (a SQL Server feature that groups related database together), and the name of the table that will be used to store session data. The connection string is the same one specified in the appsettings. Development.json file and must be copied exactly and entered on a single line. The schema argument is dbo (which is the default value used by SQL Server), and the final argument is SessionData, which specifies the name of the table that will be created.

■ **Tip** Notice that the Server setting in Listing 9-15 has only one \ character in (localdb)\MSSQLLocalDB, whereas there are two in the app settings file. The additional character in the file is required because the backslash has special meaning in JSON and must be escaped when it is used.

Configuring the ASP.NET Core MVC Application

To set up the ASP.NET Core MVC to use the session database, add the statements shown in Listing 9-16 to the Startup class.

Listing 9-16. Configuring Session Data in the Startup.cs File in the ServerApp Folder

```
using System;
using System.Collections.Generic;
using System.Linq;
using System.Threading.Tasks;
using Microsoft.AspNetCore.Builder;
using Microsoft.AspNetCore.Hosting;
using Microsoft.AspNetCore.HttpsPolicy;
using Microsoft.Extensions.Configuration;
```

```csharp
using Microsoft.Extensions.DependencyInjection;
using Microsoft.Extensions.Hosting;
using Microsoft.AspNetCore.SpaServices.AngularCli;
using ServerApp.Models;
using Microsoft.EntityFrameworkCore;

using Microsoft.OpenApi.Models;

namespace ServerApp {
    public class Startup {

        public Startup(IConfiguration configuration) {
            Configuration = configuration;
        }

        public IConfiguration Configuration { get; }

        public void ConfigureServices(IServiceCollection services) {

            string connectionString =
                Configuration["ConnectionStrings:DefaultConnection"];
            services.AddDbContext<DataContext>(options =>
                options.UseSqlServer(connectionString));

            services.AddControllersWithViews()
                .AddJsonOptions(opts => {
                    opts.JsonSerializerOptions.IgnoreNullValues = true;
                });
            services.AddRazorPages();

            services.AddSwaggerGen(options => {
                options.SwaggerDoc("v1",
                    new OpenApiInfo { Title = "SportsStore API", Version = "v1" });
            });

            services.AddDistributedSqlServerCache(options => {
                options.ConnectionString = connectionString;
                options.SchemaName = "dbo";
                options.TableName = "SessionData";
            });

            services.AddSession(options => {
                options.Cookie.Name = "SportsStore.Session";
                options.IdleTimeout = System.TimeSpan.FromHours(48);
                options.Cookie.HttpOnly = false;
                options.Cookie.IsEssential = true;
            });
        }

        public void Configure(IApplicationBuilder app, IWebHostEnvironment env,
                IServiceProvider services) {
```

```
            if (env.IsDevelopment()) {
                app.UseDeveloperExceptionPage();
            } else {
                app.UseExceptionHandler("/Home/Error");
                app.UseHsts();
            }

            app.UseHttpsRedirection();
            app.UseStaticFiles();

            app.UseSession();

            app.UseRouting();
            app.UseAuthorization();

            app.UseEndpoints(endpoints => {
                endpoints.MapControllerRoute(
                    name: "default",
                    pattern: "{controller=Home}/{action=Index}/{id?}");

                endpoints.MapControllerRoute(
                    name: "angular_fallback",
                    pattern: "{target:regex(store|cart)}/{*catchall}",
                    defaults: new { controller = "Home", action = "Index" });

                endpoints.MapRazorPages();
            });

            app.UseSwagger();
            app.UseSwaggerUI(options => {
                options.SwaggerEndpoint("/swagger/v1/swagger.json",
                    "SportsStore API");
            });

            app.UseSpa(spa => {
                string strategy = Configuration
                    .GetValue<string>("DevTools:ConnectionStrategy");
                if (strategy == "proxy") {
                    spa.UseProxyToSpaDevelopmentServer("http://127.0.0.1:4200");
                } else if (strategy == "managed") {
                    spa.Options.SourcePath = "../ClientApp";
                    spa.UseAngularCliServer("start");
                }
            });

            SeedData.SeedDatabase(services.GetRequiredService<DataContext>());
        }
    }
}
```

The AddDistributedSqlServerCache extension method tells ASP.NET Core MVC to use SQL Server as a data cache, with configuration options that correspond to the arguments used on the command line in Listing 9-15.

The AddSession extension method sets up session state and configures the cookie that will be used to identify sessions. The configuration options set the name of the cookie to SportsStore.Session, with an expiry period of 48 hours. The CookieHttpOnly property must be set to false so that it will be accessible to the Angular application. The UseSession method enables sessions in the ASP.NET Core application.

Creating the Web Service Controller

Now that ASP.NET Core MVC has been configured to use session data, it is time to create the web service that will allow the Angular application to store its cart data. Add a C# class file called SessionValuesController.cs in the ServerApp/Controllers folder and use it to define the class shown in Listing 9-17.

Listing 9-17. The Contents of the SessionValuesController.cs File in the ServerApp/Controllers Folder

```
using Microsoft.AspNetCore.Http;
using Microsoft.AspNetCore.Mvc;
using Newtonsoft.Json;
using ServerApp.Models;

namespace ServerApp.Controllers {

    [Route("/api/session")]
    [ApiController]
    public class SessionValuesController : Controller {

        [HttpGet("cart")]
        public IActionResult GetCart() {
            return Ok(HttpContext.Session.GetString("cart"));
        }

        [HttpPost("cart")]
        public void StoreCart([FromBody] ProductSelection[] products) {
            var jsonData = JsonConvert.SerializeObject(products);
            HttpContext.Session.SetString("cart", jsonData);
        }
    }
}
```

This controller defines actions that can be targeted with HTTP GET and POST requests, allowing cart data to be retrieved and stored. Within the action methods, session data is accessed through the HttpContext.Session property, with the GetString and SetString extension methods being used to read and write string data.

The StoreCart action method defines a ProductSelection array parameter that has been decorated with the FromBody attribute so that the MVC model binder will read the data from the body of the HTTP request. The data is then converted back into JSON and then stored as session data, which will be written to the SQL database. The process of parsing JSON data into a .NET object and then serializing back into JSON ensures that clients can't store arbitrary data.

Storing and Retrieving Cart Data

Now that the ASP.NET Core MVC part of the project can store cart data, I can modify the Angular application so that it sends an HTTP POST request to the server whenever the user makes a change to the cart. Add new methods to the Repository class so that it can get and create session data, as shown in Listing 9-18.

Listing 9-18. Handling Session Data in the repository.ts File in the ClientApp/src/app/models Folder

```
import { Product } from "./product.model";
import { Injectable } from "@angular/core";
import { HttpClient } from "@angular/common/http";
import { Filter, Pagination } from "./configClasses.repository";
import { Supplier } from "./supplier.model";
import { Observable } from "rxjs";

const productsUrl = "/api/products";
const suppliersUrl = "/api/suppliers";
const sessionUrl = "/api/session";

type productsMetadata = {
    data: Product[],
    categories: string[];
}

@Injectable()
export class Repository {
    product: Product;
    products: Product[];
    suppliers: Supplier[] = [];
    filter: Filter = new Filter();
    categories: string[] = [];
    paginationObject = new Pagination();

    constructor(private http: HttpClient) {
        this.filter.related = true;
    }

    // ...other methods and properties omitted for brevity...

    storeSessionData<T>(dataType: string, data: T) {
        return this.http.post(`${sessionUrl}/${dataType}`, data)
            .subscribe(response => { });
    }

    getSessionData<T>(dataType: string): Observable<T> {
        return this.http.get<T>(`${sessionUrl}/${dataType}`);
    }
}
```

The storeSessionData and getSessionData methods send requests that target the web service to store and retrieve session data. These methods are not specific to dealing with carts because I am going to use the same features to store other kinds of data later in this chapter.

■ **Tip**   The HttpClient class doesn't send a request until the subscribe method is called. This is why the subscribe method is called in the storeSessionData method in Listing 9-18, even though the result is discarded.

Make the changes to the Cart class shown in Listing 9-19 to store and retrieve cart data through the repository.

Listing 9-19. Persisting Cart Data in the cart.model.ts File in the ClientApp/src/app/models Folder

```
import { Injectable } from "@angular/core";
import { Product } from "./product.model";
import { Repository } from './repository';

@Injectable()
export class Cart {
    selections: ProductSelection[] = [];
    itemCount: number = 0;
    totalPrice: number = 0;

    constructor(private repo: Repository) {
        repo.getSessionData<ProductSelection[]>("cart").subscribe(cartData => {
            if (cartData != null) {
                cartData.forEach(item => this.selections.push(item));
                this.update(false);
            }
        });
    }

    addProduct(product: Product) {
        let selection = this.selections
            .find(ps => ps.productId == product.productId);
        if (selection) {
            selection.quantity++;
        } else {
            this.selections.push(new ProductSelection(this,
                product.productId, product.name,
                product.price, 1));
        }
        this.update();
    }

    updateQuantity(productId: number, quantity: number) {
        if (quantity > 0) {
            let selection = this.selections.find(ps => ps.productId == productId);
            if (selection) {
                selection.quantity = quantity;
            }
        } else {
            let index = this.selections.findIndex(ps => ps.productId == productId);
```

```
            if (index != -1) {
                this.selections.splice(index, 1);
            }
            this.update();
        }
    }

    clear() {
        this.selections = [];
        this.update();
    }

    update(storeData: boolean = true) {
        this.itemCount = this.selections.map(ps => ps.quantity)
            .reduce((prev, curr) => prev + curr, 0);
        this.totalPrice = this.selections.map(ps => ps.price * ps.quantity)
            .reduce((prev, curr) => prev + curr, 0);
        if (storeData) {
            this.repo.storeSessionData("cart", this.selections.map(s => {
                return {
                    productId: s.productId, name: s.name,
                    price: s.price, quantity: s.quantity
                }
            }));
        }
    }
}

export class ProductSelection {

    constructor(public cart: Cart,
        public productId?: number,
        public name?: string,
        public price?: number,
        private quantityValue?: number) { }

    get quantity() {
        return this.quantityValue;
    }

    set quantity(newQuantity: number) {
        this.quantityValue = newQuantity;
        this.cart.update();
    }
}
```

The constructor receives a Repository object through dependency injection, which is used to get any stored cart data for the user's session. If there is data available, it is used to populate the cart, and the update method is called in order to update the properties that are used in data bindings and, in doing so, trigger Angular to reevaluate those bindings to present the modified cart to the user.

The update method uses the Repository to store the cart as session data whenever there is a change. The structure of the Cart class makes it easy to use with the ngModel directive but will create a reference loop when serialized, so I use the JavaScript array map method to select the properties that should be sent to the server and stored. The Angular application doesn't check the result returned by the web service when session data is stored, producing a fire-and-forget effect.

To see the effect, restart the ASP.NET Core runtime and then use a browser to request https://localhost:5001. Use the Add To Cart buttons to select some products, click the cart icon at the top of the window, and then reload the browser window. Now that the cart data is stored using the ASP.NET Core MVC session feature, reloading the browser doesn't clear the cart, as shown in Figure 9-6. ASP.NET Core MVC adds a cookie to responses, which the browser includes in subsequent HTTP requests, allowing the Angular application to store and retrieve its cart data.

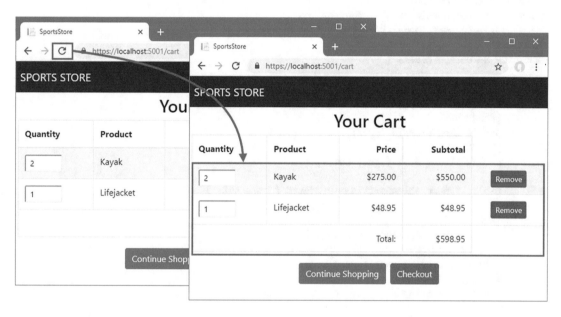

Figure 9-6. *The effect of storing cart data*

Creating the Checkout Process

In the sections that follow, I extend both the ASP.NET Core MVC and Angular parts of the project to support the checkout process and allow the user to complete an order. In a real project, this would include integration with a payment system, but for simplicity, I am going to leave a placeholder for payment in the SportsStore application. Payment systems are country-specific and typically require bank account details and anti-money laundering checks to be performed, all of which is beyond the scope of this book.

■ **Caution**   I store payment detail in the SportsStore database in the sections that follow. This won't always be allowed by your payment provider or local laws. If you do store payment data, then you should pay particular attention to security to avoid leaking sensitive data.

Extending the ASP.NET Core MVC Data Model

Most of the work for the checkout process will be done by the Angular application, but the ASP.NET Core MVC part of the project will be responsible for validating the payment details provided by the user and storing orders at the end of the checkout process.

Create a C# file called Order.cs in the ServerApp/Models folder and add the code shown in Listing 9-20 to create a model class that will represent a user's order.

Listing 9-20. The Contents of the Order.cs File in the ServerApp/Models Folder

```
using Microsoft.AspNetCore.Mvc.ModelBinding;
using System.Collections.Generic;
using System.ComponentModel.DataAnnotations;
using System.ComponentModel.DataAnnotations.Schema;

namespace ServerApp.Models {

    public class Order {

        [BindNever]
        public long OrderId { get; set; }
        [Required]
        public string Name { get; set; }

        public IEnumerable<CartLine> Products { get; set; }

        [Required]
        public string Address{ get; set; }
        [Required]
        public Payment Payment { get; set; }
        [BindNever]
        public bool Shipped { get; set; } = false;
    }

    public class Payment {
        [BindNever]
        public long PaymentId { get; set; }
        [Required]
        public string CardNumber { get; set; }
        [Required]
        public string CardExpiry { get; set; }
        [Required]
        public string CardSecurityCode { get; set; }
        [BindNever]
        [Column(TypeName = "decimal(8, 2)")]
        public decimal Total { get; set; }
        [BindNever]
        public string AuthCode { get; set; }
    }
```

```
public class CartLine {
    [BindNever]
    public long CartLineId { get; set; }
    [Required]
    public long ProductId { get; set; }
    [Required]
    public int Quantity { get; set; }
}
}
```

This is a simplified representation of an order that will let me demonstrate the process for capturing the data without getting too bogged down in the details.

■ **Tip** Notice that the CartLine class doesn't use Product objects to represent the user's selection. This is because Entity Framework Core would try to add a column to the Products table to relate Product objects to CartLine objects, which is not the relationship that the application requires since a single Product can be used in multiple CartLine objects. To avoid this problem, I store just the ProductId value, which can then be used as a key in a query for the Product data.

Creating a New Entity Framework Core Migration

Orders will be stored in the database, which means that Entity Framework Core must be configured so that it knows about Order objects. Edit the database context class to add the property shown in Listing 9-21.

Listing 9-21. Adding a Property in the DataContext.cs File in the Models Folder

```
using Microsoft.EntityFrameworkCore;

namespace ServerApp.Models {

    public class DataContext : DbContext {

        public DataContext(DbContextOptions<DataContext> opts)
            : base(opts) { }

        public DbSet<Product> Products { get; set; }
        public DbSet<Supplier> Suppliers { get; set; }
        public DbSet<Rating> Ratings { get; set; }
        public DbSet<Order> Orders { get; set; }

        protected override void OnModelCreating(ModelBuilder modelBuilder) {
            modelBuilder.Entity<Product>().HasMany<Rating>(p => p.Ratings)
                .WithOne(r => r.Product).OnDelete(DeleteBehavior.Cascade);
            modelBuilder.Entity<Product>().HasOne<Supplier>(p => p.Supplier)
                .WithMany(s => s.Products).OnDelete(DeleteBehavior.SetNull);
        }
    }
}
```

Stop the ASP.NET Core runtime and use the command prompt to run the command shown in Listing 9-22 in the ServerApp folder to create the database migration that will allow Entity Framework Core to store Order objects in the database.

Listing 9-22. Creating a Database Migration

```
dotnet ef migrations add Orders
```

The migration that this command creates will update the database schema when the ASP.NET Core MVC application is restarted and allow Order data to be stored.

Creating the ASP.NET Core MVC Web Service

To allow Order objects to be accessed by the Angular application, add a new C# class file called OrderValuesController.cs in the Controllers folder and use it to define the web service controller shown in Listing 9-23.

Listing 9-23. The Contents of the OrderValuesController.cs File in the ServerApp/Controllers Folder

```
using Microsoft.AspNetCore.Mvc;
using Microsoft.EntityFrameworkCore;
using ServerApp.Models;
using System.Collections.Generic;
using System.Linq;

namespace ServerApp.Controllers {

    [Route("/api/orders")]
    [ApiController]
    public class OrderValuesController : Controller {
        private DataContext context;

        public OrderValuesController(DataContext ctx) {
            context = ctx;
        }

        [HttpGet]
        public IEnumerable<Order> GetOrders() {
            return context.Orders
                .Include(o => o.Products).Include(o => o.Payment);
        }

        [HttpPost("{id}")]
        public void MarkShipped(long id) {
            Order order = context.Orders.Find(id);
            if (order != null) {
                order.Shipped = true;
                context.SaveChanges();
            }
        }
    }
```

```csharp
[HttpPost]
public IActionResult CreateOrder([FromBody] Order order) {
    if (ModelState.IsValid) {

        order.OrderId = 0;
        order.Shipped = false;
        order.Payment.Total = GetPrice(order.Products);

        ProcessPayment(order.Payment);
        if (order.Payment.AuthCode != null) {
            context.Add(order);
            context.SaveChanges();
            return Ok(new {
                orderId = order.OrderId,
                authCode = order.Payment.AuthCode,
                amount = order.Payment.Total
            });
        } else {
            return BadRequest("Payment rejected");
        }
    }
    return BadRequest(ModelState);
}

private decimal GetPrice(IEnumerable<CartLine> lines) {
    IEnumerable<long> ids = lines.Select(l => l.ProductId);
    IEnumerable<Product> prods
        = context.Products.Where(p => ids.Contains(p.ProductId));
    return prods.Select(p => lines
            .First(l => l.ProductId == p.ProductId).Quantity * p.Price)
        .Sum();
}

private void ProcessPayment(Payment payment) {
    // integrate your payment system here
    payment.AuthCode = "12345";
}
    }
}
```

This controller supports HTTP POST requests to create new orders in the CreateOrder method, relying on the MVC model binding feature to create an Order object, which is checked using the model validation process.

Notice that the CreateOrder method calls the GetPrice method, which queries the database to get the prices for the products selected by the user to determine the total cost of the order. It is important not to trust the client to provide critical information because it is easy for a malicious user to craft an HTTP request that contains arbitrary data, such as specifying the cost of all products as one dollar.

The CreateOrder method calls the ProcessPayment method to process payment for the order. This is where you would integrate a payment system into the project, but this method simply returns a placeholder authorization code that is returned to the client, along with the transaction amount and the ID value used to store the order in the database.

Creating the Angular Checkout Process

Now that the backend services are in place, the next step is to extend the Angular application so that it can get the data required to create an order that is submitted to the ASP.NET Core MVC part of the project. In the sections that follow, I create a model class that will represent the order. I will also create a component that uses HTML form elements to get the required data from the user and sends it using an HTTP POST request.

Extending the Angular Data Model

To describe the order that will be sent to the server, add a TypeScript file called order.model.ts in the models folder and add the code shown in Listing 9-24.

Listing 9-24. The Contents of the order.model.ts File in the ClientApp/src/app/models Folder

```
import { Injectable } from "@angular/core";
import { Cart } from "./cart.model";
import { Repository } from "./repository";

@Injectable()
export class Order {
    orderId: number;
    name: string;
    address: string;
    payment: Payment = new Payment();

    submitted: boolean = false;
    shipped: boolean = false;
    orderConfirmation: OrderConfirmation;

    constructor(private repo: Repository, public cart: Cart) { }

    get products(): CartLine[] {
        return this.cart.selections
            .map(p => new CartLine(p.productId, p.quantity));
    }

    clear() {
        this.name = null;
        this.address = null;
        this.payment = new Payment();
        this.cart.clear();
        this.submitted = false;
    }

    submit() {
        this.submitted = true;
        this.repo.createOrder(this);
    }
}
```

```
export class Payment {
    cardNumber: string;
    cardExpiry: string;
    cardSecurityCode: string;
}

export class CartLine {

    constructor(private productId: number,
        private quantity: number) { }
}

export class OrderConfirmation {

    constructor(public orderId: number,
        public authCode: string,
        public amount: number) { }
}
```

Checkout processes can be complex, and I am going to make it easier for the user by presenting them with a series of individual steps that solicit the different pieces of information required to create the order. To make this easier to code, the Order and Payment classes define properties outside of its constructor, which means that I will be able to use data bindings to build up the data gradually.

The Order class defines a submit method that will send the data to the server using a method called createOrder defined by the Repository class, which is shown in Listing 9-25.

Listing 9-25. Creating Orders in the repository.ts File in the ClientApp/src/app/models Folder

```
import { Product } from "./product.model";
import { Injectable } from "@angular/core";
import { HttpClient } from "@angular/common/http";
import { Filter, Pagination } from "./configClasses.repository";
import { Supplier } from "./supplier.model";
import { Observable } from "rxjs";
import { Order, OrderConfirmation } from "./order.model";

const productsUrl = "/api/products";
const suppliersUrl = "/api/suppliers";
const sessionUrl = "/api/session";
const ordersUrl = "/api/orders";

type productsMetadata = {
    data: Product[],
    categories: string[];
}

@Injectable()
export class Repository {
    product: Product;
    products: Product[];
    suppliers: Supplier[] = [];
```

```
    filter: Filter = new Filter();
    categories: string[] = [];
    paginationObject = new Pagination();
    orders: Order[] = [];

    constructor(private http: HttpClient) {
        this.filter.related = true;
    }

    // ...other methods omitted for brevity...

    getOrders() {
        this.http.get<Order[]>(ordersUrl)
            .subscribe(data => this.orders = data);
    }

    createOrder(order: Order) {
        this.http.post<OrderConfirmation>(ordersUrl, {
            name: order.name,
            address: order.address,
            payment: order.payment,
            products: order.products
        }).subscribe(data => {
            order.orderConfirmation = data
            order.cart.clear();
            order.clear();
        });
    }

    shipOrder(order: Order) {
        this.http.post(`${ordersUrl}/${order.orderId}`, {})
            .subscribe(() => this.getOrders())
    }
}
```

The new method sends a POST request to the /api/orders URL with a data payload that the MVC model binder will be easily able to process. The response from the web service is assigned to the orderConfirmation property of the Order object, which I will present to the user when the checkout process is complete.

To ensure that a single Order object is used through the checkout process, register a new service, as shown in Listing 9-26.

Listing 9-26. Registering a Service in the model.module.ts File in the ClientApp/src/app/models Folder

```
import { NgModule } from "@angular/core";
import { Repository } from "./repository";
import { HttpClientModule } from '@angular/common/http';
import { NavigationService } from "./navigation.service";
import { Cart } from "./cart.model";
import { Order } from './order.model';
```

```
@NgModule({
    imports: [HttpClientModule],
    providers: [Repository, NavigationService, Cart, Order]
})
export class ModelModule {}
```

The addition of the Order class to the model feature module's providers property will allow other parts of the application to declare Order constructor parameters that will be resolved using dependency injection.

Creating the Checkout Components

To provide the user with the HTML forms that will be required to complete the checkout process, I am going to create a series of Angular components, each of which will present a single set of form elements, and navigate between them using the URL routing system. In the sections that follow, I create the components and use them to build up the data required to send an order to the ASP.NET Core MVC part of the project.

Creating the Checkout Details Component

The first component will ask the user to provide their name and address. Create a ClientApp/src/app/store/checkout folder and add to it a TypeScript file called checkoutDetails.component.ts, with the code shown in Listing 9-27.

Listing 9-27. The Contents of the checkoutDetails.component.ts File in the ClientApp/src/app/store/checkout Folder

```
import { Component } from "@angular/core";
import { Router } from "@angular/router";
import { Order } from "../../models/order.model";

@Component({
    templateUrl: "checkoutDetails.component.html"
})
export class CheckoutDetailsComponent {

    constructor(private router: Router,
                public order: Order) {
        if (order.products.length == 0) {
            this.router.navigateByUrl("/cart");
        }
    }
}
```

The component defines a constructor that receives an Order object through dependency injection so that it can be accessed in the template. It also receives a Router object, which is used to navigate to the shopping cart if the user navigates directly to the component without having selected any products. To create the template for the component, add a file called checkoutDetails.component.html in the store/checkout folder, with the content shown in Listing 9-28.

Listing 9-28. The checkoutDetails.component.html File in the ClientApp/src/app/store/checkout Folder

```html
<div class="bg-dark text-white p-2">
    <div class="navbar-brand">SPORTS STORE</div>
</div>

<h2 class="text-center mt-2">Step 1: Your Details</h2>

<div class="p-2">
    <form novalidate #detailsForm="ngForm">
        <div class="form-group">
            <label>Name</label>
            <input #name="ngModel" name="name" class="form-control"
                   [(ngModel)]="order.name" required />
            <div *ngIf="name.invalid" class="text-danger">
                Please enter your name
            </div>
        </div>
        <div class="form-group">
            <label>Address</label>
            <input #address="ngModel" name="street" class="form-control"
                   [(ngModel)]="order.address" required />
            <div *ngIf="address.invalid" class="text-danger">
                Please enter your address
            </div>
        </div>
        <div class="text-center pt-2">
            <button type="button" class="btn btn-outline-primary m-1"
                    routerLink="/cart">Back</button>
            <button type="button" class="btn btn-danger m-1"
                    [disabled]="detailsForm.invalid"
                    routerLink="/checkout/step2">
                Next
            </button>
        </div>
    </form>
</div>
```

This template takes advantage of the features that Angular provides for managing HTML forms and validating the data that users enter. Two-way data bindings, defined using the ngModel directive and the banana-in-a-box brackets, tell Angular which data value should be associated with the input element, like this:

```html
...
<input #name="ngModel" name="name" class="form-control"
    [(ngModel)]="order.name" required />
...
```

This data binding creates a two-way binding on the component's order.name property, which will be used to set the value of the input element and which will be updated as the user edits the contents of the element.

To support data validation, Angular uses the standard HTML validation attributes, which are applied to input elements like this:

```
...
<input #name="ngModel" name="name" class="form-control"
    [(ngModel)]="order.name" required />
...
```

The required attribute specifies that a value is required for this input element. To allow the validation status of the input element to be inspected, the #name attribute is used to create a variable, called name and assigned the value ngModel, which can be used elsewhere in the template. In this case, a validation message is displayed alongside the element, like this:

```
...
<div *ngIf="name.invalid" class="text-danger">Please enter your name</div>
...
```

The name variable is assigned an object that defines invalid and valid properties that indicate whether the contents of the element meet the validation constraints that have been applied to it. In this case, the invalid property is used with an ngIf directive to display a message.

■ **Caution** Do not apply the ASP.NET Core MVC client-side validation attributes to HTML elements in an Angular application. Doing so will apply two different validation systems to the same content and cause errors and confusion for users.

The same approach can be used to check the validation status of the entire form. A template variable is declared on the form element like this:

```
...
<form novalidate #detailsForm="ngForm">
...
```

This attribute creates a variable called detailsForm, which is assigned ngForm to provide access to the overall validation status of the form. The same valid and invalid properties are provided, but they reflect the combined status of the individual elements in the form so that, for example, the invalid property will return true if any of the input elements in the form contains an invalid value. These properties can be accessed through the detailsForm to prevent the user from proceeding with the checkout process, like this:

```
...
<button type="button" class="btn btn-danger" [disabled]="detailsForm.invalid"
        routerLink="/checkout/step2">Next</button>
...
```

This binding sets the disabled property on the button element such that it will be disabled unless all of the input elements in the form meet the validation constraints that have been applied to them.

Creating the Checkout Payment Component

The second step in the checkout process will be to provide payment details. Add a TypeScript file called checkoutPayment.component.ts to the store/checkout folder, with the code shown in Listing 9-29.

Listing 9-29. The checkoutPayment.component.ts File in the ClientApp/src/app/store/checkout Folder

```
import { Component } from "@angular/core";
import { Router } from "@angular/router";
import { Order } from "../../models/order.model";

@Component({
    templateUrl: "checkoutPayment.component.html"
})
export class CheckoutPaymentComponent {

    constructor(private router: Router,
                public order: Order) {
        if (order.name == null || order.address == null) {
            router.navigateByUrl("/checkout/step1");
        }
    }
}
```

This component follows the same pattern as the one for the previous step in the process and defines a constructor that will provide the template with access to the Order and that will use the Router to return to the previous step if the user has navigated directly without providing a name and address.

COMPONENTS ARE THE BASIC ANGULAR UNIT

To an MVC developer, the process of creating nearly identical classes to provide support for templates can feel awkward, since it conflicts with the ASP.NET Core MVC model of a single controller class that can select multiple templates.

The architecture of Angular makes components the basic unit of application functionality, and there is no way to create interchangeable templates that correspond to the way that Razor views work. Although it can feel odd, you should embrace the Angular design philosophy and accept that each template has its own component, even if that component only exists to provide access to a shared service and is largely similar to other components in the same application.

To define the template, create an HTML file called checkoutPayment.component.html in the store/checkout folder and add the elements shown in Listing 9-30.

Listing 9-30. The checkoutPayment.component.html File in the ClientApp/src/app/store/checkout Folder

```
<div class="bg-dark text-white p-2">
    <div class="navbar-brand">SPORTS STORE</div>
</div>

<h2 class="text-center mt-1">Step 2: Payment</h2>
```

```
<div class="p-2">
    <form novalidate #paymentForm="ngForm">
        <div class="form-group">
            <label>Card Number</label>
            <input #cardNumber="ngModel" name="cardNumber" class="form-control"
                    [(ngModel)]="order.payment.cardNumber" required />
            <div *ngIf="cardNumber.invalid" class="text-danger">
                Please enter your card number
            </div>
        </div>
        <div class="form-group">
            <label>Card Expiry</label>
            <input #cardExpiry="ngModel" name="cardExpiry" class="form-control"
                    [(ngModel)]="order.payment.cardExpiry" required />
            <div *ngIf="cardExpiry.invalid" class="text-danger">
                Please enter your card expiry
            </div>
        </div>
        <div class="form-group">
            <label>Security Code</label>
            <input #cardCode="ngModel" name="cardCode" class="form-control"
                    [(ngModel)]="order.payment.cardSecurityCode" required />
            <div *ngIf="cardCode.invalid" class="text-danger">
                Please enter your security code
            </div>
        </div>
        <div class="text-center pt-2">
            <button type="button" class="btn btn-outline-primary m-1"
                    routerLink="/checkout/step1">
                Back
            </button>
            <button type="button" class="btn btn-danger m-1"
                    [disabled]="paymentForm.invalid"
                    routerLink="/checkout/step3">Next</button>
        </div>
    </form>
</div>
```

This template works in the same way as the one in Listing 9-28, except that it is the Payment object whose properties are selected by the two-way data bindings. The button elements that appear at the end of the template allow the user to navigate to the previous stage in the checkout process or progress to the next stage.

Creating the Checkout Summary Component

The third step in the checkout process presents the user with a summary of the order that is about to be placed. Create a TypeScript file called checkoutSummary.component.ts in the store/checkout folder and add the code shown in Listing 9-31.

Listing 9-31. The checkoutSummary.component.ts File in the ClientApp/src/app/store/checkout Folder

```
import { Component } from "@angular/core";
import { Router } from "@angular/router";
import { Order } from "../../models/order.model";

@Component({
    templateUrl: "checkoutSummary.component.html"
})
export class CheckoutSummaryComponent {

    constructor(private router: Router,
                public order: Order) {
        if (order.payment.cardNumber == null
            || order.payment.cardExpiry == null
            || order.payment.cardSecurityCode == null) {
            router.navigateByUrl("/checkout/step2");
        }
    }

    submitOrder() {
        this.order.submit();
        this.router.navigateByUrl("/checkout/confirmation");
    }
}
```

This component uses its constructor to receive an Order object that will be provided by dependency injection and is accessible to its template, as well as using the Route to navigate away from the summary if the values required by the previous step have not been provided. It also defines a submitOrder method, which sends the order to the web service and navigates to the final step in the process.

To create the template, add an HTML file called checkoutSummary.component.html to the store/checkout folder, with the elements shown in Listing 9-32.

Listing 9-32. The checkoutSummary.component.html File in the ClientApp/src/app/store/checkout Folder

```
<div class="bg-dark text-white p-2">
    <div class="navbar-brand">SPORTS STORE</div>
</div>

<h2 class="text-center m-1">Summary</h2>

<div class="container">
    <table class="table m-2">
        <tr><th>Name</th><td>{{order.name}}</td></tr>
        <tr><th>Address</th><td>{{order.address}}</td></tr>
        <tr><th>Products</th><td>{{order.cart.itemCount}}</td></tr>
        <tr>
            <th>Total Price</th>
            <td>{{order.cart.totalPrice | currency:"USD":"symbol" }}</td>
        </tr>
    </table>
```

```
    <div class="text-center pt-2">
        <button type="button" class="btn btn-outline-primary m-1"
                routerLink="/checkout/step2">
            Back
        </button>
        <button type="button" class="btn btn-danger m-1" (click)="submitOrder()">
            Place Order
        </button>
    </div>
</div>
```

The Place Order button uses a click event binding to invoke the component's submitOrder method to complete the checkout process.

Creating the Confirmation Component

The final component required for the checkout sequence displays a summary of the order, displaying its ID, the payment authorization code, and the price. Create a TypeScript file called orderConfirmation. component.ts in the store/checkout folder and add the code shown in Listing 9-33.

Listing 9-33. The orderConfirmation.component.ts File in the ClientApp/src/app/store/checkout Folder

```
import { Component } from "@angular/core";
import { Router } from "@angular/router";
import { Order } from "../../models/order.model";

@Component({
    templateUrl: "orderConfirmation.component.html"
})
export class OrderConfirmationComponent {

    constructor(private router: Router,
                public order: Order) {
        if (!order.submitted) {
            router.navigateByUrl("/checkout/step3");
        }
    }
}
```

This component prevents direct navigation by checking to see if the order has been submitted and navigating to the previous step if it has not. To provide the component with its template, add an HTML file called orderConfirmation.component.html to the store/checkout folder with the elements shown in Listing 9-34.

Listing 9-34. The orderConfirmation.component.html File in the ClientApp/src/app/store/checkout Folder

```
<div class="bg-dark text-white p-2">
    <div class="navbar-brand">SPORTS STORE</div>
</div>

<h2 class="text-center m-2">Order Confirmation</h2>
```

```
<div class="container">
    <table *ngIf="order.orderConfirmation; else nodata" class="table m-2">
        <tr><th>Order</th><td>{{order.orderConfirmation.orderId}}</td></tr>
        <tr><th>Price</th><td>{{order.orderConfirmation.amount}}</td></tr>
        <tr><th>Payment Code</th><td>{{order.orderConfirmation.authCode}}</td></tr>
    </table>
    <div class="text-center">
        <button class="btn btn-primary m-1" routerLink="/">Done</button>
    </div>

    <ng-template #nodata>
        <h3 class="text-center m-1">Submitting Order...</h3>
    </ng-template>
</div>
```

The template displays the confirmation data in a table, along with a Done button that navigates back to the store.

Registering the Components and Creating the Routes

To set up the checkout process, the four new components have to be registered with the store feature module, and the Angular application's URL routing configuration must be updated to include the routes that are used to navigate between them.

First, register the components so they are included in the application, as shown in Listing 9-35.

Listing 9-35. Registering Components in the store.module.ts File in the ClientApp/src/app/store Folder

```
import { NgModule } from "@angular/core";
import { BrowserModule } from '@angular/platform-browser';
import { CartSummaryComponent } from "./cartSummary.component";
import { CategoryFilterComponent } from "./categoryFilter.component";
import { PaginationComponent } from "./pagination.component";
import { ProductListComponent } from "./productList.component";
import { RatingsComponent } from "./ratings.component";
import { ProductSelectionComponent } from "./productSelection.component";
import { CartDetailComponent } from "./cartDetail.component";
import { FormsModule } from "@angular/forms";
import { RouterModule } from "@angular/router";
import { CheckoutDetailsComponent } from "./checkout/checkoutDetails.component";
import { CheckoutPaymentComponent } from "./checkout/checkoutPayment.component";
import { CheckoutSummaryComponent } from "./checkout/checkoutSummary.component";
import { OrderConfirmationComponent } from "./checkout/orderConfirmation.component";

@NgModule({
    declarations: [CartSummaryComponent, CategoryFilterComponent,
        PaginationComponent, ProductListComponent, RatingsComponent,
        ProductSelectionComponent, CartDetailComponent, CheckoutDetailsComponent,
        CheckoutPaymentComponent, CheckoutSummaryComponent, OrderConfirmationComponent],
    imports: [BrowserModule, FormsModule, RouterModule],
    exports: [ProductSelectionComponent]
})
export class StoreModule { }
```

Finally, add the routes shown in Listing 9-36, which will allow the user to work through the checkout process.

Listing 9-36. Creating Routes in the app-routing.module.ts File in the ClientApp/src/app Folder

```
import { NgModule } from '@angular/core';
import { Routes, RouterModule } from '@angular/router';
import { ProductSelectionComponent } from "./store/productSelection.component";
import { CartDetailComponent } from "./store/cartDetail.component";
import { CheckoutDetailsComponent }
    from "./store/checkout/checkoutDetails.component";
import { CheckoutPaymentComponent }
    from "./store/checkout/checkoutPayment.component";
import { CheckoutSummaryComponent }
    from "./store/checkout/checkoutSummary.component";
import { OrderConfirmationComponent }
    from "./store/checkout/orderConfirmation.component";

const routes: Routes = [
    { path: "checkout/step1", component: CheckoutDetailsComponent },
    { path: "checkout/step2", component: CheckoutPaymentComponent },
    { path: "checkout/step3", component: CheckoutSummaryComponent },
    { path: "checkout/confirmation", component: OrderConfirmationComponent },
    { path: "checkout", redirectTo: "/checkout/step1", pathMatch: "full" },
    { path: "cart", component: CartDetailComponent },
    { path: "store/:category/:page", component: ProductSelectionComponent },
    { path: "store/:categoryOrPage", component: ProductSelectionComponent },
    { path: "store", component: ProductSelectionComponent },
    { path: "", redirectTo: "/store", pathMatch: "full" }
];

@NgModule({
  imports: [RouterModule.forRoot(routes)],
  exports: [RouterModule]
})
export class AppRoutingModule { }
```

Update the fallback route used by the ASP.NET Core MVC part of the project, as shown in Listing 9-37, so that the user can navigate directly to the /checkout URL or reload the browser while the checkout is shown.

Listing 9-37. Modifying the Fallback Route in the Startup.cs File in the ServerApp Folder

```
...
app.UseEndpoints(endpoints => {
    endpoints.MapControllerRoute(
        name: "default",
        pattern: "{controller=Home}/{action=Index}/{id?}");
```

```
    endpoints.MapControllerRoute(
        name: "angular_fallback",
        pattern: "{target:regex(store|cart|checkout)}/{*catchall}",
        defaults: new  { controller = "Home", action = "Index"});

    endpoints.MapRazorPages();
});
...
```

Start the ASP.NET Core runtime, use a browser to navigate to `https://localhost:5001`, and add some items to the cart. Click the cart icon and then click the Checkout button to start the checkout process. For each step in the process, validation messages will be displayed alongside the form elements until you enter values, at which point they will disappear. When all the form elements have valid values, the button that allows you to proceed to the next step will be activated, as illustrated by Figure 9-7.

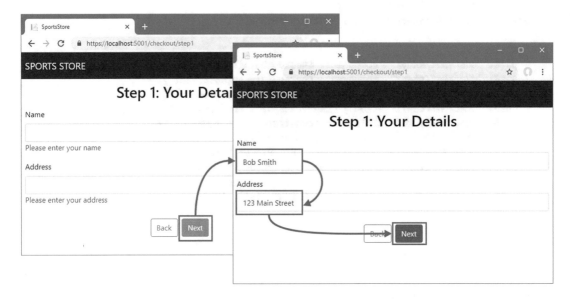

Figure 9-7. *Using Angular data validation*

Continue through the checkout process and provide the data required to create the order. When you get to the summary stage, click the Place Order button, and the Angular application will send the data to the ASP.NET Core MVC web service and present a confirmation, as shown in Figure 9-8.

Figure 9-8. *Sending an order to the web service*

Storing Checkout Details as Session Data

The data entered by the user will be lost if they reload the browser window during the checkout process, which can be especially confusing when a task is presented as a series of distinct steps. The problem can be solved by storing progress through the checkout process as session data, similar to the way that the shopping cart is stored.

Extending the Session Data Web Service

To provide the MVC model binder with a class that it can use to parse checkout data values from HTTP requests, create a C# class file called CheckoutState.cs in the Models/BindingTargets folder and add the code shown in Listing 9-38.

Listing 9-38. The Contents of the CheckoutState.cs File in the ServerApp/Models/BindingTargets Folder

```
namespace ServerApp.Models.BindingTargets {

    public class CheckoutState  {

        public string name { get; set; }
        public string address { get; set; }
        public string cardNumber { get; set; }
        public string cardExpiry { get; set; }
        public string cardSecurityCode { get; set; }
    }
}
```

The names of the properties defined by the CheckoutState class follow the JavaScript capitalization convention, which will make the data easier to handle in the Angular part of the project. To add support for storing checkout state data, add the methods shown in Listing 9-39 to the SessionValues controller.

Listing 9-39. Adding Methods in the SessionValuesController.cs File in the ServerApp/Controllers Folder

```
using Microsoft.AspNetCore.Http;
using Microsoft.AspNetCore.Mvc;
using Newtonsoft.Json;
using ServerApp.Models;
using ServerApp.Models.BindingTargets;

namespace ServerApp.Controllers {

    [Route("/api/session")]
    [ApiController]
    public class SessionValuesController : Controller {

        [HttpGet("cart")]
        public IActionResult GetCart() {
            return Ok(HttpContext.Session.GetString("cart"));
        }

        [HttpPost("cart")]
        public void StoreCart([FromBody] ProductSelection[] products) {
            var jsonData = JsonConvert.SerializeObject(products);
            HttpContext.Session.SetString("cart", jsonData);
        }

        [HttpGet("checkout")]
        public IActionResult GetCheckout() {
            return Ok(HttpContext.Session.GetString("checkout"));
        }

        [HttpPost("checkout")]
        public void StoreCheckout([FromBody] CheckoutState data) {
            HttpContext.Session.SetString("checkout",
                JsonConvert.SerializeObject(data));
        }
    }
}
```

The StoreCheckout method receives data from the client through the MVC model binder, serializes it as JSON, and stores it as session data. As with the cart data, this means that the data is received as JSON from the client, parsed to create a .NET object, and then serialized into JSON again, which is a redundant process but helps ensure that clients can't use this web service to store arbitrary data. The GetCheckout method retrieves the serialized data and returns it, as is, to the client.

Storing Checkout Data

The final change is to store the values that the user enters in the checkout process as session data. The two-way data bindings used by the Angular checkout components are updated every time that the user makes a change, which would generate too many HTTP requests if used as the trigger for HTTP requests. Instead, I am going to store data when the application navigates to a new URL that begins with checkout, which will indicate that a transition between checkout stages has occurred. The Router class, which I used in Chapter 7 to navigate within a component, generates events that can be observed to learn about routing changes. Add the code shown in Listing 9-40 to the Angular Order class to register for these events and use them to send session data to the service.

Listing 9-40. Using Session Data in the order.model.ts File in the ClientApp/src/app/models Folder

```
import { Injectable } from "@angular/core";
import { Cart } from "./cart.model";
import { Repository } from "./repository";
import { Router, NavigationStart } from "@angular/router";
import { filter } from "rxjs/operators";

type OrderSession = {
    name: string,
    address: string,
    cardNumber: string,
    cardExpiry: string,
    cardSecurityCode: string
}

@Injectable()
export class Order {
    orderId: number;
    name: string;
    address: string;
    payment: Payment = new Payment();

    submitted: boolean = false;
    shipped: boolean = false;
    orderConfirmation: OrderConfirmation;

    constructor(private repo: Repository,
        public cart: Cart,
        router: Router) {

        router.events
            .pipe(filter(event => event instanceof NavigationStart))
            .subscribe(event => {
                if (router.url.startsWith("/checkout")
                        && this.name != null && this.address != null) {
                    repo.storeSessionData<OrderSession>("checkout", {
                        name: this.name,
                        address: this.address,
                        cardNumber: this.payment.cardNumber,
                        cardExpiry: this.payment.cardExpiry,
                        cardSecurityCode: this.payment.cardSecurityCode
                    });
                }
            });
```

```
    repo.getSessionData<OrderSession>("checkout").subscribe(data => {
        if (data != null) {
            this.name = data.name;
            this.address = data.address;
            this.payment.cardNumber = data.cardNumber;
            this.payment.cardExpiry = data.cardExpiry;
            this.payment.cardSecurityCode = data.cardSecurityCode;
        }
    })
}

// ...other methods and properties omitted for brevity...
}
```

The Router.events property returns an observable for the routing events. I use the Reactive Extensions filter operator to select only the NavigationStart event so that I don't send multiple requests to the server for the same navigation change (there are corresponding event types for the end of a navigation, for example).

I use the subscribe method to handle events by sending session data to the server but only if there are values assigned to the name and address properties, which ensures that I don't try to store the data before the user has entered something into the form elements and started the checkout process.

To retrieve previously stored session data, the constructor uses the Repository.getSessionData method and uses the data that is received to populate the properties. Notice that I don't have to worry about handling the product selections, which are already stored as cart session data.

The result is that reloading the browser during the checkout process will return the user to the cart detail component but ensure that the form elements are correctly populated when they resume the checkout process. Allow the ASP.NET Core runtime to restart, navigate to https://localhost:5001, and reload the browser during the checkout process to ensure that the values you enter have been persisted, as shown in Figure 9-9.

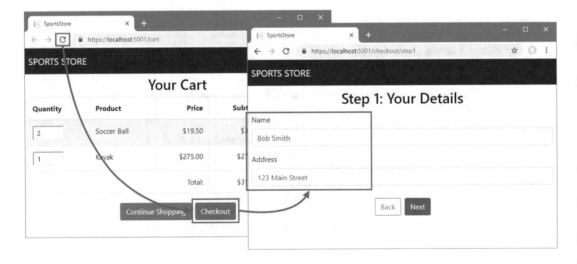

Figure 9-9. *Resuming the checkout process*

Summary

In this chapter, I showed you how to use ASP.NET Core MVC session state to store cart data, which bridges the gap between the way that Angular URL routing works and the way that the user can reload the browser or navigate directly to a URL. I also showed you how to create a multistage checkout process, which validates the data provided by the user and sends it to an ASP.NET Core MVC web service. In the next chapter, I add the administration features for the SportsStore application.

CHAPTER 10

Using Angular with Blazor

In this chapter, I provide a brief introduction to Blazor and describe the different ways it can be used alongside Angular. As I explain, Angular remains a better choice for most projects, but if you have no choice but to use both, the techniques I describe in this chapter will be helpful. Bear in mind that combining two frameworks can be brittle and prone to problems, so keep things as simple as possible and always consider if you can consolidate everything into one framework. This chapter uses a pre-release version of Blazor because the final release was not included in ASP.NET Core 3.0. I will publish an update to the GitHub repository if the final release introduces any breaking changes.

■ **Caution**   The examples in this chapter introduce another .NET project into the SportsStore folder. Pay close attention to the file names for each listing to make sure you are altering the correct file. If you don't get the expected results, compare your project to the source code for this chapter on the GitHub repository, `https://github.com/Apress/esntl-angular-for-asp.net-core-mvc-3`.

Preparing for This Chapter

This chapter uses the SportsStore project that I created in Chapter 3 and modified in the chapters since. To remove the database so that the application will use fresh seed data, open a new command prompt, navigate to the ServerApp folder, and run the commands shown in Listing 10-1.

■ **Tip**   You can download the complete project for every chapter without charge from the source code repository, `https://github.com/Apress/esntl-angular-for-asp.net-core-mvc-3`. Run `npm install` in the ClientApp folder to install the packages required for Angular development and then start the development tools as instructed.

Listing 10-1.   Resetting the Database

```
dotnet ef database drop --force
dotnet ef database update
dotnet sql-cache create "Server=(localdb)\MSSQLLocalDB;Database=EssentialApp" "dbo"
"SessionData"
```

© Adam Freeman 2019
A. Freeman, *Essential Angular for ASP.NET Core MVC 3*,
https://doi.org/10.1007/978-1-4842-5284-0_10

These commands are different from earlier chapters because Chapter 9 introduced support for session data, and the database for this must be configured from the command line.

Creating the Blazor Project

To add a Blazor project to the example, open a new command prompt, navigate to the SportsStore application, and run the command shown in Listing 10-2.

Listing 10-2. Creating a Blazor Project

```
dotnet new -i Microsoft.AspNetCore.Blazor.Templates::3.0.0-preview9.19465.2
dotnet new blazorwasm -o BlazorApp
```

Visual Studio Code will detect the new files added to the SportsStore folder automatically. If you are using Visual Studio, right-click the SportsStore solution item in the Solution Explorer, select Add ➤ Existing Project from the popup menu, select the BlazorApp.csproj file in the BlazorApp folder, and click the Open button.

Running the Angular and Blazor Applications

Use a command prompt to run the command shown in Listing 10-3 in the ServerApp folder to start the ASP. NET Core runtime and the Angular development tools.

Listing 10-3. Starting the Development Tools

```
dotnet watch run
```

Open a new browser window and navigate to https://localhost:5001; you will see the Angular application, as shown in Figure 10-1.

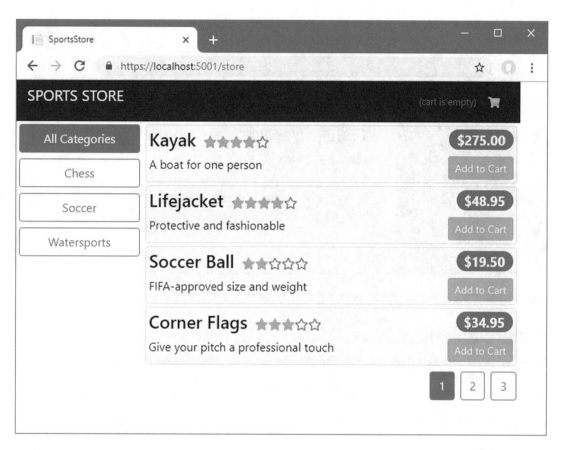

Figure 10-1. *Running the example application*

Stop the ASP.NET Core runtime and run the command shown in Listing 10-4 in the BlazorApp folder.

Listing 10-4. Starting a Server for the Blazor Project

```
dotnet watch run --urls=https://127.0.0.1:5500
```

Navigate to https://localhost:5500; you will see the placeholder content added to Blazor projects, as shown in Figure 10-2.

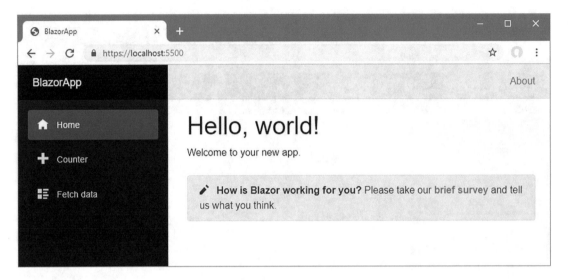

Figure 10-2. *The placeholder Blazor content*

Understanding Blazor

Blazor is a framework for writing client-side applications using C#. Like Angular, Blazor functionality is built as a series of components that are combined using HTML elements. To understand how Blazor components work, add the statement shown in Listing 10-5 to the Counter.razor file in the BlazorApp/Pages folder.

Listing 10-5. Adding a Statement in the Counter.razor File in the BlazorApp/Pages Folder

```
@page "/counter"

<h1>Counter</h1>

<p>Current count: @currentCount</p>

<button class="btn btn-primary" @onclick="@IncrementCount">Click me</button>

@code {
    int currentCount = 0;

    void IncrementCount() {
        currentCount++;
        System.Console.WriteLine("Counter: " + currentCount);
    }
}
```

Blazor components combine HTML elements and C# code in the same file. The HTML content contains expressions prefixed with @, which are used to reference the properties and methods defined in the code section.

Save the change to the component, allow the ASP.NET Core for the Blazor project to restart, and then reload the browser (there is no automatic reloading for Blazor development at the time of writing). Press

F12 to open the browser's developer tools and switch to the Console tab. In the main browser window, click Counter and then click the Click Me button, as shown in Figure 10-3.

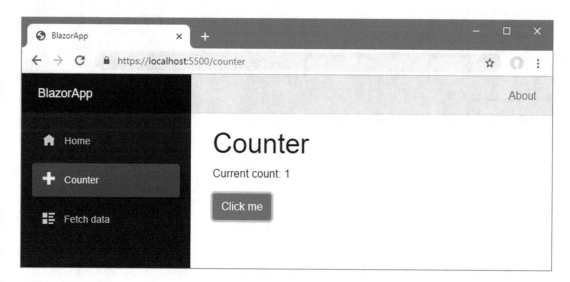

Figure 10-3. *Using a Blazor component*

Each time the button is clicked, a message will appear in the browser JavaScript console, like this:

```
...
WASM: Counter: 1
WASM: Counter: 2
WASM: Counter: 3
...
```

The C# code in Listing 10-5 has been transformed so that it can be executed by the browser, which is why the calls to the Console.WriteLine method produce messages in the F12 console window and not in the output from the ASP.NET Core runtime.

Understanding How Blazor Works

Blazor relies on WebAssembly, often abbreviated to Wasm, which is a low-level language for web applications that allows languages other than JavaScript to be compiled into a format that browsers can execute. Microsoft has created a version of the .NET Core runtime for WebAssembly, which provides the means for executing the code in Blazor components. The chain of development tools for Blazor components is the same as for regular C# classes, as shown in Figure 10-4. The difference is that the .NET Core runtime is executed by the browser through the WebAssembly feature.

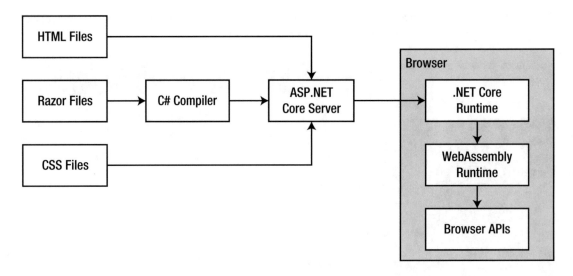

Figure 10-4. *The Blazor toolchain*

Applications running on WebAssembly have full access to the features provided by browsers, such as altering the HTML content presented to the users and sending HTTP requests. There is also interoperability with JavaScript so that Blazor components can interact with Angular, as I demonstrate later in this chapter.

When you navigated to `https://localhost:5500`, the ASP.NET Core server for the `BlazorApp` project responded with the contents of the `index.html` file in the `BlazorApp/wwwroot` folder, which contains the following elements:

```
<!DOCTYPE html>
<html>
<head>
    <meta charset="utf-8" />
    <meta name="viewport" content="width=device-width" />
    <title>BlazorApp</title>
    <base href="/" />
    <link href="css/bootstrap/bootstrap.min.css" rel="stylesheet" />
    <link href="css/site.css" rel="stylesheet" />
</head>
<body>
    <app>Loading...</app>
    <script src="_framework/blazor.webassembly.js"></script>
</body>
</html>
```

The `script` element loads the `WebAssembly` code required to run the application. The `Startup` class in the Blazor app contains a statement that identifies the app element in the HTML file as the target for the client app, like this:

```
using Microsoft.AspNetCore.Components.Builder;
using Microsoft.Extensions.DependencyInjection;

namespace BlazorApp {
    public class Startup {
```

```
        public void ConfigureServices(IServiceCollection services) {
        }

        public void Configure(IComponentsApplicationBuilder app) {
            app.AddComponent<App>("app");
        }
    }
}
```

The app element is populated with the HTML produced by the component defined in the BlazorApp/App.razor file. Blazor provides a routing system for selecting the components displayed to the user, based on the URLs specified by each component's @page directive. For the root URL, Blazor will select the Index component, which is defined in the BlazorApp/Pages/Index.razor file.

```
@page "/"

<h1>Hello, world!</h1>

Welcome to your new app.

<SurveyPrompt Title="How is Blazor working for you?" />
```

The default layout for components is specified in the Pages/_Imports.razor file, and it is this file that provides the menu and navigation links for the placeholder content. Clicking Counter, for example, triggers navigation to the /counter URL, which corresponds to the @page directive defined by the Counter component.

The HTML elements generated by Blazor components are styled using normal CSS features, just like elements created by JavaScript applications. The components in the BlazorApp project rely on the Bootstrap CSS framework and a site.css file, although if you examine the link element in the Blazor index.html file, you will see the Bootstrap file is in a different location than the one conventionally used in MVC applications.

■ **Note** Blazor also has a server-side mode, in which the browser maintains an HTTP connection back to the ASP.NET Core server. When the user interacts with the content presented by the browser, a message is sent to the server, which executes the Blazor component logic and responds with instructions for updating the HTML presented to the user. I do not describe server-side Blazor in this book.

Understanding the Limitations of Blazor

The appeal of Blazor to ASP.NET Core MVC developers is obvious: write your client-side applications in C# and avoid learning TypeScript and figuring out how Angular works. Unfortunately, Blazor has limitations that make Angular a better proposition for most projects.

The first issue is that WebAssembly is a new standard that isn't supported by older browsers. You can use Blazor if you are sure that you need to target only newer versions of Chrome, Firefox, Safari, and Edge but not if you need to support older versions or support Internet Explorer, which is still widely used for corporate desktops.

The second issue is that the browser has to download the WebAssembly version of the .NET Core runtime to execute a Blazor application, which requires about 2 MB of files at the time of writing. The files are cached by the browser, and Microsoft may be able to reduce the size in future Blazor versions, but Blazor requires a larger initial download compared to the 400 KB that an Angular application requires.

The third issue is that Blazor adoption remains uncertain. Microsoft has a history of abandoning technologies if they don't become popular. ASP.NET Core is most widely used for line-of-business applications, which will be slow to embrace Blazor because the WebAssembly dependency conflicts with the long tail of Internet Explorer use. If Blazor adoption doesn't capture enough market share to create a viable alternative to Angular, React, and Vue.js, then there is a substantial risk that Microsoft will focus resources elsewhere and Blazor will be allowed to wither.

Serving Blazor Using ASP.NET Core MVC

The simplest form of integration is to configure the ASP.NET Core runtime so that it is able to support both Angular and Blazor applications through the same set of URLs and so only one HTTP server is required. I am going to configure the project so it will deliver components from the BlazorApp project when the /blazor URL is requested.

■ **Caution** There are now two .NET projects in the SportsStore folder, and they have similar folder structures. It is important you follow the instructions closely and run the commands exactly as shown and do so in the folders specified. If you have problems creating the project, then you can download everything you need for this chapter from the GitHub repository for this book, https://github.com/Apress/esntl-angular-for-asp. net-core-mvc-3.

Changing the Blazor Root URL

The first step is to change the root URL that the Blazor application uses, as shown in Listing 10-6. This ensures that the Blazor application knows how to perform navigation relative to the URL that has been used to load it.

■ **Caution** The value of the href attribute in Listing 10-6 starts and finishes with a forward slash character. Both are required, and omitting either character will cause problems.

Listing 10-6. Changing the Root URL in the index.html File in the BlazorApp/wwwroot Folder

```
<!DOCTYPE html>
<html>
<head>
    <meta charset="utf-8" />
    <meta name="viewport" content="width=device-width" />
    <title>BlazorApp</title>
    <base href="/blazor/" />
    <link href="css/bootstrap/bootstrap.min.css" rel="stylesheet" />
    <link href="css/site.css" rel="stylesheet" />
</head>
<body>
    <app>Loading...</app>
    <script src="_framework/blazor.webassembly.js"></script>
</body>
</html>
```

Configuring the MVC Project to Serve Blazor Content

Additional configuration is required so that the Blazor functionality can be delivered through the MVC part of the application. Stop the Blazor server and use the command prompt to navigate to the ServerApp folder and run the command shown in Listing 10-7 to add a package to the MVC project.

■ **Note** These commands are run in the ServerApp folder and not in the BlazorApp folder.

Listing 10-7. Adding a Package to the MVC Project

```
dotnet add package Microsoft.AspNetCore.Blazor.Server --version 3.0.0-preview9.19465.2
```

Run the command shown in Listing 10-8 in the ServerApp folder to add a reference from the MVC project to the Blazor project so that the types in the BlazorApp project can be used in the MVC project.

Listing 10-8. Adding a Project Reference to the MVC Project

```
dotnet add reference ..\BlazorApp
```

To configure the ASP.NET Core runtime so that it will serve Blazor content, add the statements shown in Listing 10-9 to the Startup.cs file in the ServerApp folder.

Listing 10-9. Adding Support for Blazor in the Startup.cs File in the ServerApp Folder

```
using System;
using System.Collections.Generic;
using System.Linq;
using System.Threading.Tasks;
using Microsoft.AspNetCore.Builder;
using Microsoft.AspNetCore.Hosting;
using Microsoft.AspNetCore.HttpsPolicy;
using Microsoft.Extensions.Configuration;
using Microsoft.Extensions.DependencyInjection;
using Microsoft.Extensions.Hosting;
using Microsoft.AspNetCore.SpaServices.AngularCli;
using ServerApp.Models;
using Microsoft.EntityFrameworkCore;
using Microsoft.OpenApi.Models;
using Microsoft.AspNetCore.ResponseCompression;
using Microsoft.Extensions.FileProviders;
using System.IO;

namespace ServerApp {
    public class Startup {

        public Startup(IConfiguration configuration) {
            Configuration = configuration;
        }
```

```
    public IConfiguration Configuration { get; }

    public void ConfigureServices(IServiceCollection services) {

        string connectionString =
            Configuration["ConnectionStrings:DefaultConnection"];
        services.AddDbContext<DataContext>(options =>
            options.UseSqlServer(connectionString));

        services.AddControllersWithViews()
            .AddJsonOptions(opts => {
                opts.JsonSerializerOptions.IgnoreNullValues = true;
            });
        services.AddRazorPages();

        services.AddSwaggerGen(options => {
            options.SwaggerDoc("v1",
                new OpenApiInfo { Title = "SportsStore API", Version = "v1" });
        });

        services.AddDistributedSqlServerCache(options => {
            options.ConnectionString = connectionString;
            options.SchemaName = "dbo";
            options.TableName = "SessionData";
        });

        services.AddSession(options => {
            options.Cookie.Name = "SportsStore.Session";
            options.IdleTimeout = System.TimeSpan.FromHours(48);
            options.Cookie.HttpOnly = false;
            options.Cookie.IsEssential = true;
        });

        services.AddResponseCompression(opts => {
            opts.MimeTypes = ResponseCompressionDefaults.MimeTypes.Concat(
                new[] { "application/octet-stream" });
        });
    }

    public void Configure(IApplicationBuilder app, IWebHostEnvironment env,
            IServiceProvider services) {

        if (env.IsDevelopment()) {
            app.UseDeveloperExceptionPage();
        } else {
            app.UseExceptionHandler("/Home/Error");
            app.UseHsts();
        }

        app.UseHttpsRedirection();
        app.UseStaticFiles();
```

```
app.UseStaticFiles(new StaticFileOptions {
    RequestPath = "/blazor",
    FileProvider = new PhysicalFileProvider(
        Path.Combine(Directory.GetCurrentDirectory(),
            "../BlazorApp/wwwroot"))
});

app.UseSession();

app.UseRouting();
app.UseAuthorization();

app.UseEndpoints(endpoints => {
    endpoints.MapControllerRoute(
        name: "default",
        pattern: "{controller=Home}/{action=Index}/{id?}");

    endpoints.MapControllerRoute(
        name: "angular_fallback",
        pattern: "{target:regex(store|cart|checkout)}/{*catchall}",
        defaults: new { controller = "Home", action = "Index" });

    endpoints.MapFallbackToClientSideBlazor<BlazorApp
        .Startup>("blazor/{*path:nonfile}", "index.html");

    endpoints.MapRazorPages();
});

app.Map("/blazor", opts =>
    opts.UseClientSideBlazorFiles<BlazorApp.Startup>());

app.UseSwagger();
app.UseSwaggerUI(options => {
    options.SwaggerEndpoint("/swagger/v1/swagger.json",
        "SportsStore API");
});

app.UseSpa(spa => {
    string strategy = Configuration
        .GetValue<string>("DevTools:ConnectionStrategy");
    if (strategy == "proxy") {
        spa.UseProxyToSpaDevelopmentServer("http://127.0.0.1:4200");
    } else if (strategy == "managed") {
        spa.Options.SourcePath = "../ClientApp";
        spa.UseAngularCliServer("start");
    }
});

SeedData.SeedDatabase(services.GetRequiredService<DataContext>());
        }
    }
}
```

The changes add support for mapping the /blazor URL to the BlazorApp project and serving static files from the BlazorApp/wwwroot folder. The result is that a request for /blazor will return the contents of the BlazorApp/wwwroot/index.html file, which loads the Blazor app. Requests for URLs that start with /blazor will be served from the BlazorApp/wwwroot folder, if there is a matching file, or using the WebAssembly files generated for the Blazor application.

Use the PowerShell command prompt to run the command shown in Listing 10-10 in the ServerApp folder to start the ASP.NET Core runtime.

Listing 10-10. Starting the ASP.NET Core Runtime for the ServerApp Project

```
dotnet watch run
```

Once the runtime has started, navigate to https://localhost:5001/blazor; you will see the placeholder content from the BlazorApp project. The routing configuration used in Listing 10-9 allows direct navigation to URLs that are understood by the Blazor application, such as https://localhost:5001/blazor/fetchdata, which produces the content shown in Figure 10-5.

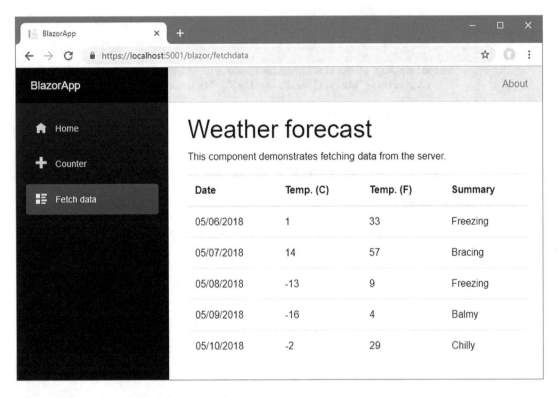

Figure 10-5. *Navigating directly to a URL for a Blazor component*

Displaying Blazor Components in an MVC Razor View

The configuration in the previous section uses ASP.NET Core for the MVC project to deliver the HTML file that loads the Blazor application. This is similar to the approach I took when using ASP.NET Core to deliver the static HTML file that loaded the Angular application. The problem in both cases is that the static HTML files don't benefit from the shared layouts used by the MVC application.

A more graceful approach is to use Razor views to deliver Blazor components, which allows the same layouts to be used for Blazor, Angular, and traditional MVC applications. To allow Angular and Blazor to share a common layout, make the changes shown in Listing 10-11 to the _Layout.cshtml file in the ServerApp/Views/Shared folder.

Listing 10-11. Preparing the Layout in the _Layout.cshtml File in the ServerApp/Views/Shared Folder

```
<!DOCTYPE html>
<html lang="en">
<head>
    <base href="@( ViewData["RootUrl"] ?? "/")">
    <meta charset="utf-8" />
    <meta name="viewport" content="width=device-width, initial-scale=1.0" />
    <title>SportsStore</title>
    <link rel="stylesheet" href="~/lib/bootstrap/dist/css/bootstrap.css" />
    <link rel="stylesheet" href="~/lib/font-awesome/css/all.css"  />
    @RenderSection("ExtraCSS", required: false)
</head>
<body>
    @RenderBody()
    @RenderSection("Scripts", required: false)
</body>
</html>
```

The additions to the view allow the root URL for the application to be specified by the view and provide a section for adding CSS files. To create a view that will render the placeholder Blazor application, add a file called Blazor.cshtml in the ServerApp/Views/Home folder, with the contents shown in Listing 10-12.

Listing 10-12. The Contents of the Blazor.cshtml File in the ServerApp/Views/Home Folder

```
@{
    ViewData["RootUrl"] = "/blazor/";
}

@section scripts {
    <script src="_framework/blazor.webassembly.js"></script>
}

@section extraCSS {
    <link href="css/site.css" rel="stylesheet" />
}
```

```
<div class="bg-dark text-white p-2">
    <div class="navbar-brand">SPORTS STORE</div>
</div>

<app>Loading...</app>
```

This view sets the root URL to /blazor/, adds a script element for the Blazor WebAssembly file, and adds a link element for the site.css file in the BlazorApp project. I have also added a SportsStore header element so that the changes to the way the Blazor app is delivered are visible.

Next, add the action shown in Listing 10-13 to the Home controller in the ServerApp/Controllers folder.

Listing 10-13. Adding an Action in the HomeController.cs File in the ServerApp/Controllers Folder

```
using Microsoft.AspNetCore.Mvc;
using ServerApp.Models;
using System.Diagnostics;
using System.Linq;

namespace ServerApp.Controllers {

    public class HomeController : Controller {
        private DataContext context;

        public HomeController(DataContext ctx) {
            context = ctx;
        }

        public IActionResult Index() {
            return View(context.Products.First());
        }

        public IActionResult Blazor() {
            return View();
        }

        public IActionResult Privacy() {
            return View();
        }

        [ResponseCache(Duration = 0, Location = ResponseCacheLocation.None,
            NoStore = true)]
        public IActionResult Error() {
            return View(new ErrorViewModel { RequestId = Activity.Current?.Id
                ?? HttpContext.TraceIdentifier });
        }
    }
}
```

To configure the ASP.NET Core runtime to direct requests for /blazor to the new action, make the changes shown in Listing 10-14 to the routing configuration defined in the Startup class in the ServerApp project.

Listing 10-14. Changing the Routing Configuration in the Startup.cs File in the ServerApp Folder

```
...
app.UseEndpoints(endpoints => {
    endpoints.MapControllerRoute(
        name: "default",
        pattern: "{controller=Home}/{action=Index}/{id?}");

    endpoints.MapControllerRoute(
        name: "angular_fallback",
        pattern: "{target:regex(store|cart|checkout)}/{*catchall}",
        defaults: new  { controller = "Home", action = "Index"});

    endpoints.MapControllerRoute(
        name: "blazor_integration",
        pattern: "/blazor/{*path:nonfile}",
        defaults: new  { controller = "Home", action = "Blazor"});

    // endpoints.MapFallbackToClientSideBlazor<BlazorApp
    //      .Startup>("/blazor/{*path:nonfile}", "index.html");

    endpoints.MapRazorPages();
});
...
```

Instead of returning the index.html file from the BlazorApp project, the new route targets the action defined in Listing 10-13. Once the ASP.NET Core runtime has restarted, navigate to https://localhost:5001/blazor; you will see the Blazor application from the BlazorApp project, delivered through a Razor view from the ServerApp project, as shown in Figure 10-6.

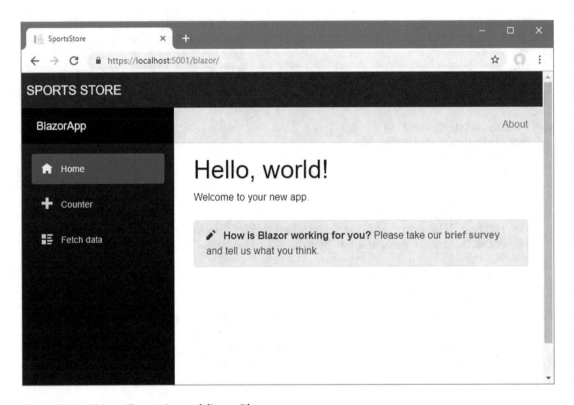

Figure 10-6. *Using a Razor view to deliver a Blazor app*

Using Angular and Blazor in the Same View

The previous sections demonstrated how to deliver a Blazor application through the ASP.NET Core MVC server, using a Razor view for consistency. That's a useful approach if you are dealing with a separate application, but Blazor can also be incorporated into the ASP.NET Core project alongside the MVC views and controllers, and Blazor components can be displayed alongside—and interoperate with—Angular applications.

■ **Caution**   This type of integration should be done only when you can't use a single framework. Getting everything to work just right can be difficult, and the results can be brittle.

Defining the Blazor Component

My focus is on Angular in this book, and this will remain the main application framework, with some additional functionality provided by Blazor. To get started, replace the contents of the App.razor file in the BlazorApp folder with those shown in Listing 10-15.

Listing 10-15. Replacing the Contents of the App.razor File in the BlazorApp Folder

```
@inject HttpClient Http

<div class="p-2 bg-info text-white">
    <EditForm Model="@search" OnValidSubmit="@HandleSearch" class="form-inline">
        <InputText class="form-control" @bind-Value="@search.searchTerm"
            placeholder="Enter search term" />
        <button type="submit" class="btn btn-primary m-1">Search</button>
        <span class="ml-3">@results</span>
    </EditForm>
</div>

@code {
    static readonly string productsUrl = "/api/products";
    SearchSettings search = new SearchSettings();
    string results = "No results to display";

    async void HandleSearch() {
        if (search.searchTerm != String.Empty) {
            Product[] prods = await Http.GetJsonAsync<Product[]>
                ($"{productsUrl}/?search={search.searchTerm}");
            decimal totalPrice = prods.Select(p => p.Price).Sum();
            results = $"{ prods.Length } products, total price is ${ totalPrice }";
            StateHasChanged();
        }
    }

    class Product {
        public decimal Price {get; set; }
    }

    class SearchSettings {
        public string searchTerm;
    }
}
```

The placeholder content in the BlazorApp project is a complete, albeit simple, application that uses URL routing to select the component presented to the user. Simplicity is key when using Blazor alongside Angular, and features like URL routing won't work because both frameworks assume they have sole responsibility for navigation, which leads to unpredictable results. The best approach is to work with applications that use a single Blazor component, such as the one in Listing 10-15. This component presents a simple search interface that sends an HTTP request to the RESTful web service and provides a summary that reports the number of products that matched the search query and their total price. Update the view that delivers the Blazor application to remove the site.css stylesheet, as shown in Listing 10-16. The stylesheet is no longer required and interferes with the layout used in Listing 10-15.

Listing 10-16. Removing a Stylesheet in the Blazor.cshtml File in the ServerApp/Views/Home Folder

```
@{
    ViewData["RootUrl"] = "/blazor/";
}

@section scripts {
    <script src="_framework/blazor.webassembly.js"></script>
}

@section extraCSS {
    <!-- <link href="css/site.css" rel="stylesheet" /> -->
}

<div class="bg-dark text-white p-2">
    <div class="navbar-brand">SPORTS STORE</div>
</div>


<app>Loading...</app>
```

Save the changes and allow the ASP.NET Core runtime to restart. Use a browser to navigate to https://localhost:5001/blazor, and you will see the new component. Enter a search term, and the component will query the web service and provide a summary of the matching items, as shown in Figure 10-7.

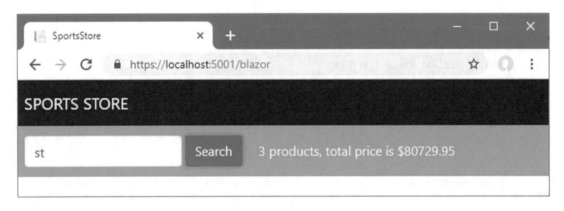

Figure 10-7. *Using the Blazor component*

Configuring ASP.NET Core

When used alone, Blazor relies on the base element in the HTML file to create the URLs for its files. The base element used earlier in the chapter specified /blazor as the root URL, which allowed the Blazor application to be delivered through the same server as the Angular application.

This is a problem for closer integration because Angular also uses the base element. This means that a configuration change is required in the Startup class of the ServerApp folder so that the files Blazor requires are served when the base element is set to /, as shown in Listing 10-17.

Listing 10-17. Updating the Blazor Configuration in the Startup.cs File in the ServerApp Folder

```
...
public void Configure(IApplicationBuilder app, IWebHostEnvironment env,
        IServiceProvider services) {

    if (env.IsDevelopment()) {
        app.UseDeveloperExceptionPage();
    } else {
        app.UseExceptionHandler("/Home/Error");
        app.UseHsts();
    }

    app.UseHttpsRedirection();
    app.UseStaticFiles();
    app.UseStaticFiles(new StaticFileOptions {
        RequestPath = "/blazor",
        FileProvider = new PhysicalFileProvider(
            Path.Combine(Directory.GetCurrentDirectory(),
                "../BlazorApp/wwwroot"))
    });

    app.UseSession();

    app.UseRouting();
    app.UseAuthorization();

    app.UseEndpoints(endpoints => {
        endpoints.MapControllerRoute(
            name: "default",
            pattern: "{controller=Home}/{action=Index}/{id?}");

        endpoints.MapControllerRoute(
            name: "angular_fallback",
            pattern: "{target:regex(store|cart|checkout)}/{*catchall}",
            defaults: new { controller = "Home", action = "Index" });

        endpoints.MapControllerRoute(
            name: "blazor_integration",
            pattern: "/blazor/{*path:nonfile}",
            defaults: new { controller = "Home", action = "Blazor" });

        //endpoints.MapFallbackToClientSideBlazor<BlazorApp
        //     .Startup>("blazor/{*path:nonfile}", "index.html");

        endpoints.MapRazorPages();
    });

    app.Map("/blazor", opts =>
        opts.UseClientSideBlazorFiles<BlazorApp.Startup>());

    app.UseClientSideBlazorFiles<BlazorApp.Startup>();
```

```
    app.UseSwagger();
    app.UseSwaggerUI(options => {
        options.SwaggerEndpoint("/swagger/v1/swagger.json",
            "SportsStore API");
    });

    app.UseSpa(spa => {
        string strategy = Configuration
            .GetValue<string>("DevTools:ConnectionStrategy");
        if (strategy == "proxy") {
            spa.UseProxyToSpaDevelopmentServer("http://127.0.0.1:4200");
        } else if (strategy == "managed") {
            spa.Options.SourcePath = "../ClientApp";
            spa.UseAngularCliServer("start");
        }
    });

    SeedData.SeedDatabase(services.GetRequiredService<DataContext>());
}
...
```

Updating the Angular Application

Including the Blazor component inside the content presented by the Angular application requires a new component. Add a file named blazorLoader.component.ts to the ClientApp/src/app/store folder and add the code shown in Listing 10-18.

Listing 10-18. The Contents of the blazorLoader.component.ts File in the ClientApp/src/app/store Folder

```
import { Component } from "@angular/core";

@Component({
    selector: "blazor",
    template: "<app></app>"
})
export class BlazorLoader {
    template: any = "";

    ngOnInit() {
        if (!document.getElementById("blazorScript")) {
            let scriptElem = document.createElement("script");
            scriptElem.type = "text/javascript";
            scriptElem.id = "blazorScript";
            scriptElem.src = "_framework/blazor.webassembly.js";
            document.getElementsByTagName("head")[0].appendChild(scriptElem);
        }
    }
}
```

Angular doesn't allow `script` elements to be defined in templates and will silently remove them as a security precaution. This is a barrier to integrating Blazor because I need to be able to load the _framework/ `blazor.webassembly.js` file. To accommodate this restriction, the component in Listing 10-18 uses the JavaScript DOM API to create a `script` element and inserts it into the `head` element of the HTML document. The component uses the `template` property to define the app element into which Blazor will render its content.

In Listing 10-19, I have registered the new component with the module for the store part of the application.

Listing 10-19. Registering a Component in the store.module.ts File in the ClientApp/src/app/store Folder

```
import { NgModule, NO_ERRORS_SCHEMA } from "@angular/core";
import { BrowserModule } from '@angular/platform-browser';
import { CartSummaryComponent } from "./cartSummary.component";
import { CategoryFilterComponent } from "./categoryFilter.component";
import { PaginationComponent } from "./pagination.component";
import { ProductListComponent } from "./productList.component";
import { RatingsComponent } from "./ratings.component";
import { ProductSelectionComponent } from "./productSelection.component";
import { CartDetailComponent } from "./cartDetail.component";
import { FormsModule } from "@angular/forms";
import { RouterModule } from "@angular/router";
import { CheckoutDetailsComponent } from "./checkout/checkoutDetails.component";
import { CheckoutPaymentComponent } from "./checkout/checkoutPayment.component";
import { CheckoutSummaryComponent } from "./checkout/checkoutSummary.component";
import { OrderConfirmationComponent } from "./checkout/orderConfirmation.component";
import { BlazorLoader } from "./blazorLoader.component";

@NgModule({
    declarations: [CartSummaryComponent, CategoryFilterComponent,
        PaginationComponent, ProductListComponent, RatingsComponent,
        ProductSelectionComponent, CartDetailComponent, CheckoutDetailsComponent,
        CheckoutPaymentComponent, CheckoutSummaryComponent,
        OrderConfirmationComponent, BlazorLoader],
    imports: [BrowserModule, FormsModule, RouterModule],
    exports: [ProductSelectionComponent],
    schemas: [NO_ERRORS_SCHEMA]
})
export class StoreModule { }
```

Listing 10-19 also adds a `schema` property to the module. By default, Angular will report an error if it encounters a custom HTML element for which there isn't a corresponding component. The NO_ERRORS_ SCHEMA option prevents Angular from reporting an error about the app element defined by the component in Listing 10-18, which is the target for Blazor. To apply the Angular component that will load the Blazor application, add the elements shown in Listing 10-20 to the template for the `ProductSelection` component.

Listing 10-20. Updating the productSelection.component.html File in the ClientApp/src/app/store Folder

```
<div class="container-fluid">
    <div class="row">
        <div class="col bg-dark text-white">
            <div class="navbar-brand">SPORTS STORE</div>
            <div class="float-right navbar-text">
```

```
                <store-cartsummary></store-cartsummary>
            </div>
        </div>
    </div>
</div>
<div class="row no-gutters">
    <div class="col"><blazor></blazor></div>
</div>
<div class="row no-gutters">
    <div class="col-3">
        <store-categoryfilter></store-categoryfilter>
    </div>
    <div class="col">
        <store-product-list></store-product-list>
        <store-pagination></store-pagination>
    </div>
</div>
```

The final step is to adjust the Angular routing configuration. Each time that a different Angular route matches the current URL, new instances of the components specified by the route are created and displayed to the user. This is a problem for the Blazor application because it requires the Blazor files to be requested from the server each time. The changes to the Angular routing configuration minimize the transitions between routes to prevent this problem, as shown in Listing 10-21.

Listing 10-21. Adjusting Routes in the app-routing.module.ts File in the ClientApp/src/app Folder

```
import { NgModule } from '@angular/core';
import { Routes, RouterModule } from '@angular/router';
import { ProductSelectionComponent } from "./store/productSelection.component";
import { CartDetailComponent } from "./store/cartDetail.component";
import { CheckoutDetailsComponent }
    from "./store/checkout/checkoutDetails.component";
import { CheckoutPaymentComponent }
    from "./store/checkout/checkoutPayment.component";
import { CheckoutSummaryComponent }
    from "./store/checkout/checkoutSummary.component";
import { OrderConfirmationComponent }
    from "./store/checkout/orderConfirmation.component";

const routes: Routes = [
    { path: "checkout/step1", component: CheckoutDetailsComponent },
    { path: "checkout/step2", component: CheckoutPaymentComponent },
    { path: "checkout/step3", component: CheckoutSummaryComponent },
    { path: "checkout/confirmation", component: OrderConfirmationComponent },
    { path: "checkout", redirectTo: "/checkout/step1", pathMatch: "full" },
    { path: "cart", component: CartDetailComponent },
    { path: "store/:category/:page", component: ProductSelectionComponent },
    { path: "store/:categoryOrPage", component: ProductSelectionComponent },
    { path: "store", redirectTo: "store/", pathMatch: "full" },
    { path: "", redirectTo: "store/", pathMatch: "full" }
];
```

```
@NgModule({
  imports: [RouterModule.forRoot(routes)],
  exports: [RouterModule]
})
export class AppRoutingModule { }
```

Save the changes, allow the runtime to restart, and then navigate to https://localhost:5001, where you will see the Blazor component is displayed inside the content presented by Angular, as shown in Figure 10-8.

■ **Tip** If you encounter an error message in the JavaScript console, then restart the ASP.NET Core runtime and reload the browser once everything has started again.

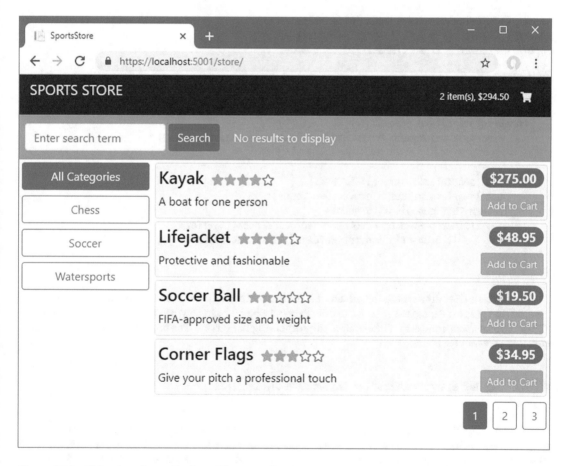

Figure 10-8. Using Angular to display a Blazor application

Adding Interoperability Between Angular and Blazor

The Angular application is displaying the Blazor application as part of its content, but that is the extent of the integration. The Blazor application makes its own HTTP requests, which are entirely independent of those made by the Angular application. In the sections that follow, I show you how to communicate between the two different applications.

Invoking an Angular Method from Blazor

A global JavaScript variable is required to create a bridge between Angular and Blazor, which allows a function to be defined that the Blazor application can invoke. Add a file named external.service.ts to the ClientApp/src/app folder and add the code shown in Listing 10-22.

Listing 10-22. The Contents of the external.service.ts File in the ClientApp/src/app Folder

```
import { Injectable } from "@angular/core";
import { Repository } from './models/repository';
import { Product } from './models/product.model';

@Injectable()
export class ExternalService {

    constructor(private repository: Repository) {
        window["angular_searchProducts"] = this.doSearch.bind(this);
    }

    doSearch(searchTerm: string): Product[] {
        let lowerTerm = searchTerm.toLowerCase();
        return this.repository.products
            .filter(p => p.name.toLowerCase().includes(lowerTerm)
                || p.description.toLowerCase().includes(lowerTerm));
    }
}
```

The ExternalService class is decorated with the @Injectable directive and defines a doSearch method that uses the Repository service to filter Product objects based on the search term. This is standard TypeScript/JavaScript and is no different from any other Angular service. The important statement is in the constructor, as shown here:

```
...
window["angular_searchProducts"] = this.doSearch.bind(this);
...
```

The window object provides access to the JavaScript runtime's global scope and allows global variables to be read and defined. This statement creates a global property named angular_searchProducts, which the Blazor application will use to locate the Angular functionality. The global variable is assigned the doSearch method, with the important use of the bind method.

```
...
window["angular_searchProducts"] = this.doSearch.bind(this);
...
```

The doSearch method uses this keyword to access its repository property and get access to the data that is required. The JavaScript value of this changes based on how a function is invoked, and, by default, this will be null when the doSearch method is invoked by the Blazor application. The bind method is used to create a JavaScript function object that has a fixed value for this, ensuring that the doSearch method works as intended. The result is a global function whose name is angular_searchProducts and that returns a filtered list of Product objects.

Registering the Angular Service

Make the changes shown in Listing 10-23 to the main Angular module to register the service.

Listing 10-23. Registering a Service in the app.module.ts File in the ClientApp/src/app Folder

```
import { BrowserModule } from '@angular/platform-browser';
import { NgModule } from '@angular/core';
import { AppRoutingModule } from './app-routing.module';
import { AppComponent } from './app.component';
import { ModelModule } from "./models/model.module";
import { FormsModule } from '@angular/forms';
import { StoreModule } from "./store/store.module";
import { ExternalService } from "./external.service";

@NgModule({
    declarations: [AppComponent],
    imports: [BrowserModule, AppRoutingModule, ModelModule,FormsModule, StoreModule],
    providers: [ExternalService],
    bootstrap: [AppComponent]
})
export class AppModule {

    constructor(external: ExternalService) {}
}
```

In addition to adding the ExternalService class to the module's providers, Listing 10-23 adds a constructor that receives an ExternalService object via dependency injection. This ensures that an ExternalService object will be created to provide Blazor with a global function to invoke.

Save the changes and allow the Angular developer tools to rebuild the application. Once the browser has restarted, open the F12 developer tools and switch to the Console tab. Enter the following code fragment at the console prompt and press the Enter key:

```
angular_searchProducts("kayak")[0].name
```

The code executes the method that Angular has made available and prints out the name property from the first object returned, producing the following output:

```
"Kayak"
```

Invoking the Angular Method from the Blazor Component

Make the changes shown in Listing 10-24 to the App.razor file in the BlazorApp folder to replace the HTTP request with a call to the method defined by the Angular service.

Listing 10-24. Calling an Angular Method in the App.razor File in the BlazorApp Folder

```
@inject HttpClient Http
@inject IJSRuntime JSRuntime

<div class="p-2 bg-info text-white">
    <EditForm Model="@search" OnValidSubmit="@HandleSearch" class="form-inline">
        <InputText class="form-control" @bind-Value="@search.searchTerm"
            placeholder="Enter search term" />
        <button type="submit" class="btn btn-primary m-1">Search</button>
        <span class="ml-3">@results</span>
    </EditForm>
</div>

@code {
    //static readonly string productsUrl = "/api/products";
    SearchSettings search = new SearchSettings();
    string results = "No results to display";

    async void HandleSearch() {
        if (search.searchTerm != String.Empty) {
            Product[] prods =
                await JSRuntime.InvokeAsync<Product[]>("angular_searchProducts",
                    search.searchTerm);
            decimal totalPrice = prods.Select(p => p.Price).Sum();
            results = $"{ prods.Length } products, total price is ${ totalPrice }";
            StateHasChanged();
        }
    }

    class Product {
        public decimal Price {get; set; }
    }

    class SearchSettings {
        public string searchTerm;
    }
}
```

Blazor provides the IJSRuntime interface for JavaScript interoperability, and global JavaScript functions can be called using the InvokeAsync method, like this:

```
...
await JSRuntime.InvokeAsync<Product[]>("angular_searchProducts", search.searchTerm);
...
```

The name of the JavaScript function is specified as a string as the first argument to the InvokeAsync method, followed by any arguments that should be passed on to the JavaScript function. The generic type argument for the InvokeAsync method tells Blazor which data type to expect as the result, which is an array of Product objects in this case.

The result is that the Blazor component receives its Product objects from the Angular object, avoiding the duplicate HTTP request to the web service.

The .NET watch mode won't detect the change to the App.razor file, so stop the runtime and run the command shown in Listing 10-25 in the ServerApp folder to start it again.

Listing 10-25. Starting the ASP.NET Core Runtime

```
dotnet watch run
```

Allow the runtime to start and then reload the browser window, click the Chess category button, enter st in the Blazor app's input element, and click the Search button. The search is performed on the Product objects that the Angular application provides, which is restricted to the Chess category. There are only two products that match the search, as shown in Figure 10-9.

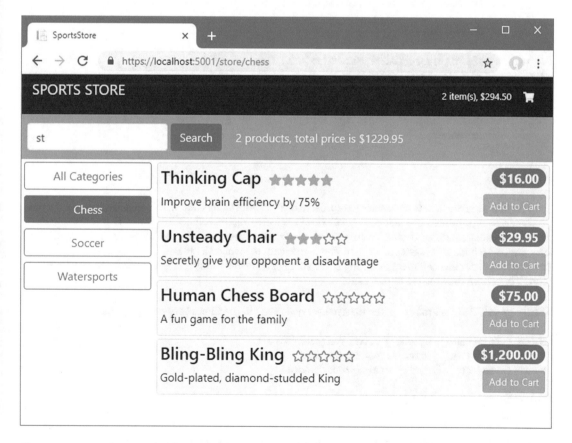

Figure 10-9. *Invoking an Angular method from Blazor*

Modifying the Angular Application State

Angular will automatically respond to changes in the application's state when those changes happen inside of the application, such as when a button is clicked. When a change is triggered from outside the application, such as when Blazor invokes a method, an additional step is required to trigger the change process.

To prepare for a change in the application state, make the changes shown in Listing 10-26 to the getProducts method of the Repository class in the Angular project so the method returns a Promise that yields the data from the web service when it resolves.

Listing 10-26. Returning a Promise in the repository.ts File in the ClientApp/src/app/models Folder

```
...
getProducts(): Promise<productsMetadata> {
    let url = `${productsUrl}?related=${this.filter.related}`;
    if (this.filter.category) {
        url += `&category=${this.filter.category}`;
    }
    if (this.filter.search) {
        url += `&search=${this.filter.search}`;
    }
    url += "&metadata=true";

    return this.http.get<productsMetadata>(url)
        .toPromise<productsMetadata>()
        .then(md => {
            this.products = md.data;
            this.categories = md.categories;
            return md;
        });
}
...
```

Angular uses the Observable class to represent one or more values that will be generated in the future, which can be represented as a standard JavaScript Promise using the toPromise object. The getProducts method has been modified so that it returns a Promise that can be used with the JavaScript async/await keywords, which makes it easier to write methods that can be invoked by Blazor. Next, update the ExternalService class as shown in Listing 10-27 so that it calls the repository getProducts method and returns data from the Promise as the result.

Listing 10-27. Using a Promise in the external.service.ts File in the ClientApp/src/app Folder

```
import { Injectable, NgZone } from "@angular/core";
import { Repository } from './models/repository';
import { Product } from './models/product.model';

@Injectable()
export class ExternalService {

    constructor(private repository: Repository, private zone: NgZone) {
        window["angular_searchProducts"] = this.doSearch.bind(this);
    }
```

```
async doSearch(searchTerm: string): Promise<Product[]> {
    return this.zone.run(async () => {
        this.repository.filter.search = searchTerm;
        return (await this.repository.getProducts()).data;
    })
}
}
```

The doSearch method passes on the search term received from the Blazor application to the repository and then calls the repository's getProducts method. This has the effect of updating the products stored by the repository, but the Angular application won't automatically respond to the new data because the change was triggered by Blazor, which is outside the scope of the Angular application. This problem is resolved using an NgZone object, which is received through the constructor and is used to execute the statements that change the Angular application state.

```
...
async doSearch(searchTerm: string): Promise<Product[]> {
    return this.zone.run(async () => {
        this.repository.filter.search = searchTerm;
        return (await this.repository.getProducts()).data;
    })
}
...
```

Once the function passed to the NgZone.run method has been executed, Angular runs its update cycle and reflects any changes that have occurred in the content that is presented to the user. In this case, the changes mean that entering a search term into the Blazor application and clicking the Search button triggers an HTTP request in the Angular application that displays only the matching items to the user, as shown in Figure 10-10.

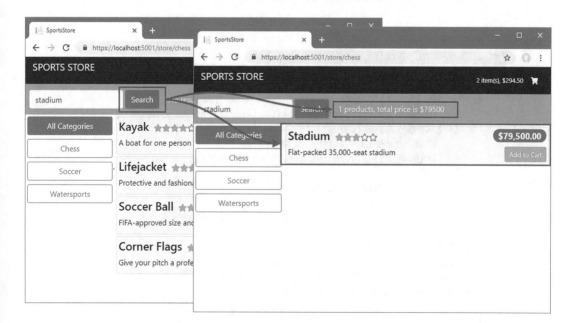

Figure 10-10. *Updating the state of the Angular application from Blazor*

Invoking a Blazor Method from Angular

The Angular application can invoke methods defined by the Blazor application, but the process is more complex. In preparation, I have added a Subject to the NavigationService class, which is an easy way to create an Observable object that provides updates to interested parties when there is a navigation change, as shown in Listing 10-28.

Listing 10-28. Adding a Subject in the navigation.service.ts File in the ClientApp/src/app/models Folder

```
import { Injectable } from "@angular/core";
import { Router, ActivatedRoute, NavigationEnd } from "@angular/router";
import { Repository } from '../models/repository';
import { filter } from "rxjs/operators";
import { Subject, Observable } from 'rxjs';

export type NavigationUpdate = {
    category: string,
    page: number
}

@Injectable()
export class NavigationService {
    private  changeSubject = new Subject<NavigationUpdate>();

    constructor(private repository: Repository, private router: Router,
            private active: ActivatedRoute) {
        router.events
            .pipe(filter(event => event instanceof NavigationEnd))
            .subscribe(ev => this.handleNavigationChange());
    }

    private handleNavigationChange() {
        let active = this.active.firstChild.snapshot;
        if (active.url.length > 0 && active.url[0].path === "store") {
            this.repository.filter.search = "";
            if (active.params["categoryOrPage"] !== undefined) {
                let value = Number.parseInt(active.params["categoryOrPage"]);
                if (!Number.isNaN(value)) {
                    this.repository.filter.category = "";
                    this.repository.paginationObject.currentPage = value;
                } else {
                    this.repository.filter.category
                        = active.params["categoryOrPage"];
                    this.repository.paginationObject.currentPage = 1;
                }
            } else {
                let category = active.params["category"];
                this.repository.filter.category = category || "";
                this.repository.paginationObject.currentPage
                    = Number.parseInt(active.params["page"]) || 1
            }
        }
```

```
        this.repository.getProducts();
        this.changeSubject.next({
            category: this.currentCategory,
            page: this.currentPage
        });
    }
}

get change(): Observable<NavigationUpdate> {
    return this.changeSubject;
}

// ...other properties omitted for brevity...
}
```

Events are generated in the Subject using the next method, and an event is provided to subscribers each time there is a navigation change. The next step is to receive and process the events in the ExternalService class and pass them on to the Blazor application, as shown in Listing 10-29.

Listing 10-29. Receiving Navigation Events in the external.service.ts File in the ClientApp/src/app Folder

```
import { Injectable, NgZone } from "@angular/core";
import { Repository } from './models/repository';
import { Product } from './models/product.model';
import { NavigationService } from "./models/navigation.service";

interface DotnetInvokable {
    invokeMethod<T>(methodName: string, ...args: any): T;
    invokeMethodAsync<T>(methodName: string, ...args: any): Promise<T>;
}

@Injectable()
export class ExternalService {
    private resetFunction: (msg: string) => {};

    constructor(private repository: Repository,
            private zone: NgZone,
            private navService: NavigationService) {

        window["angular_searchProducts"] = this.doSearch.bind(this);
        window["angular_receiveReference"] = this.receiveReference.bind(this);

        navService.change.subscribe(update => {
            if (this.resetFunction) {
                this.resetFunction("Results reset");
            }
        });
    }

    async doSearch(searchTerm: string): Promise<Product[]> {
        return this.zone.run(async () => {
```

```
                this.repository.filter.search = searchTerm;
                return (await this.repository.getProducts()).data;
            })
        }

    receiveReference(target: DotnetInvokable) {
        this.resetFunction =
            (msg: string) => target.invokeMethod("resetSearch", msg);
    }
}
```

The way the relationship between Angular and Blazor works in this example is a little odd. First, the Angular application creates a global function that receives an object from the Blazor application. This is the receiveReference method in Listing 10-29, and the object it receives is a wrapper around a .NET object, which is accessed through the invokeMethod and invokeMethodAsync methods. When the NavigationService sends an event through the Observer, the ExternalService responds by invoking the resetSearch method on the Blazor object, which it does by calling invokeMethod on the wrapper object it has received.

```
...
(msg: string) => target.invokeMethod("resetSearch", msg);
...
```

Angular can't invoke the Blazor method until Blazor calls the receiveReference method, as shown in Listing 10-30.

Listing 10-30. Providing Angular with an Object in the App.razor File in the BlazorApp/Pages Folder

```
@inject HttpClient Http
@inject IJSRuntime JSRuntime

<div class="p-2 bg-info text-white">
    <EditForm Model="@search" OnValidSubmit="@HandleSearch" class="form-inline">
        <InputText class="form-control" @bind-Value="@search.searchTerm"
            placeholder="Enter search term" />
        <button type="submit" class="btn btn-primary m-1">Search</button>
        <span class="ml-3">@results</span>
    </EditForm>
</div>

@code {
    SearchSettings search = new SearchSettings();
    string results = "No results to display";

    protected override void OnAfterRender(bool firstRender) {
        JSRuntime.InvokeAsync("angular_receiveReference",
            DotNetObjectReference.Create(this));
    }

    async void HandleSearch() {
        if (search.searchTerm != String.Empty) {
```

```
            Product[] prods =
                await JSRuntime.InvokeAsync<Product[]>("angular_searchProducts",
                    search.searchTerm);
            decimal totalPrice = prods.Select(p => p.Price).Sum();
            results = $"{ prods.Length } products, total price is ${ totalPrice }";
            StateHasChanged();
        }
    }

    [JSInvokable]
    public void resetSearch(string message) {
        search.searchTerm = "";
        results = message;
        StateHasChanged();
    }

    class Product {
        public decimal Price {get; set; }
    }

    class SearchSettings {
        public string searchTerm;
    }
}
```

Methods that can be invoked by Angular are decorated with the JSInvokable attribute, which has been applied to the resetSearch method in Listing 10-30. To provide Angular with the object to use, the OnAfterRender method invokes the angular_receiveReference function set up by Angular and uses the static DotnetObjectReference.Create method to create the wrapper object.

```
...
JSRuntime.InvokeAsync<object>("angular_receiveReference",
            DotNetObjectReference.Create(this));
...
```

So, when the Angular application starts, it creates a global function that allows it to receive the wrapper object. When the Blazor application starts, it invokes the Angular global function and provides the wrapper. The Angular application can then use the InvokeMethod method to invoke methods that have been decorated by the JSInvokable attribute.

The .NET watch mode won't detect the change to the App.razor file, so stop the runtime and run the command shown in Listing 10-31 in the ServerApp folder to start it again.

Listing 10-31. Starting the ASP.NET Core Runtime

```
dotnet watch run
```

Allow the runtime to start and then reload the browser window. You will see that clicking a category or page button in the Angular application resets the search term and results in the Blazor application, as shown in Figure 10-11.

Figure 10-11. *Invoking a Blazor method from the Angular application*

Summary

In this chapter, I showed you the different ways that Angular and Blazor can be used together, from simply serving Blazor with the same ASP.NET Core runtime as the MVC and Angular applications to invoking methods in both directions. These techniques should be used with caution, but they can be useful when you have no choice but to use both frameworks. In the next chapter, I create administration features for the SportsStore application.

CHAPTER 11

■ ■ ■

Creating Administration Features

In this chapter, I build on the Angular and ASP.NET Core MVC features from earlier chapters to create the basic administration features required by the application. To keep the example application manageable, I don't use all of the features that allowed me to demonstrate different aspects of Angular or ASP.NET Core MVC programming in earlier chapters, but I create enough new functionality to show that new additions can be assembled quickly and easily once the right foundation is in place. Table 11-1 puts this chapter in context.

Table 11-1. *Putting Administration Features in Context*

Question	Answer
What are they?	The administration features allow for the management of the application and its data.
Why are they useful?	Most applications require some kind of administration, either to manage the publicly accessible data or to manage user accounts.
How are they used?	Administration features can be built with the same techniques used for the end-user features.
Are there any pitfalls or limitations?	Depending on the complexity of the administration features, it may make sense to create a completely separate administration application. In this chapter, I have included the administration code as part of the Angular application so that it can be accessed using the /admin URL.
Are there any alternatives?	Not all applications require administration features.

Preparing for This Chapter

This chapter uses the SportsStore project that I created in Chapter 3 and modified in the chapters since. To remove the database so that the application will use fresh seed data, open a new command prompt, navigate to the ServerApp folder, and run the commands shown in Listing 11-1.

■ **Tip** You can download the complete project for every chapter without charge from the source code repository, https://github.com/Apress/esntl-angular-for-asp.net-core-mvc-3. Run npm install in the ClientApp folder to install the packages required for Angular development and then start the development tools as instructed.

Listing 11-1. Resetting the Database

```
dotnet ef database drop --force
dotnet ef database update
dotnet sql-cache create "Server=(localdb)\MSSQLLocalDB;Database=EssentialApp" "dbo"
"SessionData"
```

Use a command prompt to run the command shown in Listing 11-2 in the ServerApp folder to start the ASP.NET Core runtime and the Angular development tools.

Listing 11-2. Starting the Development Tools

```
dotnet watch run
```

Open a new browser window and navigate to https://localhost:5001; you will see the Angular application, as shown in Figure 11-1.

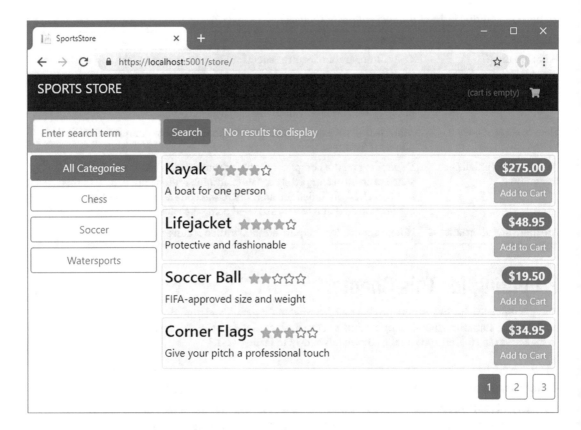

Figure 11-1. *Running the example application*

Adding Administration Features

Angular provides a number of ways to define features that will not be used by all users, although they each have different advantages and drawbacks. If you want to avoid sending the administration code and content to regular users, you can create a feature module that is loaded only when the Angular application navigates to a specific URL. This is the approach that I have taken in this book, albeit it means introducing user interface elements that allow navigation to the administration features, which not all users will use.

Alternatively, you can create an entirely separate application, which contains just the administration features. You can still use the components and content defined for the main SportsStore Angular application, but you have to create an entirely separate infrastructure, including root modules, routing configurations, and root components, which complicates the development process and is prone to errors.

■ **Tip** The choice that works for the SportsStore example application may not be the one that makes sense for your project. You should give some consideration to all of the available options, trading off the development and configuration complexity against the additional bandwidth required to deliver code and content that is unlikely to be used by most clients.

Creating the Administration Components

Create the ClientApp/src/app/admin folder and add to it a TypeScript file called admin.component.ts with the code shown in Listing 11-3. This will be the top-level component for the administration features.

Listing 11-3. The Contents of the admin.component.ts File in the ClientApp/src/app/admin Folder

```
import { Component } from "@angular/core";
import { Repository } from "../models/repository";

@Component({
    templateUrl: "admin.component.html"
})
export class AdminComponent {

    constructor(private repo: Repository) {
        repo.filter.reset();
        repo.filter.related = true;
        this.repo.getProducts();
        this.repo.getSuppliers();
        this.repo.getOrders();
    }
}
```

The constructor clears the filter used to query for product data and calls the repository's getProducts, getSuppliers, and getOrders methods to request the application data, ensuring that the administration features will have all of the data they require.

To create the template, add an HTML file called admin.component.html to the admin folder with the content shown in Listing 11-4.

Listing 11-4. The Contents of the admin.component.html File in the ClientApp/src/app/admin Folder

```
<div class="navbar bg-info mb-1">
    <a class="navbar-brand text-white">SPORTS STORE Admin</a>
</div>

<div class="col-3 fixed-bottom mb-1">
    <a class="btn btn-block btn-secondary" routerLink="/store">
        Store
    </a>
</div>

<div class="row no-gutters">
    <div class="col-3">
        <button class="btn btn-block btn-outline-info m-1" routerLink="/admin"
                routerLinkActive="active" [routerLinkActiveOptions]="{exact: true}">
            Overview
        </button>
        <button class="btn btn-block btn-outline-info m-1"
                routerLink="/admin/products" routerLinkActive="active">
            Products
        </button>
        <button class="btn btn-block btn-outline-info m-1"
                routerLink="/admin/orders" routerLinkActive="active">
            Orders
         </button>
    </div>
    <div class="col p-2">
        <router-outlet></router-outlet>
    </div>
</div>
```

The template provides a banner to make it obvious to the user that this is the administration part of the application. There are button elements that use the routerLink directive to navigate to URLs that will be managed by the routing system, combined with the routerLinkActive directive, which assigns an element to a class when the route it navigates to has been selected. In this listing, the button elements are assigned to the active class, which applies the Bootstrap CSS styles for an activated button.

The template also includes a router-outlet element, which will display components based on the current URL that are selected by clicking the button elements and managed through the URL routing system. Angular applications can have more than one router-outlet element, which allows for complex navigation schemes.

Creating the Administration Feature Components

With the top-level administration component defined, it is time to create the individual components that will be used to manage products and orders. I am going to display placeholder content so that I can focus on the structure of the application and routing configuration, before implementing the administration features later in the chapter.

The component that the administrator will see when navigating to the /admin URL will provide an overview of the data and operations available. For this component, create a TypeScript file called overview. component.ts in the admin folder, with the code shown in Listing 11-5.

Listing 11-5. The Contents of the overview.component.ts File in the ClientApp/src/app/admin Folder

```
import { Component } from "@angular/core";
import { Repository } from "../models/repository";
import { Product } from "../models/product.model";
import { Order } from "../models/order.model";

@Component({
    templateUrl: "overview.component.html"
})
export class OverviewComponent {

    constructor(private repo: Repository) { }

    get products(): Product[] {
        return this.repo.products;
    }

    get orders(): Order[] {
        return this.repo.orders;
    }
}
```

To provide the overview component with its template, create an HTML file called overview.component. html in the admin folder and add the elements shown in Listing 11-6.

Listing 11-6. The Contents of the overview.component.html File in the ClientApp/src/app/admin Folder

```
<table class="table m-1">
    <tr>
        <td>There are {{products?.length || 0}} products for sale</td>
        <td><button class="btn btn-sm btn-info btn-block"
                    routerLink="/admin/products">Manage Products</button></td>
    </tr>
    <tr>
        <td>There are {{orders?.length || 0}} orders</td>
        <td><button class="btn btn-sm btn-info btn-block"
                    routerLink="/admin/orders">Manage Orders</button></td>
    </tr>
</table>
```

The template contains a table that displays the number of products and orders and buttons that navigate to the URLs for managing each of them.

For the component that will be used to manage products, create a TypeScript file called productAdmin. component.ts in the admin folder, with the code shown in Listing 11-7.

Listing 11-7. The Contents of the productAdmin.component.ts File in the ClientApp/src/app/admin Folder

```
import { Component } from "@angular/core";

@Component({
    templateUrl: "productAdmin.component.html"
})
export class ProductAdminComponent {
}
```

Add an HTML file called `productAdmin.component.html` to the `admin` folder with the markup shown in Listing 11-8. This is placeholder content that I will replace with more useful features once the structure of the administration part of the application has been set up.

Listing 11-8. The Contents of the productAdmin.component.html File in the ClientApp/src/app/admin Folder

```
<h4 class="text-center m-2">Product Admin Placeholder</h4>
```

To create the component for managing orders, add a TypeScript file called `orderAdmin.component.ts` in the `admin` folder with the code shown in Listing 11-9.

Listing 11-9. The Contents of the orderAdmin.component.ts File in the ClientApp/add/admin Folder

```
import { Component } from "@angular/core";

@Component({
    templateUrl: "orderAdmin.component.html"
})
export class OrderAdminComponent {
}
```

To provide the component with a template, create an HTML file called `orderAdmin.component.html` in the `admin` folder and add the placeholder elements shown in Listing 11-10, which I will replace later in the chapter.

Listing 11-10. The Contents of the orderAdmin.component.html File in the ClientApp/src/app/admin Folder

```
<h4 class="text-center m-2">Order Admin Placeholder</h4>
```

Creating the Feature Module and Routing Configuration

To create a feature module that will incorporate the new components into the application, add a TypeScript file called `admin.module.ts` in the `admin` folder with the code shown in Listing 11-11.

Listing 11-11. The Contents of the admin.module.ts File in the ClientApp/src/app/admin Folder

```
import { NgModule } from "@angular/core";
import { RouterModule, Routes } from "@angular/router";
import { FormsModule } from "@angular/forms";
```

```
import { AdminComponent } from "./admin.component";
import { OverviewComponent } from "./overview.component";
import { ProductAdminComponent } from "./productAdmin.component";
import { OrderAdminComponent } from "./orderAdmin.component";

const routes: Routes = [
    {
    path: "", component: AdminComponent,
    children: [
        { path: "products", component: ProductAdminComponent },
        { path: "orders", component: OrderAdminComponent },
        { path: "overview", component: OverviewComponent },
        { path: "", component: OverviewComponent }]
    }
];

@NgModule({
    imports: [RouterModule,
        FormsModule, RouterModule.forChild(routes)],
    declarations: [AdminComponent, OverviewComponent,
        ProductAdminComponent, OrderAdminComponent]
})
export class AdminModule { }
```

The feature module follows the pattern established in earlier chapters and uses the @NgModule decorator to register the AdminComponent class in the declarations property, making it available for use in the rest of the application. The RouterModule is required for the imports property to support the URL navigation between components.

The key difference from earlier modules is that this module also defines its own routes. These routes can't be defined in the application's main routing module because that would require dependencies on the component classes, which would lead webpack to include the code in the main application bundles.

The only route that is added to the main set of routes is for the /admin URL, as shown in Listing 11-12, which loads AdminModule dynamically.

Listing 11-12. Loading a Module in the app-routing.module.ts File in the ClientApp/src/app Folder

```
import { NgModule } from '@angular/core';
import { Routes, RouterModule } from '@angular/router';
import { ProductSelectionComponent } from "./store/productSelection.component";
import { CartDetailComponent } from "./store/cartDetail.component";
import { CheckoutDetailsComponent }
    from "./store/checkout/checkoutDetails.component";
import { CheckoutPaymentComponent }
    from "./store/checkout/checkoutPayment.component";
import { CheckoutSummaryComponent }
    from "./store/checkout/checkoutSummary.component";
import { OrderConfirmationComponent }
    from "./store/checkout/orderConfirmation.component";
```

```
const routes: Routes = [
    {
        path: "admin",
        loadChildren: () =>
            import("./admin/admin.module").then(module => module.AdminModule),
    },
    { path: "checkout/step1", component: CheckoutDetailsComponent },
    { path: "checkout/step2", component: CheckoutPaymentComponent },
    { path: "checkout/step3", component: CheckoutSummaryComponent },
    { path: "checkout/confirmation", component: OrderConfirmationComponent },
    { path: "checkout", redirectTo: "/checkout/step1", pathMatch: "full" },
    { path: "cart", component: CartDetailComponent },
    { path: "store/:category/:page", component: ProductSelectionComponent },
    { path: "store/:categoryOrPage", component: ProductSelectionComponent },
    { path: "store", redirectTo: "store/", pathMatch: "full" },
    { path: "", redirectTo: "store/", pathMatch: "full" }
];

@NgModule({
  imports: [RouterModule.forRoot(routes)],
  exports: [RouterModule]
})
export class AppRoutingModule { }
```

The new route uses a dynamic import statement that will load the bundle file for the administration module only when the application first navigates to the /admin URL. To allow for that navigation, add the element shown in Listing 11-13 to the template for the ProductSelection component in the store part of the application.

Listing 11-13. Elements in the productSelection.component.html File in the ClientApp/src/app/store Folder

```
<div class="container-fluid">
    <div class="row">
        <div class="col bg-dark text-white">
            <div class="navbar-brand">SPORTS STORE</div>
            <div class="float-right navbar-text">
                <store-cartsummary></store-cartsummary>
            </div>
        </div>
    </div>
</div>

<div class="col-3 fixed-bottom mb-1">
    <a class="btn btn-block btn-secondary" routerLink="/admin">
        Administration
    </a>
</div>

<div class="row no-gutters">
    <div class="col"><blazor></blazor></div>
</div>
```

```
<div class="row no-gutters">
    <div class="col-3">
        <store-categoryfilter></store-categoryfilter>
    </div>
    <div class="col">
        <store-product-list></store-product-list>
        <store-pagination></store-pagination>
    </div>
</div>
```

The final change is to expand the set of routes that the ASP.NET Core MVC application will direct to the Home controller to accommodate the new URL, as shown in Listing 11-14.

Listing 11-14. Configuring Routes in the Startup.cs File in the ServerApp Folder

```
...
app.UseEndpoints(endpoints => {
    endpoints.MapControllerRoute(
        name: "default",
        pattern: "{controller=Home}/{action=Index}/{id?}");

    endpoints.MapControllerRoute(
        name: "angular_fallback",
        pattern: "{target:regex(admin|store|cart|checkout):nonfile}/{*catchall}",
        defaults: new  { controller = "Home", action = "Index"});

    endpoints.MapControllerRoute(
        name: "blazor_integration",
        pattern: "/blazor/{*path:nonfile}",
        defaults: new  { controller = "Home", action = "Blazor"});

    endpoints.MapRazorPages();
});
...
```

The nonfile filter is required because the name of the file that will be requested when the new Angular module is dynamically loaded is admin-admin-module.js, and care must be taken not to direct requests for this file to the MVC controller.

Save the changes, wait until the runtime has restarted, and then navigate to https://localhost:5001. Click the Administration button; the new module will be loaded, and the content shown in Figure 11-2 will be displayed.

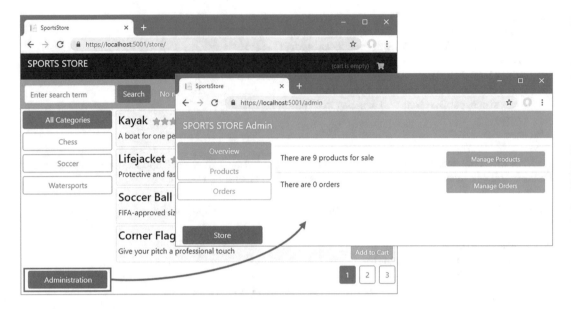

Figure 11-2. *Loading the administration module*

Clicking the buttons provided by the administration interface will navigate to URLs handled by the routes defined in Listing 11-12. For example, clicking the Manage Products button will navigate to the / admin/products URL, as shown in Figure 11-3.

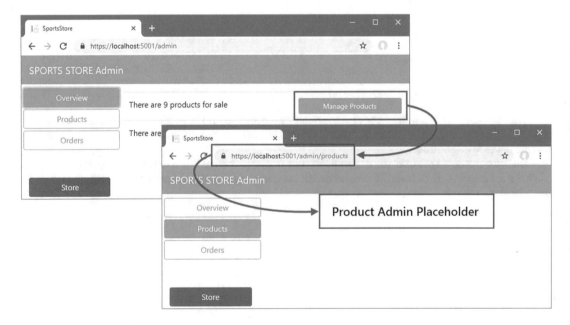

Figure 11-3. *Navigating within the administration interface*

Administering Products

Now that the basic structure is in place, I can start to define the features that an administrator will require, starting with the ability to manage the product available for sale. As you will see in the sections that follow, most of the heavy lifting has been done in earlier chapters, and the administration features can take advantage of the data model and the repository that mediates access to the ASP.NET Core MVC web service.

Creating the Editor Component

First, create a new TypeScript file called productEditor.component.ts in the admin folder and add the code shown in Listing 11-15. This component will be used to present a set of fields to the user so they can create or edit products.

Listing 11-15. The Contents of the productEditor.component.ts File in the ClientApp/src/app/admin Folder

```typescript
import { Component } from "@angular/core";
import { Repository } from "../models/repository";
import { Product } from "../models/product.model";
import { Supplier } from "../models/supplier.model";

@Component({
    selector: "admin-product-editor",
    templateUrl: "productEditor.component.html"
})
export class ProductEditorComponent {

    constructor(private repo: Repository) { }

    get product(): Product {
        return this.repo.product;
    }

    get suppliers(): Supplier[] {
        return this.repo.suppliers;
    }

    compareSuppliers(s1: Supplier, s2: Supplier) {
        return s1 && s2 && s1.name == s2.name;
    }
}
```

This component provides access to the currently edited Product object through its product property. The selection of the Product object and the actions that are performed on it are left to other components. The job of this component is only to provide access to the data so that the same set of HTML form fields can be presented without duplication to support both editing and creating data. The suppliers property and the compareSuppliers method support editing the relationship between a product and its supplier, which I describe shortly.

To provide the component with its template, add an HTML file called productEditor.component.html in the admin folder with the elements shown in Listing 11-16.

Listing 11-16. The Contents of the productEditor.component.html File in the ClientApp/src/app/admin Folder

```html
<div class="form-group">
    <label>Name</label>
    <input class="form-control" [(ngModel)]="product.name" />
</div>
<div class="form-group">
    <label>Category</label>
    <input class="form-control" [(ngModel)]="product.category" />
</div>
<div class="form-group">
    <label>Supplier</label>
    <select class="form-control" [(ngModel)]="product.supplier"
            [compareWith]="compareSuppliers">
        <option *ngFor="let s of suppliers" [ngValue]="s">{{s.name}}</option>
    </select>
</div>
<div class="form-group">
    <label>Description</label>
    <textarea class="form-control" [(ngModel)]="product.description"></textarea>
</div>
<div class="form-group">
    <label>Price</label>
    <input type="number" class="form-control" [(ngModel)]="product.price" />
</div>
```

The template uses two-way data bindings and the ngModel directive to allow the user to edit the properties of the Product object. Most of the properties are simple input or textarea elements, but some extra work is required to get the select element working correctly.

The ngModel directive on the select element works with the ngValue directive on the option elements to ensure that the appropriate option is selected by default, which is done by comparing the model value and the option value. If the two values are the same, then the option is selected in order to display the current value to the user.

A common problem when working with complex data obtained from an ASP.NET Core MVC web service is that the objects that are being compared are obtained using separate HTTP requests. In this case, the Supplier objects returned by the Product.supplier properties were created by parsing the response to a GET request sent to the /api/products URL. However, the Supplier objects that are used to create the option elements were created by parsing the response to a GET request sent to the /api/suppliers URL. This means that the ngModel directive has to compare objects from two different sources, which prevents the select element from correctly displaying the current value. To work around this problem, the compareWith directive is used to provide Angular with a method defined by the component that can be used to determine whether two objects are equal. In this case, the compareSuppliers method is specific, which compares Supplier objects using the value of the name property.

Make the changes shown in Listing 11-17 to register the new component in the administration feature module, along with the CommonModule, which contains the directives used in the next section.

Listing 11-17. Registering a Component in the admin.module.ts File in the ClientApp/src/app/admin Folder

```
import { NgModule } from "@angular/core";
import { RouterModule, Routes } from "@angular/router";
import { FormsModule } from "@angular/forms";
import { AdminComponent } from "./admin.component";
import { OverviewComponent } from "./overview.component";
import { ProductAdminComponent } from "./productAdmin.component";
import { OrderAdminComponent } from "./orderAdmin.component";
import { ProductEditorComponent } from "./productEditor.component";
import { CommonModule } from '@angular/common';

const routes: Routes = [
    {
    path: "", component: AdminComponent,
    children: [
        { path: "products", component: ProductAdminComponent },
        { path: "orders", component: OrderAdminComponent },
        { path: "overview", component: OverviewComponent },
        { path: "", component: OverviewComponent }]
    }
];

@NgModule({
    imports: [RouterModule,
        FormsModule, RouterModule.forChild(routes), CommonModule],
    declarations: [AdminComponent, OverviewComponent,
        ProductAdminComponent, OrderAdminComponent, ProductEditorComponent]
})
export class AdminModule { }
```

Creating the Product Table

The next step is to complete the main product administration component so that it will present the user with a list of products and support creating, editing, and deleting them. Add the code shown in Listing 11-18 to the ProductAdminComponent class.

Listing 11-18. Adding Features to the productAdmin.component.ts File in the ClientApp/src/app/admin Folder

```
import { Component } from "@angular/core";
import { Repository } from "../models/repository";
import { Product } from "../models/product.model";
import { Supplier } from "../models/supplier.model";

@Component({
    templateUrl: "productAdmin.component.html"
})
export class ProductAdminComponent {
```

```
    constructor(private repo: Repository) {}

    tableMode: boolean = true;

    get product(): Product {
        return this.repo.product;
    }

    selectProduct(id: number) {
        this.repo.getProduct(id);
    }

    saveProduct() {
        if (this.repo.product.productId == null) {
            this.repo.createProduct(this.repo.product);
        } else {
            this.repo.replaceProduct(this.repo.product);
        }
        this.clearProduct()
        this.tableMode = true;
    }

    deleteProduct(id: number) {
        this.repo.deleteProduct(id);
    }

    clearProduct() {
        this.repo.product = new Product();
        this.tableMode = true;
    }

    get products(): Product[] {
        return this.repo.products;
    }
}
```

The properties and methods defined by the component provide access to the product data to allow a product to be selected for editing and send changes to the web service. There is also a `tableMode` property that will be used to display the editor fields when the user creates a new product. To present the content, replace the elements in the component's template with those shown in Listing 11-19.

Listing 11-19. Displaying Data in the productAdmin.component.html File in the ClientApp/src/app/admin Folder

```html
<table *ngIf="tableMode; else create" class="table table-sm table-striped">
    <tbody>
        <tr>
            <th>ID</th><th>Name</th><th>Category</th><th>Supplier</th>
            <th>Price</th><th></th>
        </tr>
```

```
            <tr *ngFor="let p of products">
                <ng-template [ngIf]="product?.productId != p.productId"
                        [ngIfElse]="edit">
                    <td>{{p.productId}}</td>
                    <td>{{p.name}}</td>
                    <td>{{p.category}}</td>
                    <td>{{p.supplier?.name || '(None)'}}</td>
                    <td>{{p.price | currency:"USD":"symbol"}}</td>
                    <td>
                        <button class="btn btn-sm btn-primary"
                                (click)="selectProduct(p.productId)">Edit</button>
                        <button class="btn btn-sm btn-danger ml-1"
                                (click)="deleteProduct(p.productId)">Delete</button>
                    </td>
                </ng-template>
            </tr>
        </tbody>
        <tfoot>
            <tr>
                <td colspan="6" class="text-center">
                    <button class="btn btn-primary"
                        (click)="clearProduct(); tableMode = false">Create</button>
                </td>
            </tr>
        </tfoot>
    </table>

<ng-template #edit>
    <td colspan="6" class="bg-light border p-3">
        <admin-product-editor></admin-product-editor>
        <div class="text-center">
            <button class="btn btn-sm btn-primary" (click)="saveProduct()">
                Save
            </button>
            <button class="btn btn-sm btn-info ml-1" (click)="clearProduct()">
                Cancel
            </button>
        </div>
    </td>
</ng-template>

<ng-template #create>
    <div class="m-2">
        <admin-product-editor></admin-product-editor>
        <button class="btn btn-primary" (click)="saveProduct()">
            Save
        </button>
        <button class="btn btn-info ml-1" (click)="clearProduct()">
            Cancel
        </button>
    </div>
</ng-template>
```

The centerpiece of the template is a table that contains a row for each product, which you can see by reloading the application and navigating to https://localhost:5001/admin/products. Each row contains Edit and Delete buttons, as shown in Figure 11-4.

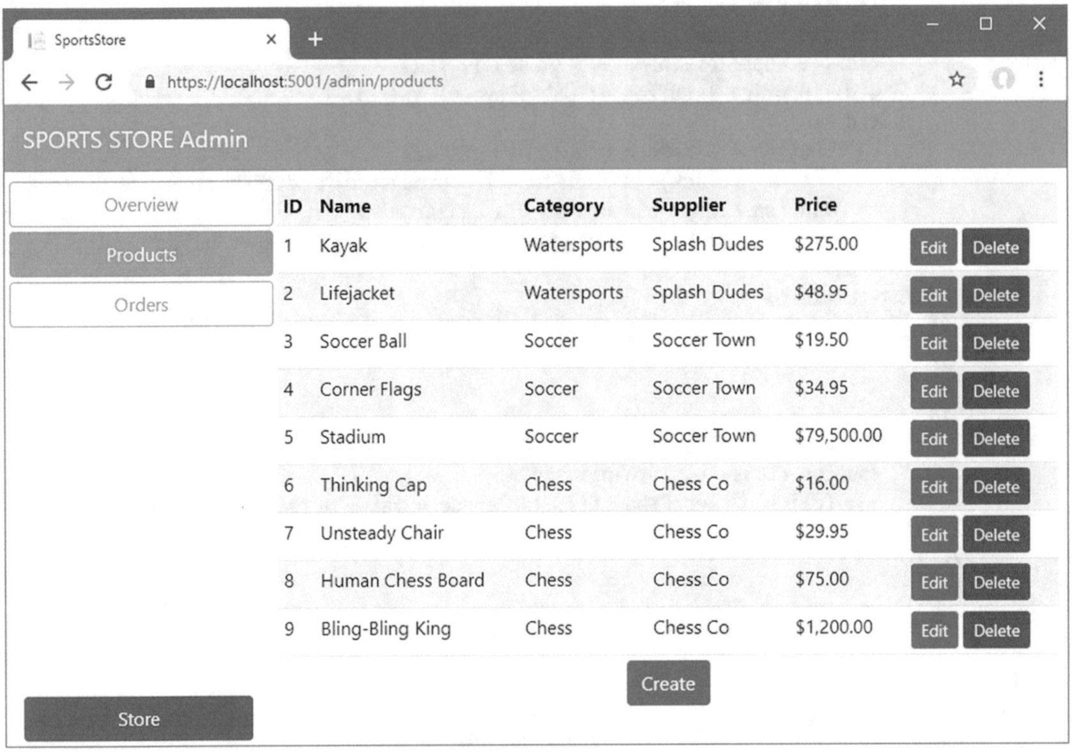

Figure 11-4. *The product administration table*

If you click one of the Edit buttons, the table row is replaced with an inline editor that allows the property values to be changed, as shown in Figure 11-5, which also shows how the same editor is used when the Create button is clicked.

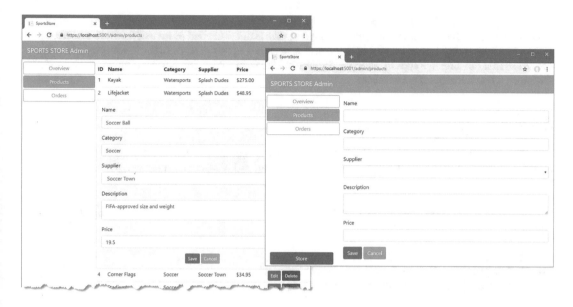

Figure 11-5. *Using the product editor*

In most situations, the concise syntax for structural directives is more convenient because it allows the directive to applied directly to the element. In Listing 11-19, the concise syntax for the ngIf directive is used to display the table of products or the editor for creating new products, like this:

```
...
<table *ngIf="tableMode; else create" class="table table-sm table-striped">
...
```

The concise syntax can't be used when there isn't a suitable element to apply it to. The template changes the contents of a table row so that different sets of td elements are used in a table row when the user is editing a product. The ngIf directive can't be applied to the tr element because the contents of each row will be different for each product and there is no suitable intermediate element between the tr and td elements that should be displayed. In this situation, the full syntax can be used, like this:

```
...
<ng-template [ngIf]="product?.productId != p.productId" [ngIfElse]="edit">
    <td>{{p.productId}}</td>
    <td>{{p.name}}</td>
    <td>{{p.category}}</td>
    <td>{{p.supplier?.name || '(None)'}}</td>
    <td>{{p.price | currency:USD:true}}</td>
    <td>
        <button class="btn btn-sm btn-primary"
            (click)="selectProduct(p.productId)">Edit</button>
        <button class="btn btn-sm btn-danger"
            (click)="deleteProduct(p.productId)">Delete</button>
    </td>
</ng-template>
...
```

The ng-template element allows the ngIf directive to be applied without changing the structure of the table. When using the full syntax, the name of the directive is not preceded by an asterisk, and a different set of data bindings is required to control how the directive works. In this case, the ngIf binding specifies the condition that the directive should evaluate, and the ngIfElse binding specifies the template that should be displayed when the expression is false.

Administering Orders

The process for dealing with orders follows the same basic pattern for products and relies on the data model and repository created in earlier chapters. Replace the OrderAdminComponent class with the code shown in Listing 11-20.

Listing 11-20. Adding Features in the orderAdmin.component.ts File in the ClientApp/src/app/admin Folder

```
import { Component } from "@angular/core";
import { Repository } from "../models/repository";
import { Order } from "../models/order.model";

@Component({
    templateUrl: "orderAdmin.component.html"
})
export class OrderAdminComponent {

    constructor(private repo: Repository) {}

    get orders(): Order[] {
        return this.repo.orders;
    }

    markShipped(order: Order) {
        this.repo.shipOrder(order);
    }
}
```

The component receives a Repository object through dependency injection and uses it to provide its template with the orders data and a method that will mark an order as shipped. To use these members, replace the contents of the component's template with the contents shown in Listing 11-21.

Listing 11-21. Managing Orders in the orderAdmin.component.html File in the ClientApp/src/app/admin Folder

```
<table *ngIf="orders?.length > 0; else nodata" class="table table-striped">
    <tbody>
        <tr>
            <th>Customer</th><th>Address</th><th>Products</th>
            <th>Total</th><th></th>
        </tr>
```

```
        <tr *ngFor="let o of orders">
            <td>{{o.name}}</td>
            <td>{{o.address}}</td>
            <td>{{o.products.length}}</td>
            <td>{{o.payment.total | currency:"USD":"symbol"}}</td>
            <td *ngIf="!o.shipped; else shipped">
                <button class="btn btn-sm btn-primary"
                        (click)="markShipped(o)">
                    Ship
                </button>
            </td>
        </tr>
    </tbody>
</table>

<ng-template #shipped>
    <td>Shipped</td>
</ng-template>

<ng-template #nodata>
    <h3 class="text-center">There are no orders</h3>
</ng-template>
```

There are no new Angular features used in this template. There is a table that is displayed only when there are orders available, managed using the ngIf directive. Within the table, rows are generated for each order using the ngFor directive. Each row contains a button element that uses a click event binding to invoke the component's markShipped method, which causes the repository to send an HTTP POST request to the ASP.NET Core MVC to update the order and then send an HTTP GET request to refresh the data.

To see the result, use the store section of the SportsStore application to create one or more orders and then navigate to https://localhost:5001/admin/orders to manage them, as shown in Figure 11-6.

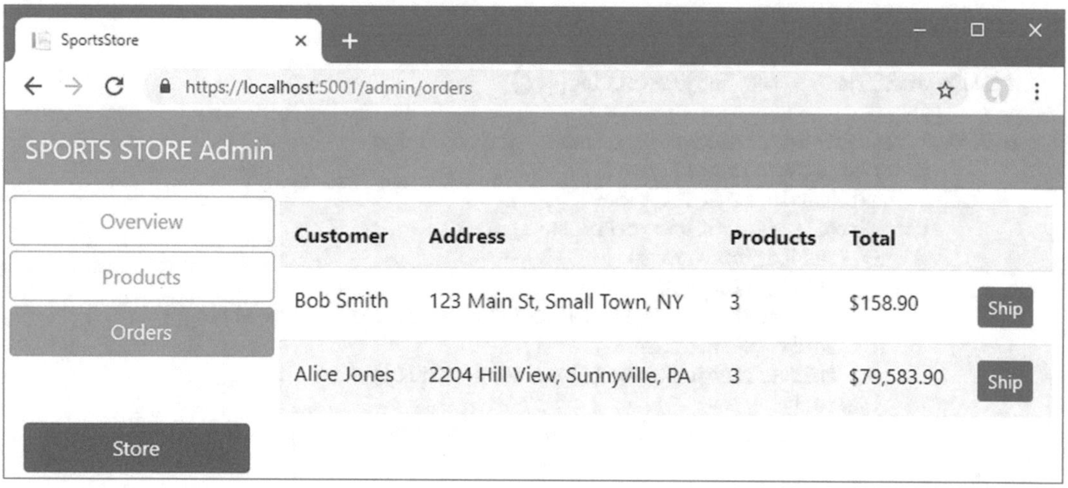

Figure 11-6. Administering orders

Dealing with Request Errors

Not all HTTP requests will produce a successful result, especially when dealing with data entered by a user, which may not pass the ASP.NET Core MVC model validation process.

Ideally, when an application receives an error response, it will deal with it in such a way that the user is able to understand what has gone wrong and is put in a position to correct the problem with the minimum of effort and lost work. But this can be hard to achieve in a real project without adding a lot of complexity to the application, which presents its own risk of errors.

For most projects, the best compromise is to try to avoid errors but simply display them to the user when they occur and then try to return the application to a known good state. Avoiding errors is most effectively done by using the Angular data validation features, which were used in Chapter 9 to ensure that the user provided all of the data values required by the checkout process. The Angular validation features can be awkward to work with, but they are effective and can be customized to handle custom validation requirements.

Angular also makes it easy to determine when an error has occurred and display it to the user, which is the focus of this part of the chapter. In the sections that follow, I create a component that displays errors and then integrate it into the application.

Creating the Error Handling and Distribution Service

Angular makes it easy to change the way that errors are handled by defining a new service. Add a TypeScript file called errorHandler.service.ts in the app folder and use it to define the class shown in Listing 11-22.

Listing 11-22. The Contents of the errorHandler.service.ts File in the ClientApp/src/app Folder

```
import { Injectable } from "@angular/core";
import { HttpEvent, HttpInterceptor, HttpHandler,
         HttpRequest, HttpErrorResponse } from "@angular/common/http";
import { Observable, throwError, Subject } from "rxjs";
import { catchError } from "rxjs/operators"

@Injectable()
export class ErrorHandlerService implements HttpInterceptor {
    private errSubject = new Subject<string[]>();

    intercept(request: HttpRequest<any>, next: HttpHandler):
            Observable<HttpEvent<any>> {
        return next.handle(request).pipe(
            catchError((resp: HttpErrorResponse) => {
                if (resp.error.errors) {
                    this.errSubject
                        .next([...Object.values(resp.error.errors) as string[]]);
                } else if (resp.error.title) {
                    this.errSubject.next([resp.error.title]);
                } else {
                    this.errSubject.next(["An HTTP error occurred"]);
                }
                return throwError(resp);
            })
        );
    }
}
```

```
    get errors(): Observable<string[]> {
        return this.errSubject;
    }
}
```

The HttpClient class that Angular provides for making HTTP requests supports interceptors, which are classes that receive requests and responses and can alter them before they are processed. Interceptors can also be used to receive HTTP errors, which is what the code in Listing 11-22 does. The ErrorHandlerService provides an Observable that produces error messages when they arise and has particular support for processing validation messages from the ASP.NET Core MVC controller so they can be easily displayed to the user.

In Listing 11-23, I have registered the service as an interceptor in the main application module, which means that it will receive all of the HTTP requests made in the application.

Listing 11-23. Registering an Interceptor in the app.module.ts File in the ClientApp/src/app Folder

```
import { BrowserModule } from '@angular/platform-browser';
import { NgModule, ErrorHandler } from '@angular/core';
import { AppRoutingModule } from './app-routing.module';
import { AppComponent } from './app.component';
import { ModelModule } from "./models/model.module";
import { FormsModule } from '@angular/forms';
import { StoreModule } from "./store/store.module";
import { ExternalService } from "./external.service";
import { HTTP_INTERCEPTORS } from "@angular/common/http";
import { ErrorHandlerService } from "./errorHandler.service";

@NgModule({
    declarations: [AppComponent],
    imports: [BrowserModule, AppRoutingModule, ModelModule, FormsModule,
        StoreModule],
    providers: [ExternalService, ErrorHandlerService,
        { provide: HTTP_INTERCEPTORS,
            useExisting: ErrorHandlerService, multi: true}],
    bootstrap: [AppComponent],

})
export class AppModule {

    constructor(external: ExternalService) {}
}
```

The ErrorHandlerService requires two registrations. The first allows the service to be consumed through regular dependency injection, and the second uses the HTTP_INTERCEPTORS token, which tells Angular that the service should intercept HTTP request and responses.

Displaying Errors

To provide access to the errors that occur in the application, add the statements shown in Listing 11-24 to the root component. (This class contains methods and properties from an earlier chapter, which I have removed for the sake of brevity.)

Listing 11-24. Accessing Errors in the app.component.ts File in the ClientApp/src/app Folder

```
import { Component } from '@angular/core';
import { ErrorHandlerService } from "./errorHandler.service";

@Component({
    selector: 'app-root',
    templateUrl: './app.component.html',
    styleUrls: ['./app.component.css']
})
export class AppComponent {
    private lastError: string[];

    constructor(errorService: ErrorHandlerService) {
        errorService.errors.subscribe(error => {
            this.lastError = error;
        });
    }

    get error(): string[] {
        return this.lastError;
    }

    clearError() {
        this.lastError = null;
    }
}
```

To display errors to the user, add the elements shown in Listing 11-25 to the root component's template.

Listing 11-25. Displaying Errors in the app.component.html File in the ClientApp/src/app Folder

```
<div class="bg-danger text-white text-center p-2 m-2" *ngIf="error != null">
    <h6 *ngFor="let e of error">{{e}}</h6>
    <button class="btn btn-warning" (click)="clearError()">OK</button>
</div>
<router-outlet></router-outlet>
```

There is a div element that is displayed only when there is an error; it contains h6 elements that are generated for each string required to describe the error. An error will be displayed until the user clicks the button element, which has a click event binding that calls the error handler's clearError method.

To see the result, reload the application in the browser, navigate to the https://localhost:5001/admin URL, and click the Products button to display the list of products. Click the Create button and then click the Save button without entering values into any of the fields. The HTTP request that is sent to the web service fails the MVC model binding process and produces the error messages shown in Figure 11-7.

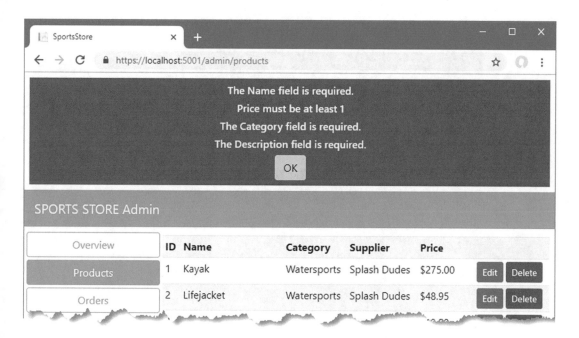

Figure 11-7. *Displaying validation errors*

Bear in mind that the asynchronous nature of the HTTP request means that the response from the ASP. NET Core MVC web service is received after the Angular application has navigated to another URL. It is for this reason that Angular form validation should be used to avoid this kind of error being generated and that handling errors like this should be a last resort.

Summary

In this chapter, I created the administration features for the application, building on the features created in earlier chapters. I also added support for displaying errors to the user, which provides a last-resort technique for problems that cannot be handled in the application code and that could not be avoided using features such as form validation. In the next chapter, I explain how to secure the application so that the administration features can be used only by authorized users.

CHAPTER 12

■ ■ ■

Securing the Application

In this chapter, I finish the SportsStore application by setting up authentication and authorization so that administrative tasks, such as modifying or deleting data, can be done by approved users only. I explain how to restrict access to web services, how to use ASP.NET Core Identity to provide security services, and how to authenticate users using Angular. Table 12-1 puts application security in context.

Table 12-1. *Putting Application Security in Context*

Question	Answer
What is it?	Application security prevents unauthorized users from using sensitive web service actions.
Why is it useful?	Without authorization, any user can administer the application.
How is it used?	ASP.NET Core Identity is used to manage users and roles and can be combined with the built-in features of ASP.NET Core MVC to authenticate or authorize users.
Are there any pitfalls or limitations?	You must take care to protect the parts of the API that are required for administration, while ensuring that the parts required for the publicly accessible features are open to anonymous access.
Are there any alternatives?	Not all applications require authorization and authentication, especially if there are no administration features.

Preparing for This Chapter

This chapter uses the SportsStore project that I created in Chapter 3 and modified in the chapters since. To remove the database so that the application will use fresh seed data, open a new command prompt, navigate to the ServerApp folder, and run the commands shown in Listing 12-1.

■ **Tip** You can download the complete project for every chapter without charge from the source code repository, `https://github.com/Apress/esntl-angular-for-asp.net-core-mvc-3`. Run `npm install` in the ClientApp folder to install the packages required for Angular development and then start the development tools as instructed.

© Adam Freeman 2019
A. Freeman, *Essential Angular for ASP.NET Core MVC 3*,
https://doi.org/10.1007/978-1-4842-5284-0_12

Listing 12-1. Resetting the Database

```
dotnet ef database drop --force
dotnet ef database update
dotnet sql-cache create "Server=(localdb)\MSSQLLocalDB;Database=EssentialApp" "dbo"
"SessionData"
```

Use a command prompt to run the command shown in Listing 12-2 in the ServerApp folder to start the ASP.NET Core runtime and the Angular development tools.

Listing 12-2. Starting the Development Tools

```
dotnet watch run
```

Open a new browser window and navigate to https://localhost:5001; you will see the Angular application, as shown in Figure 12-1.

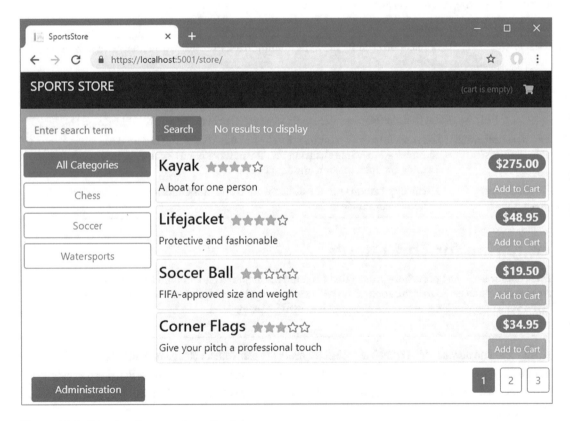

Figure 12-1. *Running the example application*

Restricting Access to Action Methods

Restricting access to the sensitive web service features requires applying the Authorize attribute, which specifies the authorization policy for an ASP.NET Core MVC controller or action method. For the SportsStore application, I am going to restrict access to the administration features to authenticated users who have been assigned a role called Administrator.

Restricting Access to Suppliers

To begin with something simple, apply the Authorize attribute to the SupplierValuesController class, as shown in Listing 12-3, to restrict access to all of the action methods used to deal with supplier data.

Listing 12-3. Restricting Access in the SupplierValuesController.cs File in the ServerApp/Controllers Folder

```
using Microsoft.AspNetCore.Mvc;
using ServerApp.Models;
using ServerApp.Models.BindingTargets;
using System.Collections.Generic;
using Microsoft.AspNetCore.Authorization;

namespace ServerApp.Controllers {

    [Route("api/suppliers")]
    [Authorize(Roles = "Administrator")]
    public class SupplierValuesController : Controller {
        private DataContext context;

        // ...methods omitted for brevity...
    }
}
```

Applying the Authorize attribute to the class affects all the action methods defined by the controller. The effect of the attribute in Listing 12-3 is to restrict all actions that operate on Supplier objects from being accessed except by authenticated users who have been assigned the Administrator role.

Restricting Access to Orders

Access to the action methods defined by the OrderValuesController class is a little more complex: all users should be able to create orders, but the ability to retrieve and modify orders should be restricted. Add the attributes shown in Listing 12-4 to set up the authorization policy on this controller.

Listing 12-4. Restricting Access in the OrderValuesController.cs File in the ServerApp/Controllers Folder

```
using Microsoft.AspNetCore.Mvc;
using Microsoft.EntityFrameworkCore;
using ServerApp.Models;
using System.Collections.Generic;
using System.Linq;
using Microsoft.AspNetCore.Authorization;
```

```
namespace ServerApp.Controllers {

    [Route("/api/orders")]
    [Authorize(Roles = "Administrator")]
    public class OrderValuesController : Controller {
        private DataContext context;

        // ...other methods omitted for brevity...

        [HttpPost]
        [AllowAnonymous]
        public IActionResult CreateOrder([FromBody] Order order) {
            if (ModelState.IsValid) {

                order.OrderId = 0;
                order.Shipped = false;
                order.Payment.Total = GetPrice(order.Products);

                ProcessPayment(order.Payment);
                if (order.Payment.AuthCode != null) {
                    context.Add(order);
                    context.SaveChanges();
                    return Ok(new {
                        orderId = order.OrderId,
                        authCode = order.Payment.AuthCode,
                        amount = order.Payment.Total
                    });
                } else {
                    return BadRequest("Payment rejected");
                }
            }
            return BadRequest(ModelState);
        }
    }
}
```

Applying the Authorize attribute restricts access to all of the action methods, but this policy is overridden by the AllowAnonymous attribute, which ensures that the CreateOrder action can be targeted by any users.

Restricting Access to Products

The final controller to secure is the ProductValuesController class, which should allow all users to view the data but allow only administrators to make changes. Some additional work is required for this controller to ensure that access to related data is handled consistently with the policy provided by the other controllers to avoid providing backdoor access to data that is restricted elsewhere. To implement the authorization policy, make the changes shown in Listing 12-5.

Listing 12-5. Restricting Access in the ProductValuesController.cs File in the ServerApp/Controllers Folder

```
using Microsoft.AspNetCore.Mvc;
using ServerApp.Models;
using Microsoft.EntityFrameworkCore;
using System.Linq;
using System.Collections.Generic;
using ServerApp.Models.BindingTargets;
using Microsoft.AspNetCore.JsonPatch;
using System.Text.Json;
using System.Reflection;
using System.ComponentModel;
using Microsoft.AspNetCore.Authorization;

namespace ServerApp.Controllers {

    [Route("api/products")]
    [ApiController]
    [Authorize(Roles = "Administrator")]
    public class ProductValuesController : Controller {
        private DataContext context;

        public ProductValuesController(DataContext ctx) {
            context = ctx;
        }

        [HttpGet("{id}")]
        [AllowAnonymous]
        public Product GetProduct(long id) {
            IQueryable<Product> query = context.Products
                .Include(p => p.Ratings);

            if (HttpContext.User.IsInRole("Administrator")) {
                query = query.Include(p => p.Supplier)
                    .ThenInclude(s => s.Products);
            }

            Product result = query.First(p => p.ProductId == id);

            if (result != null) {
                if (result.Supplier != null) {
                    result.Supplier.Products = result.Supplier.Products.Select(p =>
                        new Product {
                            ProductId = p.ProductId,
                            Name = p.Name,
                            Category = p.Category,
                            Description = p.Description,
                            Price = p.Price,
                        });
                }
```

```
            if (result.Ratings != null) {
                foreach (Rating r in result.Ratings) {
                    r.Product = null;
                }
            }
        }
    }
    return result;
}


[HttpGet]
[AllowAnonymous]
public IActionResult GetProducts(string category, string search,
        bool related = false, bool metadata = false) {
    IQueryable<Product> query = context.Products;

    if (!string.IsNullOrWhiteSpace(category)) {
        string catLower = category.ToLower();
        query = query.Where(p => p.Category.ToLower().Contains(catLower));
    }
    if (!string.IsNullOrWhiteSpace(search)) {
        string searchLower = search.ToLower();
        query = query.Where(p => p.Name.ToLower().Contains(searchLower)
            || p.Description.ToLower().Contains(searchLower));
    }

    if (related && HttpContext.User.IsInRole("Administrator")) {
        query = query.Include(p => p.Supplier).Include(p => p.Ratings);
        List<Product> data = query.ToList();
        data.ForEach(p => {
            if (p.Supplier != null) {
                p.Supplier.Products = null;
            }
            if (p.Ratings != null) {
                p.Ratings.ForEach(r => r.Product = null);
            }
        });
        return metadata ? CreateMetadata(data) : Ok(data);
    } else {
        return metadata ? CreateMetadata(query) : Ok(query);
    }
}

// ...other methods omitted for brevity...
    }
}
```

The Authorize attribute has been applied to the entire class but has been overridden by the AllowAnonymous attribute so that anyone can send requests to the GetProduct or GetProducts method. Within these methods, the role membership of the user is checked to make sure that only authorized users will receive the Supplier data that is related to a Product object.

Testing the Restrictions

To see the effect of the attributes applied to the controllers, use a browser to navigate to `https://localhost:5001`. The store part of the Angular project will work normally because it depends on web service action methods that can be accessed anonymously.

However, if you click the Administration button, you will see that the administration features are a different story. Click the Products button, for example, and you will see that the list of products is displayed but that all of them are shown with (None) in the Supplier column because access is restricted to related data, as shown in Figure 12-2.

Figure 12-2. *The effect of authorization restrictions*

The error message is displayed because some of the HTTP requests made by the administration features have failed completely. When the administration features are first displayed, requests are sent to the web service to get the product, supplier, and order data. The product request succeeds (although without related data), but the supplier and order requests fail, which produces the error shown in the figure.

If you look at the output from the ASP.NET Core MVC application, you will see that these requests have produced exceptions like this:

```
...
No authenticationScheme was specified, and there was no DefaultChallengeScheme found
...
```

The `Authorize` attribute tells ASP.NET Core MVC to restrict access to action methods but the application hasn't been configured with any way to establish the identity of users or provided with a database of users and roles. In the next section, I'll set up ASP.NET Core Identity and configure it to provide the missing functionality.

Installing and Configuring ASP.NET Core Identity

I am going to use ASP.NET Core Identity to provide ASP.NET Core MVC with the backend support it needs for managing authentication and authorization. In the sections that follow, I add the ASP.NET Core Identity packages to the project and add the configuration that is required for a conventional MVC application. Once the pieces are in place, I explain how Identity can be used to support Angular applications through a RESTful web service.

Installing the ASP.NET Core Identity NuGet Package

To install the NuGet package for ASP.NET Core Identity, use a command prompt to run the command shown in Listing 12-6 in the ServerApp folder.

Listing 12-6. Installing NuGet Packages

```
dotnet add package Microsoft.AspNetCore.Identity.EntityFrameworkCore --version 3.0.0
```

Creating the Identity Context Class and Seed Data

The ASP.NET Core Identity system depends on Entity Framework Core for access to its data, which means that a database context class is required. Add a C# class file called IdentityDataContext.cs in the ServerApp/Models folder, with the code shown in Listing 12-7.

Listing 12-7. The Contents of the IdentityDataContext.cs File in the ServerApp/Models Folder

```
using Microsoft.AspNetCore.Identity;
using Microsoft.AspNetCore.Identity.EntityFrameworkCore;
using Microsoft.EntityFrameworkCore;

namespace ServerApp.Models {

    public class IdentityDataContext : IdentityDbContext<IdentityUser> {

        public IdentityDataContext(DbContextOptions<IdentityDataContext> options)
            : base(options) { }
    }
}
```

The IdentityDbContext base class provides the properties through which the data is accessed, and creating a subclass allows the Identity features to be customized and extended. I am using all of the default options for this book, which are suitable for most projects, so the main benefit of creating a context class is that it is easier to create and apply the migration that sets up the database schema, which I do later in this chapter.

When setting up Identity, it is helpful to seed the database with a user account. Add a C# class file called IdentitySeedData.cs in the ServerApp/Models folder and add the code shown in Listing 12-8.

■ **Tip** You must ensure that the seed data uses a password that meets the Identity password policy, which requires a mix of uppercase and lowercase characters, symbols, and digits. The database will not be seeded if you do not comply with the policy.

Listing 12-8. The Contents of the IdentitySeedData.cs File in the ServerApp/Models Folder

```
using System;
using System.Linq;
using System.Threading.Tasks;
using Microsoft.AspNetCore.Identity;
using Microsoft.EntityFrameworkCore;
using Microsoft.Extensions.DependencyInjection;

namespace ServerApp.Models {

    public static class IdentitySeedData {
        private const string adminUser = "admin";
        private const string adminPassword = "MySecret123$";
        private const string adminRole = "Administrator";

        public static async Task SeedDatabase(IServiceProvider provider) {
            provider.GetRequiredService<IdentityDataContext>().Database.Migrate();

            UserManager<IdentityUser> userManager
                = provider.GetRequiredService<UserManager<IdentityUser>>();
            RoleManager<IdentityRole> roleManager
                = provider.GetRequiredService<RoleManager<IdentityRole>>();

            IdentityRole role = await roleManager.FindByNameAsync(adminRole);
            IdentityUser user = await userManager.FindByNameAsync(adminUser);

            if (role == null) {
                role = new IdentityRole(adminRole);
                IdentityResult result = await roleManager.CreateAsync(role);
                if (!result.Succeeded) {
                    throw new Exception("Cannot create role: "
                        + result.Errors.FirstOrDefault());
                }
            }

            if (user == null) {
                user = new IdentityUser(adminUser);
                IdentityResult result
                    = await userManager.CreateAsync(user, adminPassword);
                if (!result.Succeeded) {
                    throw new Exception("Cannot create user: "
                        + result.Errors.FirstOrDefault());
                }
            }
```

```
                if (! await userManager.IsInRoleAsync(user, adminRole)) {
                    IdentityResult result
                        = await userManager.AddToRoleAsync(user, adminRole);
                    if (!result.Succeeded) {
                        throw new Exception("Cannot add user to role: "
                            + result.Errors.FirstOrDefault());
                    }
                }
            }
        }
    }
}
```

The static SeedDatabase method defined in the listing receives a parameter that defines the IServiceProvider interface, which will be provided by the Startup class and which can be used to access the services that have been defined during the application's configuration. This is used to get a database context object for the Identity database to ensure that the migrations have been applied and to ensure that there is an admin user in the database that has a password of MySecret123 and that is a member of the Administrator role.

■ **Note**   When you rely on a user account seeded in the database, it is good practice to change the password when the application has been deployed into production.

Adding Identity to the Application Configuration

To set up ASP.NET Core Identity so that it is integrated with the rest of the ASP.NET Core application, add the configuration statements shown in Listing 12-9 to the Startup class in the ServerApp folder.

Listing 12-9. Configuring Identity in the Startup.cs File in the ServerApp Folder

```
using System;
using System.Collections.Generic;
using System.Linq;
using System.Threading.Tasks;
using Microsoft.AspNetCore.Builder;
using Microsoft.AspNetCore.Hosting;
using Microsoft.AspNetCore.HttpsPolicy;
using Microsoft.Extensions.Configuration;
using Microsoft.Extensions.DependencyInjection;
using Microsoft.Extensions.Hosting;
using Microsoft.AspNetCore.SpaServices.AngularCli;
using ServerApp.Models;
using Microsoft.EntityFrameworkCore;
using Microsoft.OpenApi.Models;
using Microsoft.AspNetCore.ResponseCompression;
using Microsoft.Extensions.FileProviders;
using System.IO;
using Microsoft.AspNetCore.Identity;
```

```
namespace ServerApp {
    public class Startup {

        public Startup(IConfiguration configuration) {
            Configuration = configuration;
        }

        public IConfiguration Configuration { get; }

        public void ConfigureServices(IServiceCollection services) {

            string connectionString =
                Configuration["ConnectionStrings:DefaultConnection"];
            services.AddDbContext<DataContext>(options =>
                options.UseSqlServer(connectionString));

            services.AddDbContext<IdentityDataContext>(options =>
                options.UseSqlServer(Configuration["ConnectionStrings:Identity"]));
            services.AddIdentity<IdentityUser, IdentityRole>()
                .AddEntityFrameworkStores<IdentityDataContext>();

            services.AddControllersWithViews()
                .AddJsonOptions(opts => {
                    opts.JsonSerializerOptions.IgnoreNullValues = true;
                });
            services.AddRazorPages();

            services.AddSwaggerGen(options => {
                options.SwaggerDoc("v1",
                    new OpenApiInfo { Title = "SportsStore API", Version = "v1" });
            });

            services.AddDistributedSqlServerCache(options => {
                options.ConnectionString = connectionString;
                options.SchemaName = "dbo";
                options.TableName = "SessionData";
            });

            services.AddSession(options => {
                options.Cookie.Name = "SportsStore.Session";
                options.IdleTimeout = System.TimeSpan.FromHours(48);
                options.Cookie.HttpOnly = false;
                options.Cookie.IsEssential = true;
            });

            services.AddResponseCompression(opts => {
                opts.MimeTypes = ResponseCompressionDefaults.MimeTypes.Concat(
                    new[] { "application/octet-stream" });
            });
        }
```

```
public void Configure(IApplicationBuilder app, IWebHostEnvironment env,
        IServiceProvider services) {

    if (env.IsDevelopment()) {
        app.UseDeveloperExceptionPage();
    } else {
        app.UseExceptionHandler("/Home/Error");
        app.UseHsts();
    }

    app.UseHttpsRedirection();
    app.UseStaticFiles();
    app.UseStaticFiles(new StaticFileOptions {
        RequestPath = "/blazor",
        FileProvider = new PhysicalFileProvider(
            Path.Combine(Directory.GetCurrentDirectory(),
                "../BlazorApp/wwwroot"))
    });

    app.UseSession();

    app.UseRouting();
    app.UseAuthentication();
    app.UseAuthorization();

    app.UseEndpoints(endpoints => {
        endpoints.MapControllerRoute(
            name: "default",
            pattern: "{controller=Home}/{action=Index}/{id?}");

        endpoints.MapControllerRoute(
            name: "angular_fallback",
            pattern:
            "{target:regex(admin|store|cart|checkout):nonfile}/{*catchall}",
            defaults: new { controller = "Home", action = "Index" });

        endpoints.MapControllerRoute(
            name: "blazor_integration",
            pattern: "/blazor/{*path:nonfile}",
            defaults: new { controller = "Home", action = "Blazor" });

        //endpoints.MapFallbackToClientSideBlazor<BlazorApp
        //      .Startup>("blazor/{*path:nonfile}", "index.html");

        endpoints.MapRazorPages();
    });

    app.Map("/blazor", opts =>
        opts.UseClientSideBlazorFiles<BlazorApp.Startup>());

    app.UseClientSideBlazorFiles<BlazorApp.Startup>();
```

```
app.UseSwagger();
app.UseSwaggerUI(options => {
    options.SwaggerEndpoint("/swagger/v1/swagger.json",
        "SportsStore API");
});

app.UseSpa(spa => {
    string strategy = Configuration
        .GetValue<string>("DevTools:ConnectionStrategy");
    if (strategy == "proxy") {
        spa.UseProxyToSpaDevelopmentServer("http://127.0.0.1:4200");
    } else if (strategy == "managed") {
        spa.Options.SourcePath = "../ClientApp";
        spa.UseAngularCliServer("start");
    }
});

SeedData.SeedDatabase(services.GetRequiredService<DataContext>());
IdentitySeedData.SeedDatabase(services).Wait();
        }
    }
}
```

The AddDbContext method called in ConfigureServices registers the Identity database context class with Entity Framework Core, while the AddIdentity method tells Identity to use the default classes to represent users and roles and to store the data through the context class. The call to the Wait method ensures that the database context remains available while the database is seeded.

To provide the connection string that tells Entity Framework Core where to store the Identity data, add the configuration entries shown in Listing 12-10 to the appsettings.Development.json file, ensuring that the connection string is on a single line.

Listing 12-10. Adding a Connection String in the appsettings.Development.json File in the ServerApp Folder

```
{
  "Logging": {
    "LogLevel": {
      "Default": "Debug",
      "System": "Information",
      "Microsoft": "Information"
    }
  },
  "DevTools": {
    "ConnectionStrategy": "managed"
  },
  "ConnectionStrings": {
    "DefaultConnection": "Server=(localdb)\\MSSQLLocalDB;Database=EssentialApp;
    MultipleActiveResultSets=true",
    "Identity": "Server=(localdb)\\MSSQLLocalDB;Database=EssentialAppIdentity;
    MultipleActiveResultSets=true"
  }
}
```

The connection string uses the same SQL Server container that is storing the rest of the SportsStore data but uses a database called `EssentialAppIdentity`.

Creating the Database Migration

To create the database migration, stop the ASP.NET Core MVC runtime and use a command prompt to run the command shown in Listing 12-11 in the `ServerApp` folder.

Listing 12-11. Creating a Database Migration

```
dotnet ef migrations add Identity --context IdentityDataContext
```

The next time the application is started, the migration will be applied to the database before it is seeded with the `admin` user, which will be assigned the `Administrator` role.

Creating the Authentication Controller and View

Although ASP.NET Core Identity provides all of the plumbing required to support authentication and authorization, it requires the addition of a controller to present users with a login screen when they try to access a restricted action method. Create a C# class file called `AccountController.cs` in the `ServerApp/Controllers` folder and add the code shown in Listing 12-12.

Listing 12-12. The Contents of the AccountController.cs File in the ServerApp/Controllers Folder

```
using Microsoft.AspNetCore.Identity;
using Microsoft.AspNetCore.Mvc;
using System.ComponentModel.DataAnnotations;
using System.Threading.Tasks;

namespace ServerApp.Controllers {

    public class AccountController : Controller {
        private UserManager<IdentityUser> userManager;
        private SignInManager<IdentityUser> signInManager;

        public AccountController(UserManager<IdentityUser> userMgr,
                            SignInManager<IdentityUser> signInMgr) {
            userManager = userMgr;
            signInManager = signInMgr;
        }

        [HttpGet]
        public IActionResult Login(string returnUrl) {
            ViewBag.returnUrl = returnUrl;
            return View();
        }
```

```
[HttpPost]
public async Task<IActionResult> Login(LoginViewModel creds,
        string returnUrl) {

    if (ModelState.IsValid) {
        if (await DoLogin(creds)) {
            return Redirect(returnUrl ?? "/");
        } else {
            ModelState.AddModelError("", "Invalid username or password");
        }
    }
    return View(creds);
}

[HttpPost]
public async Task<IActionResult> Logout(string redirectUrl) {
    await signInManager.SignOutAsync();
    return Redirect(redirectUrl ?? "/");
}

private async Task<bool> DoLogin(LoginViewModel creds) {
    IdentityUser user = await userManager.FindByNameAsync(creds.Name);
    if (user != null) {
        await signInManager.SignOutAsync();
        Microsoft.AspNetCore.Identity.SignInResult result =
            await signInManager.PasswordSignInAsync(user, creds.Password,
                false, false);
        return result.Succeeded;
    }
    return false;
}
}

public class LoginViewModel {
    [Required]
    public string Name {get; set;}
    [Required]
    public string Password { get; set;}
}
}
```

The Login action method that accepts GET requests renders a Razor view that will prompt the user for their credentials. The POST Login action method validates the credentials and signs the user in. The authentication is performed in the DoLogin method, which I have defined so I can use the same code for web service authentication later in the chapter.

To provide the view that will prompt the user for their credentials, create a ServerApp/Views/Account folder and add to it a Razor file called Login.cshtml, with the content shown in Listing 12-13.

Listing 12-13. The Contents of the Login.cshtml File in the ServerApp/Views/Account Folder

```
@model ServerApp.Controllers.LoginViewModel

<div class="m-3">
    <h3 class="bg-primary p-2 text-white">Log In</h3>
    <div class="text-danger" asp-validation-summary="All"></div>
    <form asp-action="Login" method="post">
        <input type="hidden" name="returnUrl" value="@ViewBag.returnUrl" />
        <div class="form-group">
            <label>Name</label>
            <input asp-for="Name" class="form-control" />
        </div>
        <div class="form-group">
            <label>Password</label>
            <input type="password" asp-for="Password" class="form-control" />
        </div>
        <div class="text-center">
            <button class="btn btn-primary" type="submit">Log In</button>
        </div>
    </form>
</div>
```

The view contains an HTML form that uses input elements to collect the username and password and send them to the Account controller.

Understanding the Conventional Authentication Flow

The controller and view in Listings 12-13 and 12-14 are the standard way to deal with authentication for traditional round-trip applications. To see how the flow of requests is handled, add the action method shown in Listing 12-14 to the Home controller so that there is a round-trip action method to target using the browser.

Listing 12-14. Adding an Action Method in the HomeController.cs File in the ServerApp/Controllers Folder

```
using Microsoft.AspNetCore.Mvc;
using ServerApp.Models;
using System.Diagnostics;
using System.Linq;
using Microsoft.AspNetCore.Authorization;

namespace ServerApp.Controllers {

    public class HomeController : Controller {
        private DataContext context;

        public HomeController(DataContext ctx) {
            context = ctx;
        }
```

```
public IActionResult Index() {
    return View(context.Products.First());
}

public IActionResult Blazor() {
    return View();
}

public IActionResult Privacy() {
    return View();
}

[ResponseCache(Duration = 0, Location = ResponseCacheLocation.None,
    NoStore = true)]
public IActionResult Error() {
    return View(new ErrorViewModel { RequestId = Activity.Current?.Id
        ?? HttpContext.TraceIdentifier });
}

[Authorize]
public string Protected() {
    return "You have been authenticated";
}
    }
}
```

The new action method is called Protected, and it has been decorated with the Authorize attribute, which means that any authenticated user will be able to access the action. Use a command prompt to run the command shown in Listing 12-15 in the ServerApp folder to start the ASP.NET Core runtime.

Listing 12-15. Starting the ASP.NET Core Runtime

```
dotnet watch run
```

Once the runtime has started, use a browser to request the URL https://localhost:5001/home/ protected. When prompted for credentials, enter admin into the Name field and MySecret123$ into the Password field and click the Log In button to see the message produced by the protected action method, as shown in Figure 12-3.

Figure 12-3. *Round-trip authentication*

When ASP.NET Core MVC finds that the `Authorize` attribute has been applied to an action method, the browser is redirected to the `/account/login` URL so that the user can enter credentials. When the user submits their name and password, the sign-in process redirects the user back to the URL for the protected action method. This second redirection includes a cookie that the browser will include in subsequent HTTP requests and that is used to identify the user without needing to prompt them for credentials again.

The use of the cookie means that the Angular application benefits from the login process, too. Navigate to `https://localhost:5001/admin/products` using the same browser tab with which you authenticated yourself, and you will see that the administration features work and that related data is displayed for each product. This happens because the browser automatically includes the authentication cookie in the HTTP requests sent by the Angular application, which means that authenticating using the round-trip part of the application also has the effect of authenticating for the web service part of the application, too.

Authenticating Directly in Angular

As things stand, the user needs to know that they have to authenticate themselves before starting the Angular application to use the administration features, which is far from ideal. But, with a little work, it is possible to allow the user to authenticate themselves directly within the Angular application so that the round-trip authentication system isn't required.

Creating a Web Service Authentication Method

The first step is to create an ASP.NET Core MVC action method that will allow clients to authenticate without trying to redirect them to a URL or return an HTML response, as well as a corresponding action that will end an authenticated session. Add the methods shown in Listing 12-16 to the `Account` controller.

Listing 12-16. Adding Action Methods in the AccountController.cs File in the Controllers Folder

```
using Microsoft.AspNetCore.Identity;
using Microsoft.AspNetCore.Mvc;
using System.ComponentModel.DataAnnotations;
using System.Threading.Tasks;
```

```
namespace ServerApp.Controllers {

    public class AccountController : Controller {
        private UserManager<IdentityUser> userManager;
        private SignInManager<IdentityUser> signInManager;

        public AccountController(UserManager<IdentityUser> userMgr,
                              SignInManager<IdentityUser> signInMgr) {
            userManager = userMgr;
            signInManager = signInMgr;
        }

        // ...other methods omitted for brevity...

        [HttpPost("/api/account/login")]
        public async Task<IActionResult> Login([FromBody] LoginViewModel creds) {
            if (ModelState.IsValid && await DoLogin(creds)) {
                return Ok("true");
            }
            return BadRequest();
        }

        [HttpPost("/api/account/logout")]
        public async Task<IActionResult> Logout() {
            await signInManager.SignOutAsync();
            return Ok();
        }
    }

    public class LoginViewModel {
        [Required]
        public string Name {get; set;}
        [Required]
        public string Password { get; set;}
    }
}
```

The new methods are simplified versions of the actions for round-trip clients, providing support for just authentication, without redirection or the need to provide HTML content to get the user's credentials.

Creating the Repository Methods

The next step is to add methods to the Angular Repository class so that the client can perform authentication, as shown in Listing 12-17.

Listing 12-17. Performing Authentication in the repository.ts File in the ClientApp/src/app/models Folder

```
import { Product } from "./product.model";
import { Injectable } from "@angular/core";
import { HttpClient } from "@angular/common/http";
import { Filter, Pagination } from "./configClasses.repository";
```

```
import { Supplier } from "./supplier.model";
import { Observable } from "rxjs";
import { Order, OrderConfirmation } from "./order.model";

const productsUrl = "/api/products";
const suppliersUrl = "/api/suppliers";
const sessionUrl = "/api/session";
const ordersUrl = "/api/orders";

type productsMetadata = {
    data: Product[],
    categories: string[];
}

@Injectable()
export class Repository {
    product: Product;
    products: Product[];
    suppliers: Supplier[] = [];
    filter: Filter = new Filter();
    categories: string[] = [];
    paginationObject = new Pagination();
    orders: Order[] = [];

    constructor(private http: HttpClient) {
        this.filter.related = true;
    }

    // ...other methods omitted for brevity...

    login(name: string, password: string) : Observable<boolean> {
        return  this.http.post<boolean>("/api/account/login",
            { name: name, password: password});
    }

    logout() {
        this.http.post("/api/account/logout", null).subscribe(response => {});
    }
}
```

The login method sends an HTTP POST request to the web service, and unlike the other methods in the repository, it returns an Observable<Response>, which will allow the outcome of the authentication request to be monitored. Unlike the data-related operations that the SportsStore supports, authentication requires immediate feedback to the user and so updates cannot be left to the normal Angular update system. The logout method also sends an HTTP POST request to the web service but doesn't allow the response to be observed (but calls the subscribe method, without which the request will not be sent).

Creating the Authentication Service

The simplest way to manage authentication in an Angular application is with a simple service, which can provide access to the repository methods and provide a consistent view of whether the user is currently authenticated. Create the ClientApp/src/app/auth folder and add to it a TypeScript file called authentication.service.ts to the ClientApp/src/app/auth folder with the code shown in Listing 12-18.

Listing 12-18. The Contents of the authentication.service.ts File in the ClientApp/src/app/auth Folder

```typescript
import { Injectable } from "@angular/core";
import { Repository } from "../models/repository";
import { Observable, of } from "rxjs";
import { Router } from "@angular/router";
import { map, catchError } from 'rxjs/operators';

@Injectable()
export class AuthenticationService {

    constructor(private repo: Repository,
                private router: Router) { }

    authenticated: boolean = false;
    name: string;
    password: string;
    callbackUrl: string;

    login() : Observable<boolean> {
        this.authenticated = false;
        return this.repo.login(this.name, this.password).pipe(
            map(response => {
                if (response) {
                    this.authenticated = true;
                    this.password = null;
                    this.router.navigateByUrl(this.callbackUrl || "/admin/overview");
                }
                return this.authenticated;
            }),
            catchError(e => {
                this.authenticated = false;
                return of(false);
            }));
    }

    logout() {
        this.authenticated = false;
        this.repo.logout();
        this.router.navigateByUrl("/admin/login");
    }
}
```

The service packages up access to the repository methods and provides an authenticated property that can be used to determine whether the user is currently authenticated. The login method uses the repository to send an HTTP request to the web service and observes the response to generate an observable true or false outcome.

Creating the Authentication Component

To create a component that will prompt the user for their credentials, add a TypeScript file called authentication.component.ts to the ClientApp/src/app/auth folder with the code shown in Listing 12-19.

Listing 12-19. The Contents of the authentication.component.ts File in the ClientApp/src/app/auth Folder

```
import {Component } from "@angular/core";
import { AuthenticationService } from "./authentication.service";

@Component({
    templateUrl: "authentication.component.html"
})
export class AuthenticationComponent {

    constructor(public authService: AuthenticationService) {}

    showError: boolean = false;

    login() {
        this.showError = false;
        this.authService.login().subscribe(result => {
            this.showError = !result;
        });
    }
}
```

The component uses its constructor to receive an AuthenticationService object through dependency injection so that it can be accessed from the template. It also defines a showError property that will signal to the template when an error message will be displayed, and there is a login method that starts the login process and uses the result to set the showError property.

To define the template, add an HTML file called authentication.component.html to the auth folder with the elements shown in Listing 12-20.

Listing 12-20. The Contents of the authentication.component.html File in the ClientApp/src/app/auth Folder

```
<div class="navbar bg-info mb-1">
    <a class="navbar-brand text-white">SPORTS STORE Admin</a>
</div>

<h4 *ngIf="showError" class="p-2 bg-danger text-white">
    Invalid username or password
</h4>
```

```
<form novalidate #authForm="ngForm" class="m-3">
    <div class="form-group">
        <label>Name:</label>
        <input #name="ngModel" name="name" class="form-control"
                [(ngModel)]="authService.name" required />
        <div *ngIf="name.invalid" class="text-danger">
            Please enter your user name
        </div>
    </div>
    <div class="form-group">
        <label>Password:</label>
        <input type="password" #password="ngModel" name="password"
                class="form-control" [(ngModel)]="authService.password" required />
        <div *ngIf="password.invalid" class="text-danger">
            Please enter your password
        </div>
    </div>
    <div class="text-center pt-2">
        <button class="btn btn-primary" [disabled]="authForm.invalid"
                (click)="login()">Login</button>
    </div>
</form>
```

The template presents form elements to the user to obtain their credentials, which Angular validation uses to ensure that the form cannot be submitted until values are provided. The component's showError property is used with the ngIf directive to show an error to the user when there is an authentication problem.

Creating the Authentication Route Guard

The Angular route guard feature is used to prevent navigation to a URL route until a specific condition is met, which will be authentication in this case. To create a route guard, add a TypeScript file called authentication.guard.ts in the auth folder and add the code shown in Listing 12-21.

Listing 12-21. The Contents of the authentication.guard.ts File in the ClientApp/src/app/auth Folder

```
import { Injectable } from "@angular/core";
import { Router, ActivatedRouteSnapshot, RouterStateSnapshot }
    from "@angular/router";
import { AuthenticationService } from "./authentication.service";

@Injectable()
export class AuthenticationGuard {

    constructor(private router: Router,
                private authService: AuthenticationService) {}

    canActivateChild(route: ActivatedRouteSnapshot,
            state: RouterStateSnapshot): boolean {
        if (this.authService.authenticated) {
            return true;
```

```
        } else {
            this.authService.callbackUrl = route.url.toString();
            this.router.navigateByUrl("/admin/login");
            return false;
        }
    }
}
```

The `canActivateChild` method is called when the user tries to navigate to a child URL protected by the guard. The `canActivateChild` method returns `true` if the user has been authenticated, which allows the navigation to proceed. If the user has not been authenticated, then the application is instructed to navigate to /admin/login, which will allow them to authenticate. The guard uses the value of the target URL to set the `callbackUrl` property defined by the authentication service, which is automatically navigated to when authentication succeeds, reproducing the redirection scheme used for round-trip clients described earlier in the chapter.

Creating and Registering the Authentication Feature Module

Add a TypeScript file called `auth.module.ts` in the `auth` folder and use it to define the Angular feature module shown in Listing 12-22, which will allow the authentication service, component, and guard to be used in the result of the application.

Listing 12-22. The Contents of the auth.module.ts File in the ClientApp/src/app/auth Folder

```
import { NgModule } from "@angular/core";
import { FormsModule } from '@angular/forms';
import { RouterModule } from "@angular/router";
import { CommonModule } from '@angular/common';
import { AuthenticationService } from "./authentication.service";
import { AuthenticationComponent } from "./authentication.component";
import { AuthenticationGuard } from "./authentication.guard";

@NgModule({
    imports: [RouterModule, FormsModule, CommonModule],
    declarations: [AuthenticationComponent],
    providers: [AuthenticationService, AuthenticationGuard],
    exports: [AuthenticationComponent]
})
export class AuthModule { }
```

To register the new feature module, add the statements shown in Listing 12-23 to the module for the administration feature.

Listing 12-23. Registering a Module in the admin.module.ts File in the ClientApp/src/app/admin Folder

```
import { NgModule } from "@angular/core";
import { RouterModule, Routes } from "@angular/router";
import { FormsModule } from "@angular/forms";
import { AdminComponent } from "./admin.component";
import { OverviewComponent } from "./overview.component";
import { ProductAdminComponent } from "./productAdmin.component";
```

```
import { OrderAdminComponent } from "./orderAdmin.component";
import { ProductEditorComponent } from "./productEditor.component";
import { CommonModule } from '@angular/common';
import { AuthModule } from '../auth/auth.module';
import { AuthenticationComponent } from '../auth/authentication.component';
import { AuthenticationGuard } from '../auth/authentication.guard';

const routes: Routes = [
    { path: "login", component: AuthenticationComponent },
    {
        path: "", component: AdminComponent,
        canActivateChild: [AuthenticationGuard],
        children: [
            { path: "products", component: ProductAdminComponent },
            { path: "orders", component: OrderAdminComponent },
            { path: "overview", component: OverviewComponent },
            { path: "", component: OverviewComponent }
        ]
    }
];

@NgModule({
    imports: [RouterModule,
        FormsModule, RouterModule.forChild(routes), CommonModule, AuthModule],
    declarations: [AdminComponent, OverviewComponent,
        ProductAdminComponent, OrderAdminComponent, ProductEditorComponent]
})
export class AdminModule { }
```

The changes set up the /admin/login URL for handling authentication and apply the route guard to prevent any of the other administration routes from being activated until authentication has been performed.

Creating the Logout Button

It is important to allow users to terminate a session, especially when they have access to administration functions. Add the code shown in Listing 12-24 to prepare to display a logout button to the user.

Listing 12-24. Preparing for Logout in the admin.component.ts File in the ClientApp/src/app/admin Folder

```
import { Component } from "@angular/core";
import { Repository } from "../models/repository";
import { AuthenticationService } from "../auth/authentication.service";

@Component({
    templateUrl: "admin.component.html"
})
export class AdminComponent {
```

```
constructor(private repo: Repository,
                public authService: AuthenticationService) {
    repo.filter.reset();
    repo.filter.related = true;
    this.repo.getProducts();
    this.repo.getSuppliers();
    this.repo.getOrders();
}
}
```

The changes receive the authentication service via dependency injection so that it can be accessed through the template. To create the logout button, add the elements shown in Listing 12-25 to the component's template.

Listing 12-25. Adding a Button in the admin.component.html File in the ClientApp/src/app/admin Folder

```
<div class="navbar bg-info mb-1">
    <a class="navbar-brand text-white">SPORTS STORE Admin</a>
    <div class="float-right navbar-text">
        <button class="btn btn-sm btn-warning"
                (click)="authService.logout()">
            Log Out
        </button>
    </div>
</div>

<div class="col-3 fixed-bottom mb-1">
    <a class="btn btn-block btn-secondary" routerLink="/store">
        Store
    </a>
</div>

<div class="row no-gutters">
    <div class="col-3">
        <button class="btn btn-block btn-outline-info m-1" routerLink="/admin"
                routerLinkActive="active" [routerLinkActiveOptions]="{exact: true}">
            Overview
        </button>
        <button class="btn btn-block btn-outline-info m-1"
                routerLink="/admin/products" routerLinkActive="active">
            Products
        </button>
        <button class="btn btn-block btn-outline-info m-1"
                routerLink="/admin/orders" routerLinkActive="active">
            Orders
        </button>
    </div>
    <div class="col p-2">
        <router-outlet></router-outlet>
    </div>
</div>
```

The new button calls the logout method provided by the authentication service, which will send an HTTP request to the web service to end the user's session and prevent the user from accessing any of the administration features until they have authenticated again.

Testing the Client Authentication Process

Restart the ASP.NET Core MVC application and use the browser to navigate to https://localhost:5001/admin. The Angular application will load and display the /admin/login URL. Enter admin into the Name field and MySecret123$ into the Password field and click the Log In button. The Angular application will use the web service for authentication and then navigate to the administration overview. Click the Log Out button, and you will be returned to the login prompt, as shown in Figure 12-4.

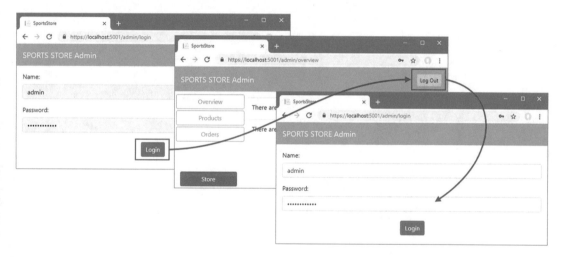

Figure 12-4. *Authenticating using the Angular application*

Authenticating the user within the Angular application provides a more integrated experience for the user but uses the same authentication system as for round-trip clients. When the Angular application provides valid credentials to the authentication web service, ASP.NET Core Identity adds a cookie to the response, which the browser automatically includes in future requests, which allows the identity of the user to be established and satisfies the restrictions applied using the Authorize attribute.

Summary

In this chapter, I explained how to use ASP.NET Core MVC and ASP.NET Core Identity to secure an application that has an Angular client. I showed you how to apply the Authorize attribute to restrict access to action methods and how to set up ASP.NET Core Identity to manage users and their roles. In the next chapter, I show you how to prepare the application for deployment.

CHAPTER 13

Preparing for Deployment

There are lots of ways to deploy an ASP.NET Core MVC application, and I don't get into the options in this book, but there are some changes that are required regardless of how the application is hosted.

In this chapter, I show how to secure the web service against cross-site forgery attacks, using a feature that can be disruptive during development but that is essential for production applications. I also show you how to disable the developer-friendly features that have ensured that the database is kept up-to-date, that the TypeScript files are automatically compiled, and that changes in the Angular application are sent to the browser automatically. These are all useful features for the developer, but they should not be left enabled for production applications.

Preparing for This Chapter

This chapter uses the SportsStore project that I created in Chapter 3 and modified in the chapters since. To remove the database so that the application will use fresh seed data, open a new command prompt, navigate to the ServerApp folder, and run the commands shown in Listing 13-1.

■ **Tip** You can download the complete project for every chapter without charge from the source code repository, `https://github.com/Apress/esntl-angular-for-asp.net-core-mvc-3`. Run `npm install` in the ClientApp folder to install the packages required for Angular development and then start the development tools as instructed.

Listing 13-1. Resetting the Database

```
dotnet ef database drop --force --context DataContext
dotnet ef database drop --force --context IdentityDataContext
dotnet ef database update --context DataContext
dotnet ef database update --context IdentityDataContext
dotnet sql-cache create "Server=(localdb)\MSSQLLocalDB;Database=EssentialApp" "dbo"
"SessionData"
```

These commands are different from earlier chapters because Chapter 12 introduced support for ASP. NET Core Identity.

Use a command prompt to run the command shown in Listing 13-2 in the ServerApp folder to start the ASP.NET Core runtime and the Angular development tools.

© Adam Freeman 2019

A. Freeman, *Essential Angular for ASP.NET Core MVC 3*,
https://doi.org/10.1007/978-1-4842-5284-0_13

Listing 13-2. Starting the Development Tools

```
dotnet watch run
```

Open a new browser window and navigate to `https://localhost:5001`; you will see the SportsStore application, as shown in Figure 13-1.

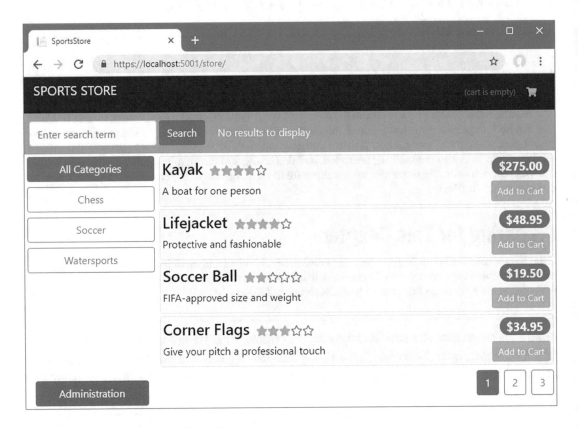

Figure 13-1. *Running the example application*

Preventing Cross-Site Request Forgery Attacks

Whenever you use cookies to identify a user, you must take care to protect your application from cross-site request forgery (CSRF) attacks. The idea of a CSRF attack is to trick the user into loading a malicious web page and sending an HTTP request to your application. The browser will automatically include any cookies it has received from your application in the request, which allows the attacker to perform operations while impersonating the user, typically to grant the attacker access to the application or to change or delete the application's data.

Protecting against CSRF attacks requires including a random cryptographic token in HTTP responses from the application and requiring that the client includes the same token in subsequent HTTP requests. For round-trip applications, the token is usually included as a hidden form field, but for Angular clients, the token is sent as a cookie. Angular detects the cookie and uses it to set the value of a header in HTTP requests, which is something that CSRF attacks cannot do, which identifies a request as coming from the Angular application and not from an attack. ASP.NET Core MVC includes built-in support for anti-CSRF tokens but requires some additional work to use them in a way that works with Angular, as described in the sections that follow.

Enabling Anti-CSRF Tokens

The first step to protecting against CSRF is to apply the attribute that tells ASP.NET Core MVC to accept requests only when they contain a valid cryptographic token. The simplest way to protect the application is to apply the `AutoValidateAntiforgeryToken` attribute to a controller that tells ASP.NET Core MVC to accept only those requests with valid tokens. Apply the attribute as shown in Listing 13-3 to protect the product API controller.

■ **Tip** You can apply the `IgnoreAntiforgeryToken` attribute to an action method if you want to exclude it from the anti-CSRF policy created by a class-wide attribute.

Listing 13-3. Requiring Tokens in the ProductValuesController.cs File in the ServerApp/Controllers Folder

```
using Microsoft.AspNetCore.Mvc;
using ServerApp.Models;
using Microsoft.EntityFrameworkCore;
using System.Linq;
using System.Collections.Generic;
using ServerApp.Models.BindingTargets;
using Microsoft.AspNetCore.JsonPatch;
using System.Text.Json;
using System.Reflection;
using System.ComponentModel;
using Microsoft.AspNetCore.Authorization;

namespace ServerApp.Controllers {

    [Route("api/products")]
    [Authorize(Roles = "Administrator")]
    [AutoValidateAntiforgeryToken]
    public class ProductValuesController : Controller {
        private DataContext context;

        public ProductValuesController(DataContext ctx) {
            context = ctx;
        }

        // ...methods omitted for brevity...
    }
}
```

Apply the same attribute to the session API controller, as shown in Listing 13-4, so that session data can be stored using only the requests that contain a valid anti-CSRF token.

Listing 13-4. Requiring Tokens in the SessionValuesController.cs File in the ServerApp/Controllers Folder

```
using Microsoft.AspNetCore.Http;
using Microsoft.AspNetCore.Mvc;
using Newtonsoft.Json;
using ServerApp.Models;
using ServerApp.Models.BindingTargets;

namespace ServerApp.Controllers {

    [Route("/api/session")]
    [AutoValidateAntiforgeryToken]
    public class SessionValuesController : Controller {

        // ...methods omitted for brevity...
    }
}
```

Apply the attribute to the controller for supplier data, as shown in Listing 13-5.

Listing 13-5. Requiring Tokens in the SupplierValuesController.cs File in the ServerApp/Controllers Folder

```
using Microsoft.AspNetCore.Mvc;
using ServerApp.Models;
using ServerApp.Models.BindingTargets;
using System.Collections.Generic;
using Microsoft.AspNetCore.Authorization;

namespace ServerApp.Controllers {

    [Route("api/suppliers")]
    [Authorize(Roles = "Administrator")]
    [AutoValidateAntiforgeryToken]
    public class SupplierValuesController : Controller {
        private DataContext context;

        public SupplierValuesController(DataContext ctx) {
            context = ctx;
        }

        // ...methods omitted for brevity...
    }
}
```

Apply the attribute to the controller for order data, as shown in Listing 13-6.

Listing 13-6. Requiring Tokens in the OrderValuesController.cs File in the ServerApp/Controllers Folder

```
using Microsoft.AspNetCore.Mvc;
using Microsoft.EntityFrameworkCore;
using ServerApp.Models;
```

```
using System.Collections.Generic;
using System.Linq;
using Microsoft.AspNetCore.Authorization;

namespace ServerApp.Controllers {

    [Route("/api/orders")]
    [Authorize(Roles = "Administrator")]
    [AutoValidateAntiforgeryToken]
    public class OrderValuesController : Controller {
        private DataContext context;

        public OrderValuesController(DataContext ctx) {
            context = ctx;
        }

        // ...methods omitted for brevity...
    }
}
```

As a result of these changes, all the web service action methods can be accessed only if the request includes a token that has been provided by the application. Restart the ASP.NET Core MVC application, navigate to https://localhost:5001, and click the Add to Cart button; you will see that the request fails, as shown in Figure 13-2.

Figure 13-2. *The effect of requiring anti-CSRF tokens*

Sending and Receiving Anti-CSRF Tokens

Angular looks for a cookie with the name XSRF-TOKEN in HTTP responses and will automatically use the cookie value to set a header called X-XSRF-TOKEN in subsequent requests. To provide the Angular client with the cookie and tell ASP.NET Core MVC about the header that Angular uses, add the statements shown in Listing 13-7 to the Startup class.

Listing 13-7. Using Anti-Forgery Tokens in the Startup.cs.cs File in the ServerApp Folder

```
using System;
using System.Collections.Generic;
using System.Linq;
using System.Threading.Tasks;
using Microsoft.AspNetCore.Builder;
using Microsoft.AspNetCore.Hosting;
using Microsoft.AspNetCore.HttpsPolicy;
using Microsoft.Extensions.Configuration;
using Microsoft.Extensions.DependencyInjection;
using Microsoft.Extensions.Hosting;
using Microsoft.AspNetCore.SpaServices.AngularCli;
using ServerApp.Models;
using Microsoft.EntityFrameworkCore;
using Microsoft.OpenApi.Models;
using Microsoft.AspNetCore.ResponseCompression;
using Microsoft.Extensions.FileProviders;
using System.IO;
using Microsoft.AspNetCore.Identity;
using Microsoft.AspNetCore.Antiforgery;
using Microsoft.AspNetCore.Http;

namespace ServerApp {
    public class Startup {

        public Startup(IConfiguration configuration) {
            Configuration = configuration;
        }

        public IConfiguration Configuration { get; }

        public void ConfigureServices(IServiceCollection services) {

            // ...other statements omitted for brevity...

            services.AddAntiforgery(options => {
                options.HeaderName = "X-XSRF-TOKEN";
            });
        }

        public void Configure(IApplicationBuilder app, IWebHostEnvironment env,
            IServiceProvider services, IAntiforgery antiforgery) {

            if (env.IsDevelopment()) {
                app.UseDeveloperExceptionPage();
            } else {
                app.UseExceptionHandler("/Home/Error");
                app.UseHsts();
            }
```

```
app.UseHttpsRedirection();
app.UseStaticFiles();
app.UseStaticFiles(new StaticFileOptions {
    RequestPath = "/blazor",
    FileProvider = new PhysicalFileProvider(
        Path.Combine(Directory.GetCurrentDirectory(),
            "../BlazorApp/wwwroot"))
});

app.UseSession();

app.UseRouting();
app.UseAuthentication();
app.UseAuthorization();

app.Use(nextDelegate => context => {
    string path = context.Request.Path.Value;
    string[] directUrls = { "/admin", "/store", "/cart", "checkout" };
    if (path.StartsWith("/api") || string.Equals("/", path)
            || directUrls.Any(url => path.StartsWith(url))) {
        var tokens = antiforgery.GetAndStoreTokens(context);
        context.Response.Cookies.Append("XSRF-TOKEN",
            tokens.RequestToken, new CookieOptions() {
                HttpOnly = false, Secure = false, IsEssential = true
            });
    }
    return nextDelegate(context);
});

app.UseEndpoints(endpoints => {
    endpoints.MapControllerRoute(
        name: "default",
        pattern: "{controller=Home}/{action=Index}/{id?}");

    endpoints.MapControllerRoute(
        name: "angular_fallback",
        pattern:
        "{target:regex(admin|store|cart|checkout):nonfile}/{*catchall}",
        defaults: new { controller = "Home", action = "Index" });

    endpoints.MapControllerRoute(
        name: "blazor_integration",
        pattern: "/blazor/{*path:nonfile}",
        defaults: new { controller = "Home", action = "Blazor" });

    //endpoints.MapFallbackToClientSideBlazor<BlazorApp
    //      .Startup>("blazor/{*path:nonfile}", "index.html");

    endpoints.MapRazorPages();
});
```

```
            app.Map("/blazor", opts =>
                opts.UseClientSideBlazorFiles<BlazorApp.Startup>());

            app.UseClientSideBlazorFiles<BlazorApp.Startup>();

            app.UseSwagger();
            app.UseSwaggerUI(options => {
                options.SwaggerEndpoint("/swagger/v1/swagger.json",
                    "SportsStore API");
            });

            app.UseSpa(spa => {
                string strategy = Configuration
                    .GetValue<string>("DevTools:ConnectionStrategy");
                if (strategy == "proxy") {
                    spa.UseProxyToSpaDevelopmentServer("http://127.0.0.1:4200");
                } else if (strategy == "managed") {
                    spa.Options.SourcePath = "../ClientApp";
                    spa.UseAngularCliServer("start");
                }
            });

            SeedData.SeedDatabase(services.GetRequiredService<DataContext>());
            IdentitySeedData.SeedDatabase(services).Wait();
        }
    }
}
```

The new statements in the ConfigureServices method tell ASP.NET Core MVC to look for the anti-CSRF token in the HTTP header called X-XSRF-TOKEN. The new statements in the Configure method add a token to requests for the / URL, for any of the top-level URLs that the user might navigate to directly, and for URLs that start with /api.

Save the changes, restart the ASP.NET Core MVC application, and navigate to https://localhost:5001. Now that Angular is receiving and sending the tokens, ASP.NET Core MVC will process its requests, as illustrated by Figure 13-3.

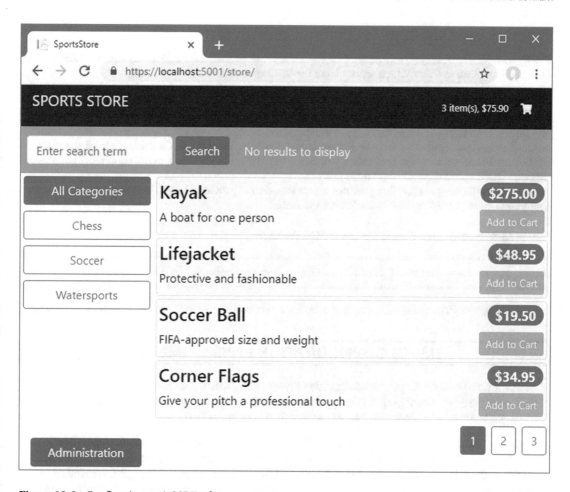

Figure 13-3. *Configuring anti-CSRF tokens*

Preparing for Deployment

The project is configured for development with features that make it easy to see the effect of code changes but that should not be used in production. In the sections that follow, I prepare the application for deployment.

■ **Note** This chapter doesn't show you how to deploy the application because there are too many different deployment options to cover. If you don't have an existing platform on which to deploy, then I recommend considering using containers, such as those provided by Docker, which can be deployed and managed on most hosted platforms or on local servers. See docker.com for details.

Creating the Database Migration Command

Throughout this book, I relied on Entity Framework Core to apply database migrations when the ASP.NET Core MVC application starts, which ensured that the database schema was up-to-date.

You should not automatically apply migrations when your application is in production because schema changes can cause data loss when tables or columns are dropped and re-created. It is still useful to be able to initialize the database, but it is important to do so explicitly, rather than every time the ASP.NET Core MVC application starts. The way that I approach this is to add support for a configuration setting that can be supplied as an environment variable or as a command-line argument. When the setting is true, the database will be initialized, and then the application will exit. When the setting is false, or not supplied, then the ASP.NET Core MVC application will start up as normal.

To add the NuGet package that provides access to variables provided by via the command line, run the commands shown in Listing 13-8 in the ServerApp folder.

Listing 13-8. Installing the Command-Line NuGet Package

```
dotnet add package Microsoft.Extensions.Configuration.CommandLine --version 3.0.0
```

To add support for configuration option, add the statements shown in Listing 13-9 to the Startup class.

USING CONFIGURATION ENVIRONMENTS

ASP.NET Core provides support for configuration environments, where a configuration setting is used to specify the environment in which the application runs and which can be used to load different configuration files or to branch to different configuration code in the Startup class.

This is a feature that requires care and should be used with caution because few project teams have the capability or discipline to test the effect of the production settings before deploying the application, which leads to deployment failures and rollbacks. I recommend going through an explicit preparation process before each deployment and rely on environments only to deal with settings such as database connection strings.

Listing 13-9. Adding Explicit Database Initialization in the Startup.cs File in the ServerApp Folder

```
using System;
using System.Collections.Generic;
using System.Linq;
using System.Threading.Tasks;
using Microsoft.AspNetCore.Builder;
using Microsoft.AspNetCore.Hosting;
using Microsoft.AspNetCore.HttpsPolicy;
using Microsoft.Extensions.Configuration;
using Microsoft.Extensions.DependencyInjection;
using Microsoft.Extensions.Hosting;
using Microsoft.AspNetCore.SpaServices.AngularCli;
using ServerApp.Models;
using Microsoft.EntityFrameworkCore;
```

```
using Microsoft.OpenApi.Models;
using Microsoft.AspNetCore.ResponseCompression;
using Microsoft.Extensions.FileProviders;
using System.IO;
using Microsoft.AspNetCore.Identity;
using Microsoft.AspNetCore.Antiforgery;
using Microsoft.AspNetCore.Http;

namespace ServerApp {
    public class Startup {

        public Startup(IWebHostEnvironment env) {
            var builder = new ConfigurationBuilder()
                .SetBasePath(env.ContentRootPath)
                .AddJsonFile("appsettings.json", optional: false, reloadOnChange: true)
                .AddJsonFile($"appsettings.{env.EnvironmentName}.json", optional: true)
                .AddEnvironmentVariables()
                .AddCommandLine(System.Environment.GetCommandLineArgs()
                    .Skip(1).ToArray());
            Configuration = builder.Build();
        }

        public IConfiguration Configuration { get; }

        public void ConfigureServices(IServiceCollection services) {

            // ...statements omitted for brevity...
        }

        public void Configure(IApplicationBuilder app, IWebHostEnvironment env,
            IServiceProvider services, IAntiforgery antiforgery,
            IHostApplicationLifetime lifetime) {

            // ...statements omitted for brevity...

            //SeedData.SeedDatabase(services.GetRequiredService<DataContext>());
            //IdentitySeedData.SeedDatabase(services).Wait();

            if ((Configuration["INITDB"] ?? "false") == "true") {
                System.Console.WriteLine("Preparing Database...");
                SeedData.SeedDatabase(services.GetRequiredService<DataContext>());
                IdentitySeedData.SeedDatabase(services).Wait();
                System.Console.WriteLine("Database Preparation Complete");
                lifetime.StopApplication();
            }
        }
    }
}
```

If there is a configuration setting called INITDB and it is true, then the databases will be migrated and seeded. After the databases have been prepared, the application will exit.

Building the Angular Application for Production

The Angular development server has been responsible for building the Angular application during the development process. To prepare for deployment, the Angular build tools are used to create an optimized version of the application that doesn't include features such as automatic browser reloading.

Creating the Dummy Module

The compilation for production is strict and reports errors that are not flagged during production. In Chapter 7, I added components to the project to demonstrate the structure of an Angular application. The components are not part of the final project and won't be included in the optimized build, but the Angular compiler will report an error when components are not associated with a module. I could delete the components, but this is a common issue for projects where the same code base is used to produce different applications and where deleting files is not ideal. To work around the issue, I am going to add a dummy module that will satisfy the compiler without needing to remove files from the project. Add a file named dummy.module.ts in the ClientApp/src/app/structure folder with the code shown in Listing 13-10.

Listing 13-10. The Contents of the dummy.module.ts File in the ClientApp/src/app/structure Folder

```
import { NgModule } from '@angular/core';
import { CommonModule } from "@angular/common";
import { RouterModule } from "@angular/router";
import { CategoryFilterComponent } from "./categoryFilter.component";
import { ProductDetailComponent } from "./productDetail.component";
import { ProductTableComponent } from "./productTable.component";

@NgModule({
    declarations: [CategoryFilterComponent, ProductDetailComponent, ProductTableComponent],
    imports: [CommonModule, RouterModule]
})
export class DummyModule {}
```

To create the production build of the Angular application, run the command shown in Listing 13-11 in the ClientApp folder.

Listing 13-11. Creating the Production Angular Build

```
ng build --prod --output-path ../ServerApp/wwwroot/app --output-hashing none
```

This command creates optimized versions of the JavaScript files that contain the Angular application and runtime and puts them in the ServerApp/wwwroot/app folder, from which they will be served to the browser.

■ **Note** The output-hashing argument is used to prevent the build process from adding a checksum to the generated file names, which I have done to simplify the example. In real projects, this argument can be omitted to produce file names that change based on their contents, which is a useful trick for preventing caching problems, although you must then use those file names when updating the script elements shown in Listing 13-12.

Updating the Script Elements

To use the production Angular files, change the `script` elements in the Razor view that delivers the Angular application to the browser, as shown in Listing 13-12.

Listing 13-12. Changing File Locations in the Index.cshtml File in the ServerApp/Views/Home Folder

```
@section scripts {
    <script src="runtime-es2015.js" type="module"></script>
    <script src="polyfills-es2015.js" type="module"></script>
    <script src="main-es2015.js" type="module"></script>
    <script src="runtime-es5.js" nomodule></script>
    <script src="polyfills-es5.js" nomodule></script>
    <script src="main-es5.js" nomodule></script>
}

<!-- <div id="data" class="p-1 bg-warning">
  @Json.Serialize(Model)
</div> -->

<app-root></app-root>
```

The new locations specified in the `src` attribute will select the files that were created by the Angular build command in Listing 13-11. The build processes two sets of JavaScript files to support a process known as differential loading, which allows modern browsers to be targeted with smaller files because they don't need to work around missing JavaScript features. Older browsers are still supported but will receive larger JavaScript files containing additional code. The selection of files is driven by the `type` and `nomodule` attributes that are added to the `script` elements in Listing 13-12.

Configuring ASP.NET Core for Production

The `Startup` class for the ASP.NET Core part of the project sets up features that are useful in development but not production. To prepare for deployment, I have commented out the sections that added support for working with the Angular development server and for checking the web service, as shown in Listing 13-13. I have also added a new static file handler that will serve the files in the `wwwroot/app` folder, which will ensure that the `script` elements defined in Listing 13-12 will work and allow the Angular application to load the administration module when it is required.

Listing 13-13. Preparing for Deployment in the Startup.cs File in the ServerApp Folder

```
using System;
using System.Collections.Generic;
using System.Linq;
using System.Threading.Tasks;
using Microsoft.AspNetCore.Builder;
using Microsoft.AspNetCore.Hosting;
using Microsoft.AspNetCore.HttpsPolicy;
using Microsoft.Extensions.Configuration;
using Microsoft.Extensions.DependencyInjection;
using Microsoft.Extensions.Hosting;
using Microsoft.AspNetCore.SpaServices.AngularCli;
```

```csharp
using ServerApp.Models;
using Microsoft.EntityFrameworkCore;
using Microsoft.OpenApi.Models;
using Microsoft.AspNetCore.ResponseCompression;
using Microsoft.Extensions.FileProviders;
using System.IO;
using Microsoft.AspNetCore.Identity;
using Microsoft.AspNetCore.Antiforgery;
using Microsoft.AspNetCore.Http;

namespace ServerApp {
    public class Startup {

        public Startup(IWebHostEnvironment env) {
            var builder = new ConfigurationBuilder()
                .SetBasePath(env.ContentRootPath)
                .AddJsonFile("appsettings.json", optional: false, reloadOnChange: true)
                .AddJsonFile($"appsettings.{env.EnvironmentName}.json", optional: true)
                .AddEnvironmentVariables()
                .AddCommandLine(System.Environment.GetCommandLineArgs()
                    .Skip(1).ToArray());
            Configuration = builder.Build();
        }

        public IConfiguration Configuration { get; }

        public void ConfigureServices(IServiceCollection services) {

            string connectionString =
                Configuration["ConnectionStrings:DefaultConnection"];
            services.AddDbContext<DataContext>(options =>
                options.UseSqlServer(connectionString));

            services.AddDbContext<IdentityDataContext>(options =>
                options.UseSqlServer(Configuration["ConnectionStrings:Identity"]));
            services.AddIdentity<IdentityUser, IdentityRole>()
                .AddEntityFrameworkStores<IdentityDataContext>();

            services.AddControllersWithViews()
                .AddJsonOptions(opts => {
                    opts.JsonSerializerOptions.IgnoreNullValues = true;
                });
            services.AddRazorPages();

            //services.AddSwaggerGen(options => {
            //    options.SwaggerDoc("v1",
            //        new OpenApiInfo { Title = "SportsStore API", Version = "v1" });
            //});
```

```
        services.AddDistributedSqlServerCache(options => {
            options.ConnectionString = connectionString;
            options.SchemaName = "dbo";
            options.TableName = "SessionData";
        });

        services.AddSession(options => {
            options.Cookie.Name = "SportsStore.Session";
            options.IdleTimeout = System.TimeSpan.FromHours(48);
            options.Cookie.HttpOnly = false;
            options.Cookie.IsEssential = true;
        });

        services.AddResponseCompression(opts => {
            opts.MimeTypes = ResponseCompressionDefaults.MimeTypes.Concat(
                new[] { "application/octet-stream" });
        });

        services.AddAntiforgery(options => {
            options.HeaderName = "X-XSRF-TOKEN";
        });
    }

    public void Configure(IApplicationBuilder app, IWebHostEnvironment env,
        IServiceProvider services, IAntiforgery antiforgery,
        IHostApplicationLifetime lifetime) {

        if (env.IsDevelopment()) {
            app.UseDeveloperExceptionPage();
        } else {
            app.UseExceptionHandler("/Home/Error");
            app.UseHsts();
        }

        app.UseHttpsRedirection();
        app.UseStaticFiles();
        app.UseStaticFiles(new StaticFileOptions {
            RequestPath = "/blazor",
            FileProvider = new PhysicalFileProvider(
                Path.Combine(Directory.GetCurrentDirectory(),
                    "../BlazorApp/wwwroot"))
        });
        app.UseStaticFiles(new StaticFileOptions {
            RequestPath = "",
            FileProvider = new PhysicalFileProvider(
                Path.Combine(Directory.GetCurrentDirectory(),
                    "./wwwroot/app"))
        });

        app.UseSession();
```

```
        app.UseRouting();
        app.UseAuthentication();
        app.UseAuthorization();

        app.Use(nextDelegate => context => {
            string path = context.Request.Path.Value;
            string[] directUrls = { "/admin", "/store", "/cart", "checkout" };
            if (path.StartsWith("/api") || string.Equals("/", path)
                    || directUrls.Any(url => path.StartsWith(url))) {
                var tokens = antiforgery.GetAndStoreTokens(context);
                context.Response.Cookies.Append("XSRF-TOKEN",
                    tokens.RequestToken, new CookieOptions() {
                        HttpOnly = false, Secure = false, IsEssential = true
                    });
            }
            return nextDelegate(context);
        });

        app.UseEndpoints(endpoints => {
            endpoints.MapControllerRoute(
                name: "default",
                pattern: "{controller=Home}/{action=Index}/{id?}");

            endpoints.MapControllerRoute(
                name: "angular_fallback",
                pattern:
                "{target:regex(admin|store|cart|checkout):nonfile}/{*catchall}",
                defaults: new { controller = "Home", action = "Index" });

            endpoints.MapControllerRoute(
                name: "blazor_integration",
                pattern: "/blazor/{*path:nonfile}",
                defaults: new { controller = "Home", action = "Blazor" });

            endpoints.MapRazorPages();
        });

        //app.Map("/blazor", opts =>
        //    opts.UseClientSideBlazorFiles<BlazorApp.Startup>());

        app.UseClientSideBlazorFiles<BlazorApp.Startup>();

        //app.UseSwagger();
        //app.UseSwaggerUI(options => {
        //    options.SwaggerEndpoint("/swagger/v1/swagger.json",
        //        "SportsStore API");
        //});

        //app.UseSpa(spa => {
        //    string strategy = Configuration
        //        .GetValue<string>("DevTools:ConnectionStrategy");
```

```
//      if (strategy == "proxy") {
//          spa.UseProxyToSpaDevelopmentServer("http://127.0.0.1:4200");
//      } else if (strategy == "managed") {
//          spa.Options.SourcePath = "../ClientApp";
//          spa.UseAngularCliServer("start");
//      }
//});

if ((Configuration["INITDB"] ?? "false") == "true") {
    System.Console.WriteLine("Preparing Database...");
    SeedData.SeedDatabase(services.GetRequiredService<DataContext>());
    IdentitySeedData.SeedDatabase(services).Wait();
    System.Console.WriteLine("Database Preparation Complete");
    lifetime.StopApplication();
}

        }
    }
}
```

Performing the Production Dry Run

The final step is to perform a dry run and ensure everything works as expected following the changes in the previous sections.

Preparing the Database

The first check is to make sure that the changes from Listing 13-9 allow the databases to be initialized and seeded from the command line. Start by running the commands shown in Listing 13-14 in the ServerApp folder to remove the existing databases.

Listing 13-14. Resetting the Databases

```
dotnet ef database drop --force --context DataContext
dotnet ef database drop --force --context IdentityDataContext
```

Run the command shown in Listing 13-15 in the ServerApp folder to initialize the databases for storing the application and identity data.

Listing 13-15. Preparing the Databases

```
dotnet run -- --INITDB=true
```

Next, run the command shown in Listing 13-16 in the ServerApp folder so that session data can be stored.

Listing 13-16. Preparing the Database for Session Data

```
dotnet sql-cache create "Server=(localdb)\MSSQLLocalDB;Database=EssentialApp" "dbo"
"SessionData"
```

Starting the ASP.NET Core MVC Application

The final step is to start the application by running the command shown in Listing 13-17 in the SportsStore folder.

Listing 13-17. Running the ASP.NET Core MVC Application

```
dotnet run
```

Once the application has started, use a browser to navigate to https://localhost:5001; you should see the list of products illustrated in Figure 13-4. Navigate to https://localhost:5001/admin and authenticate using admin as the username and MySecret123$ as the password to make sure that the integration with ASP. NET Core Identity is working, also shown in Figure 13-4.

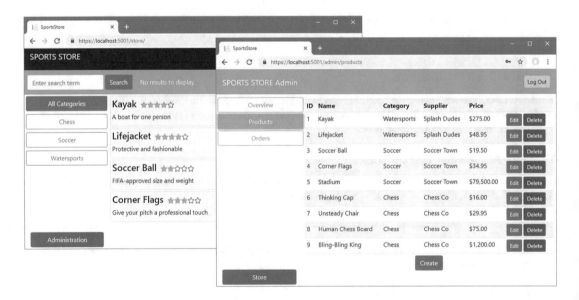

Figure 13-4. *Checking that the application works*

If everything works, you can make any final adjustments required, such as new database connection strings, and package the application for deployment.

Summary

In this chapter, I showed you how to prepare the application for deployment. I demonstrated how to add validation tokens to guard against cross-site request forgery, how to prepare the database using the command line, and how to disable the developer features.

That is all I have to teach you about using Angular and ASP.NET Core MVC together. I started by creating a project containing both Angular and ASP.NET Core MVC and showed you how to get them to work together, how to share data between them, and how to create and use web services. Along the way, I showed you how to use the core Angular building blocks to structure a client-side application and how Angular and Blazor can be used together.

I wish you every success in your Angular/ASP.NET Core MVC projects, and I can only hope that you have enjoyed reading this book as much as I enjoyed writing it.

Index

© Adam Freeman 2019
A. Freeman, *Essential Angular for ASP.NET Core MVC 3*,
https://doi.org/10.1007/978-1-4842-5284-0

Printed in the United States
By Bookmasters